THE VICTORIES™
METAHUMAN

STORY AND ART
Michael Avon Oeming

COLORS Nick Filardi
LETTERS Aaron Walker

FEATURING AGNES GARBOWSKA
AND TAKI SOMA

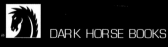

DARK HORSE BOOKS

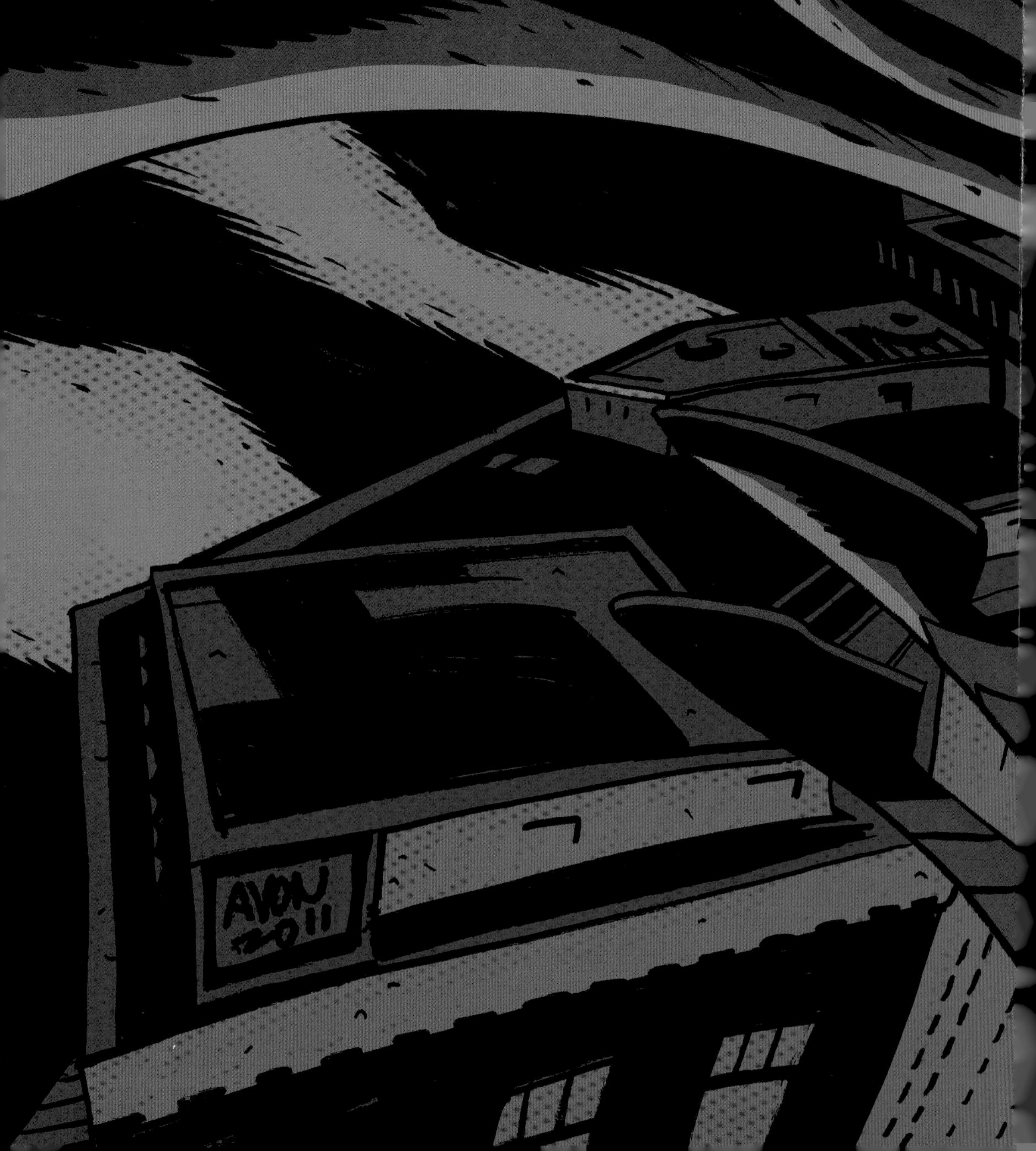

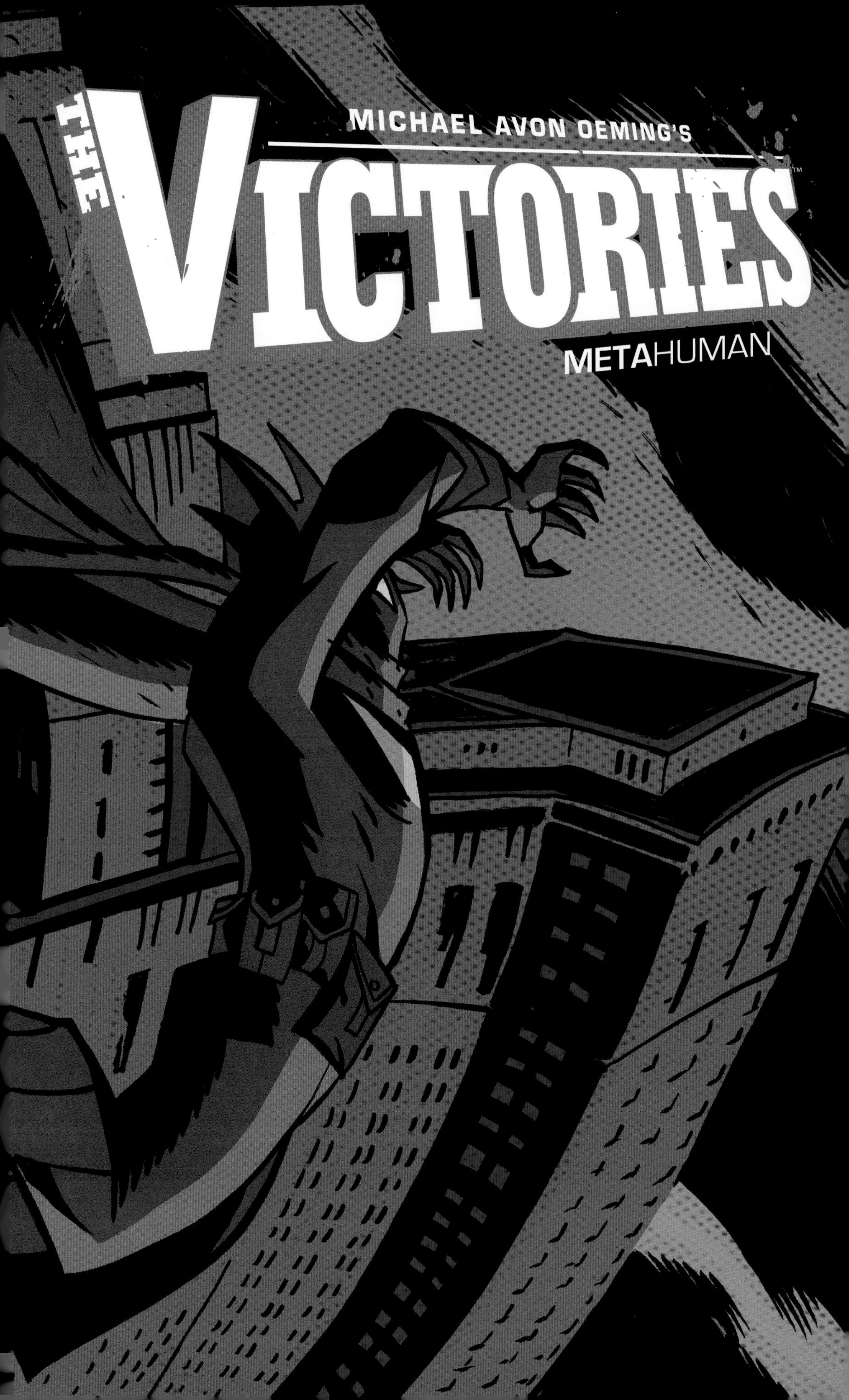
MICHAEL AVON OEMING'S
THE VICTORIES™
METAHUMAN

DESIGNER Rick DeLucco
ASSISTANT EDITOR Shantel LaRocque
EDITOR Scott Allie
PUBLISHER Mike Richardson

Mike Richardson, President and Publisher | Neil Hankerson, Executive Vice President |
Tom Weddle, Chief Financial Officer | Randy Stradley, Vice President of Publishing | Michael
Martens, Vice President of Book Trade Sales | Scott Allie, Editor in Chief | Matt Parkinson,
Vice President of Marketing | David Scroggy, Vice President of Product Development | Dale
LaFountain, Vice President of Information Technology | Darlene Vogel, Senior Director of
Print, Design, and Production | Ken Lizzi, General Counsel | Davey Estrada, Editorial Director
| Chris Warner, Senior Books Editor | Diana Schutz, Executive Editor | Cary Grazzini, Director
of Print and Development | Lia Ribacchi, Art Director | Cara Niece, Director of Scheduling |
Mark Bernardi, Director of Digital Publishing

Published by Dark Horse Books
A division of Dark Horse Comics, Inc.
10956 SE Main Street
Milwaukie, OR 97222

First edition: January 2015
ISBN 978-1-61655-517-7

10 9 8 7 6 5 4 3 2 1
Printed in China

International Licensing: (503) 905-2377
Comic Shop Locator Service: (888) 266-4226

This volume collects issues #11 through #15 of *The Victories*.

MICHAEL AVON OEMING'S THE VICTORIES™

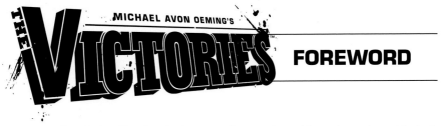

FOREWORD

Jason Martell is an expert in the Ancient Aliens hypothesis, renowned as an author, public speaker, and one of the hosts of *Ancient Aliens* on the H2 channel, and was kind enough to give us some insight into my *Victories* mythology. Thank you, Jason!

—Michael Avon Oeming

Earth's First Civilization: Sumer

My research has led me back almost six thousand years in our history to the oldest civilization we have on record. At that time, we would have found this civilization established in a fertile strip of land between the Tigris and Euphrates valleys known as Sumer. Almost overnight, from right out of the Stone Age, "Sumerian Civilization" emerged into the land that is now southern Iraq. It has been called Mesopotamia and it has been called Babylon—but the first culture located here were the Sumerians.

What is amazing about the Sumerian culture is that over one hundred of the firsts needed for an advanced civilization can be attributed to them. Keep in mind that this is a civilization nearly six thousand years old. The question we must continually ask ourselves is: did they do it alone?

The Anunnaki: Those Who from Heaven to Earth Came

In the early 1900s, British archaeologists started doing excavations in the ancient Sumerian city of Ur. Many of the artifacts and tablets spoke of beings called the Anunnaki and depicted these beings with wings. Why did ancient man depict the Anunnaki with wings? This seems very similar to angels in the modern Bible. The answer is quite simple if we look at more modern references. In ancient times, man did not understand technology. So anything flying in the skies of Earth had to be alive. Depicting the Anunnaki with wings leads me to believe the Sumerians were trying to say that the Anunnaki had the power of flight. Since ancient man did not understand technology, they gave the Anunnaki wings to symbolically represent their power of flight.

We find references to this same phenomenon in other ancient cultural records—beings who were clearly others, who had arrived from the sky. And we must not forget the astronaut and the other images constructed upon the Nazca plain—images that could only have come if the designer had an aerial viewpoint.

If you look at modern references to when we landed the first Apollo mission on the moon, the words used to mark that event were, "Houston, the *Eagle* has landed." Even the Apollo symbol was an eagle. Does this mean six thousand years from now people will wonder why we were landing birds on the moon?

As archaeologists over the years have gone over the cuneiform tablets left by the Sumerians, they have found countless references to these Anunnaki—which in Sumerian means literally, "those who from heaven to Earth came." In these writings, they were described as beings who came from the sky, who had the power of flight, who taught them things, who gave them resources and information. As you might imagine, most of the tablets describing the Anunnaki were thrown into a big "myth" pile and basically left untouched to this day. What is truly stunning is how the Sumerian stories relating to the Anunnaki are similar to so many other "myths" we find in the study of other ancient cultures.

Finally, with regard to the Sumerian cuneiform tablets, something remarkable happened. The assistant curators of the museum found a set of tablets and began to decipher a very familiar story. On this ancient stone tablet was recorded a story about how a Sumerian man is chosen by God to build a great ship. He is instructed to take his family and animals and even plants onto the boat because there is going to be a great flood—and he must preserve their lives on his boat while everything on land is swept away. Sound familiar? This tablet was thousands of years older than any other biblical source of information. Clearly, they had found the original source for Noah's ark.

The curator ran out of the room with his hands in the air, shouting, "I can't believe it, I can't believe it!"

The Epic of Gilgamesh is widely known today. The first modern translation of the epic was published in the early 1870s by George Smith. More recent translations into English include one undertaken by the American novelist John Gardner and John Maier, published in 1984. In 2001, Benjamin Foster produced a reading in the Norton Critical Edition Series that fills in many of the blanks of the standard edition with previous material.

Scholars found many tablets that seem to parallel stories found in our modern biblical texts. But since Sumer is the oldest recorded civilization, did we find the original source of biblical information?

What really makes the Sumerian versions of these seemingly biblical stories different is the remarkable fact that they so often speak of these Anunnaki. It is clear that the Anunnaki are not another people like themselves—no, instead they are living gods to the Sumerians. They speak about how they came from heaven and live among them. Even though they live among them, there is still a sense of worship and an understanding that these Anunnaki are advanced.

The Sumerians left behind much more evidence of the Anunnaki than just the cuneiform tablets. They also took the trouble to produce a number of wall carvings depicting their interaction with these beings. They always drew the Anunnaki with wings on their backs, or coming down from heaven on a winged disk.

Of course, when British archaeologists in the early 1900s were uncovering all this information, they considered it mythology. But why is it that so many of the images and stories left behind by other ancient cultures across the globe share so many similar echoes?

Jason Martell
July 2014
XFacts.com

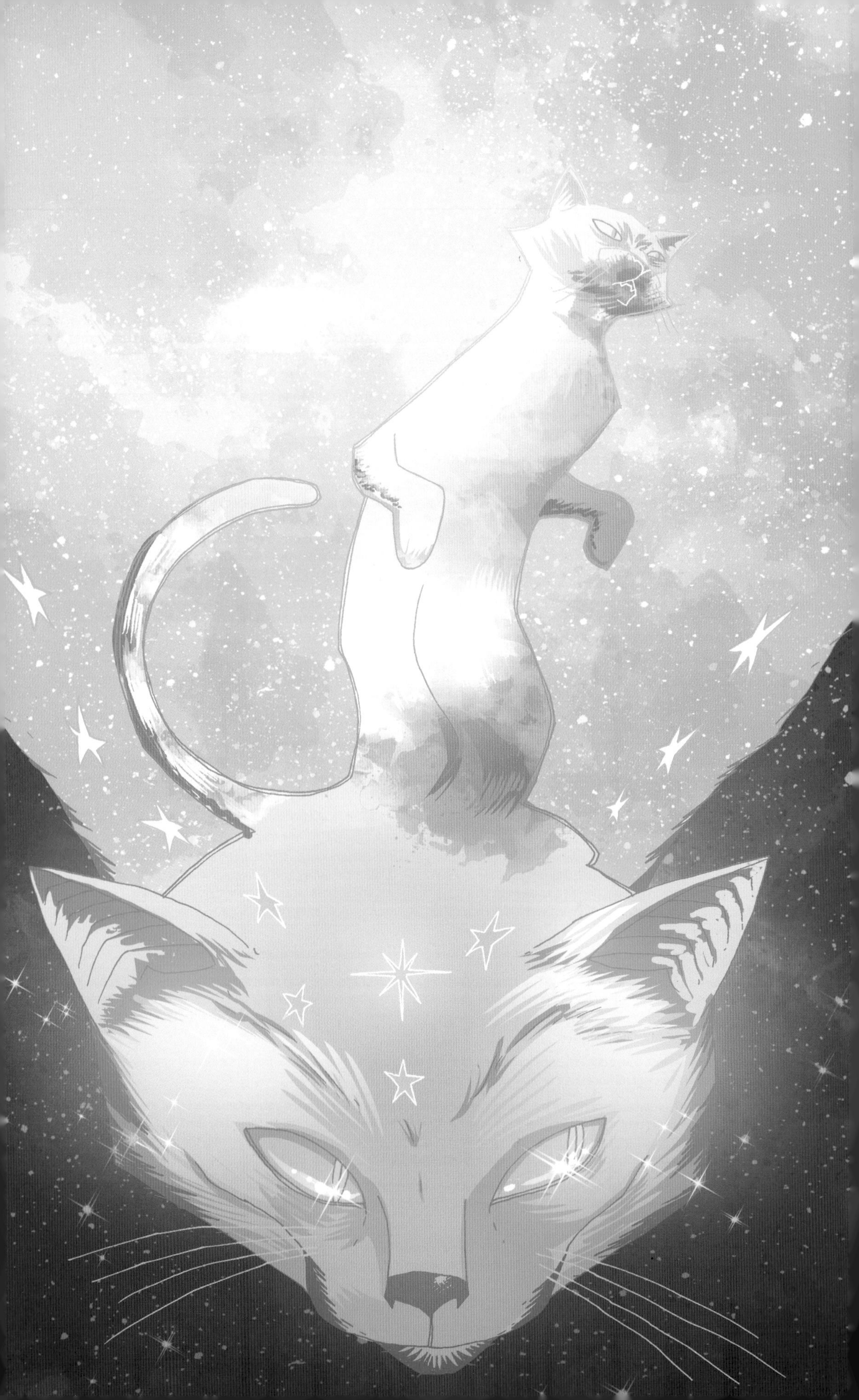

CHAPTER ONE

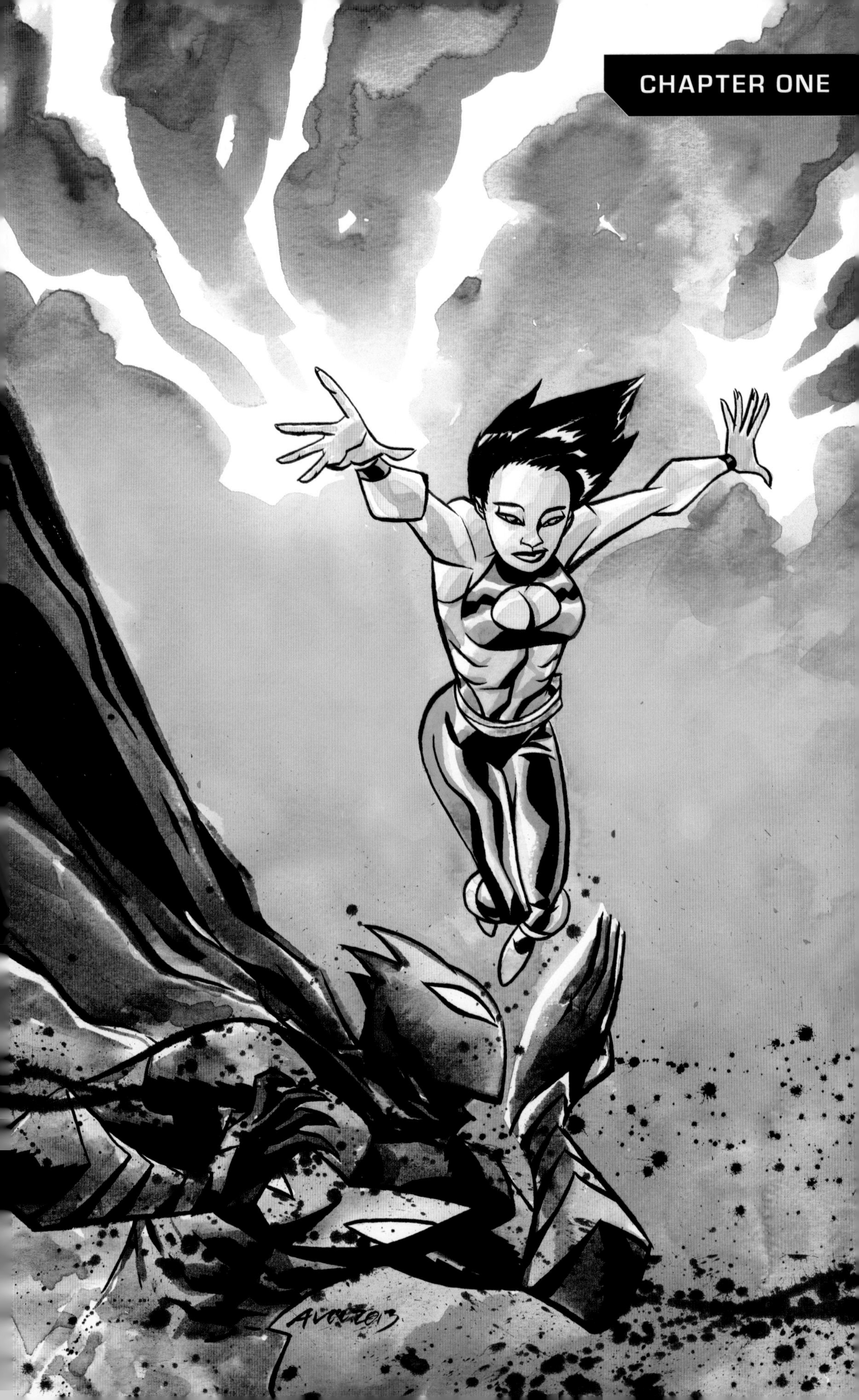

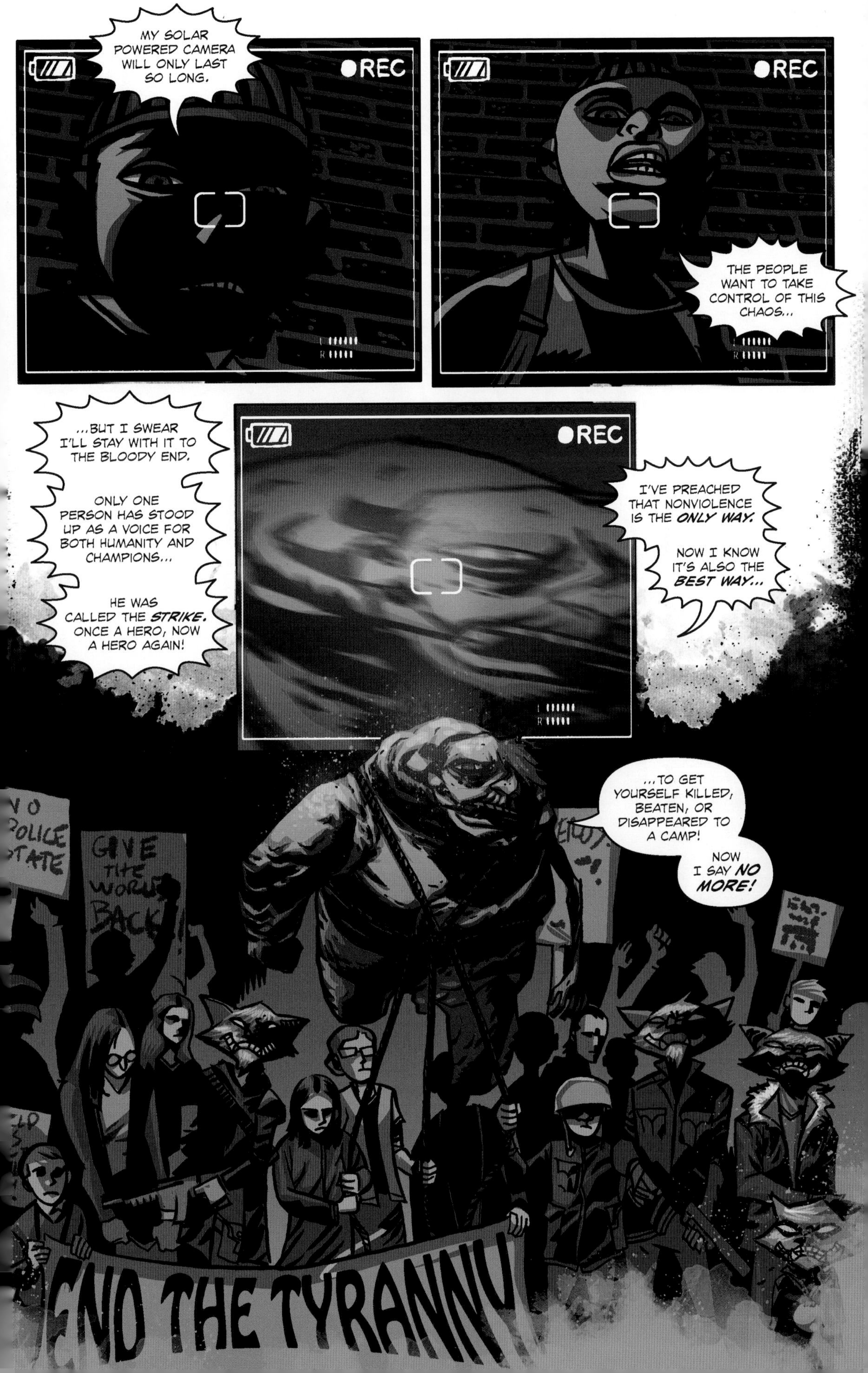
REC
MY SOLAR POWERED CAMERA WILL ONLY LAST SO LONG.
REC
THE PEOPLE WANT TO TAKE CONTROL OF THIS CHAOS...
...BUT I SWEAR I'LL STAY WITH IT TO THE BLOODY END.
ONLY ONE PERSON HAS STOOD UP AS A VOICE FOR BOTH HUMANITY AND CHAMPIONS...
HE WAS CALLED THE STRIKE. ONCE A HERO, NOW A HERO AGAIN!
REC
I'VE PREACHED THAT NONVIOLENCE IS THE ONLY WAY.
NOW I KNOW IT'S ALSO THE BEST WAY...
...TO GET YOURSELF KILLED, BEATEN, OR DISAPPEARED TO A CAMP!
NOW I SAY NO MORE!
NO POLICE STATE
GIVE THE WORLD BACK
END THE TYRANNY

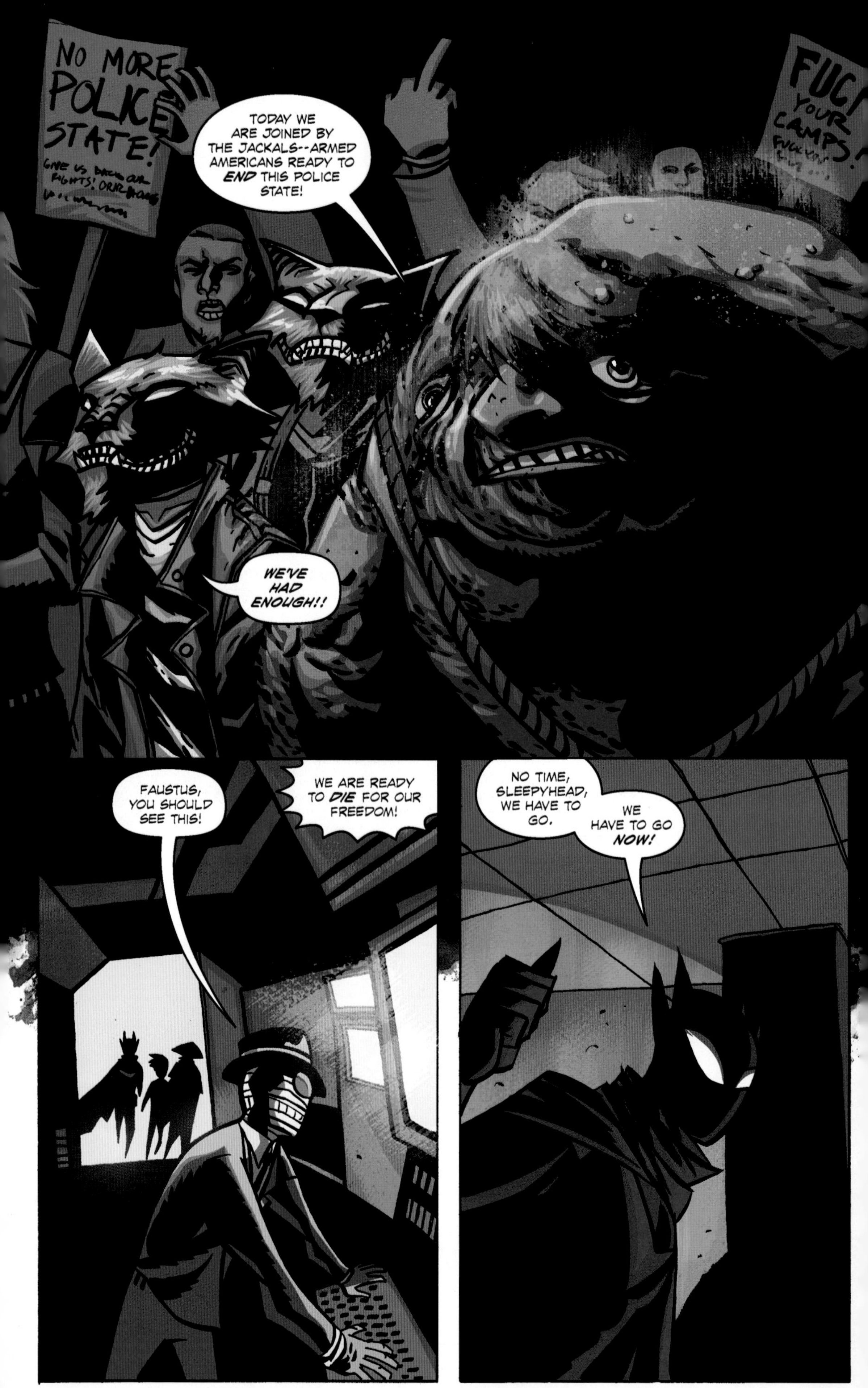
NO MORE POLICE STATE!
TODAY WE ARE JOINED BY THE JACKALS--ARMED AMERICANS READY TO *END* THIS POLICE STATE!
YOUR CAMPS
WE'VE HAD ENOUGH!!
FAUSTUS, YOU SHOULD SEE THIS!
WE ARE READY TO *DIE* FOR OUR FREEDOM!
NO TIME, SLEEPYHEAD, WE HAVE TO GO.
WE HAVE TO GO *NOW!*

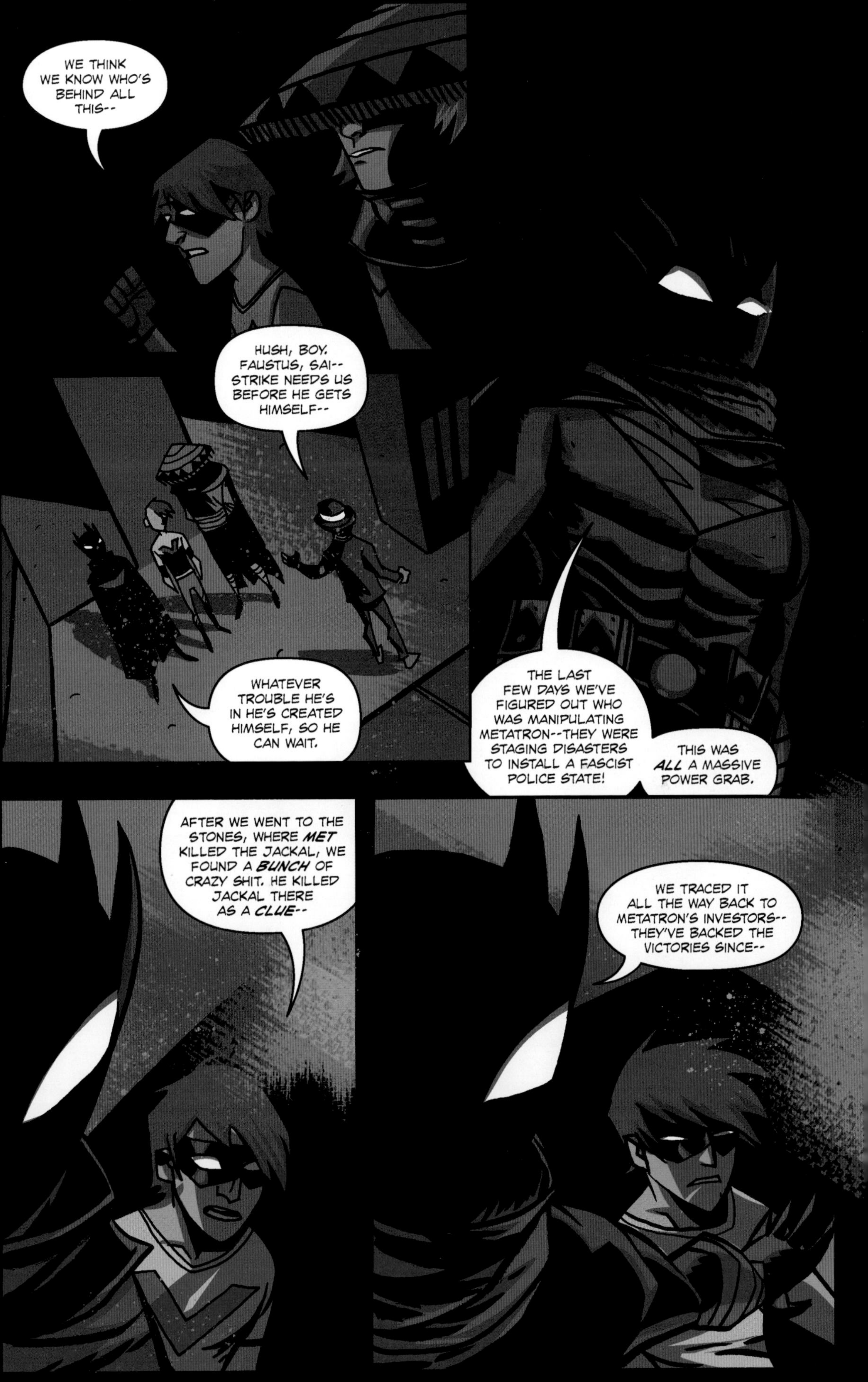
WE THINK WE KNOW WHO'S BEHIND ALL THIS--
HUSH, BOY. FAUSTUS, SAI-- STRIKE NEEDS US BEFORE HE GETS HIMSELF--
WHATEVER TROUBLE HE'S IN HE'S CREATED HIMSELF, SO HE CAN WAIT.
THE LAST FEW DAYS WE'VE FIGURED OUT WHO WAS MANIPULATING METATRON--THEY WERE STAGING DISASTERS TO INSTALL A FASCIST POLICE STATE!
THIS WAS ALL A MASSIVE POWER GRAB.
AFTER WE WENT TO THE STONES, WHERE MET KILLED THE JACKAL, WE FOUND A BUNCH OF CRAZY SHIT. HE KILLED JACKAL THERE AS A CLUE--
WE TRACED IT ALL THE WAY BACK TO METATRON'S INVESTORS-- THEY'VE BACKED THE VICTORIES SINCE--

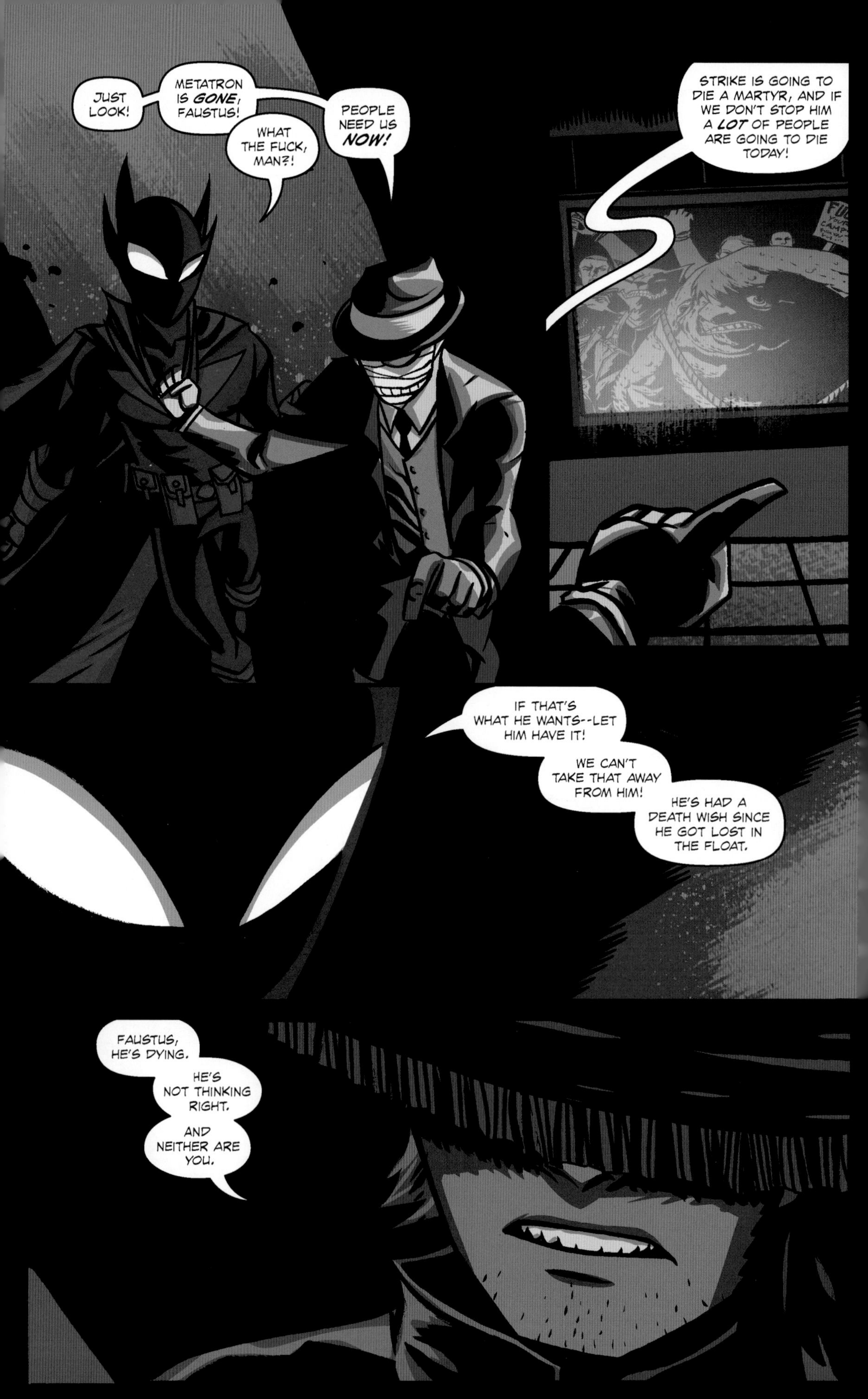
JUST LOOK!
METATRON IS GONE, FAUSTUS!
WHAT THE FUCK, MAN?!
PEOPLE NEED US NOW!
STRIKE IS GOING TO DIE A MARTYR, AND IF WE DON'T STOP HIM A LOT OF PEOPLE ARE GOING TO DIE TODAY!
IF THAT'S WHAT HE WANTS--LET HIM HAVE IT!
WE CAN'T TAKE THAT AWAY FROM HIM!
HE'S HAD A DEATH WISH SINCE HE GOT LOST IN THE FLOAT.
FAUSTUS, HE'S DYING.
HE'S NOT THINKING RIGHT.
AND NEITHER ARE YOU.

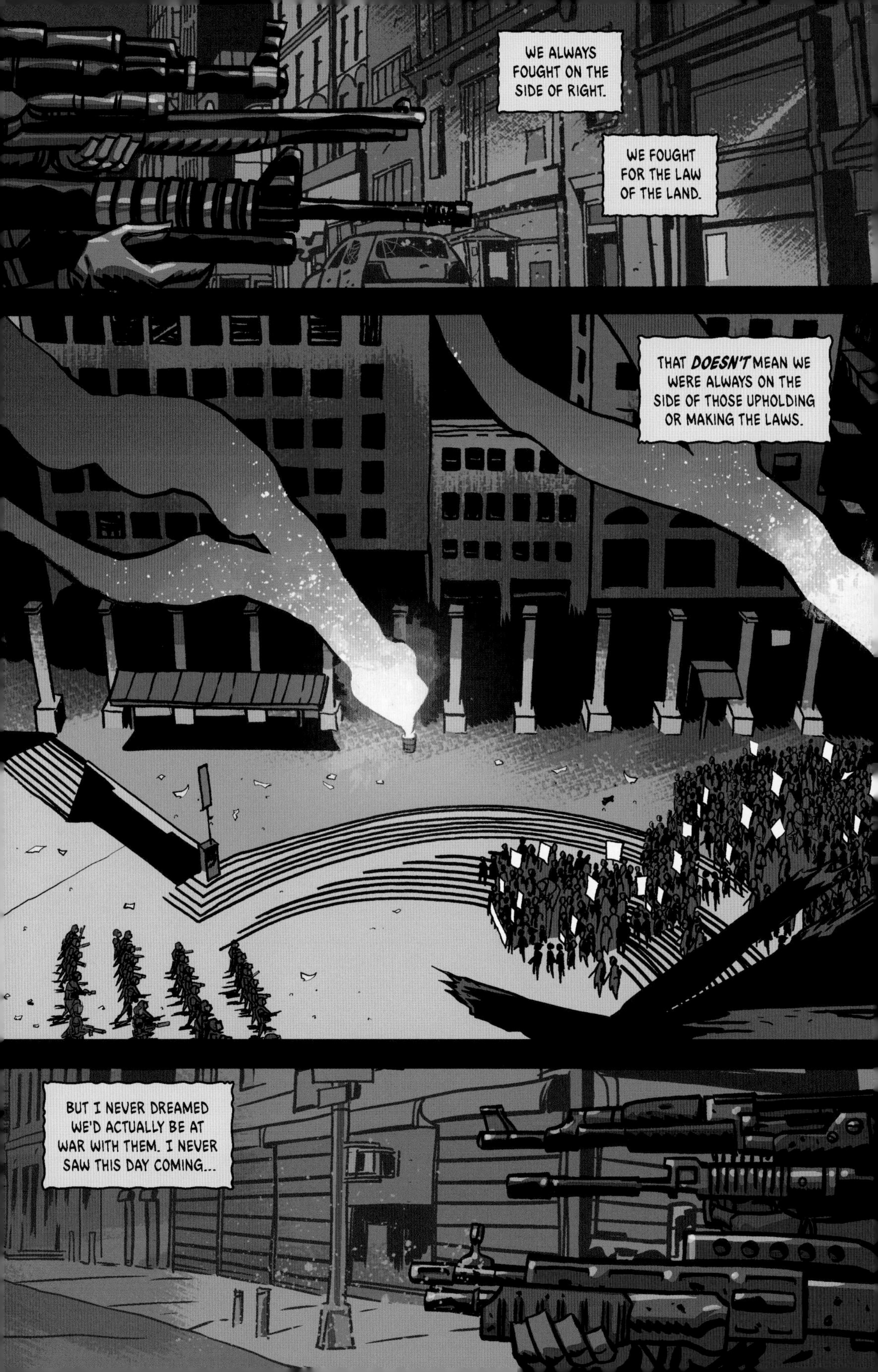
WE ALWAYS FOUGHT ON THE SIDE OF RIGHT.
WE FOUGHT FOR THE LAW OF THE LAND.
THAT DOESN'T MEAN WE WERE ALWAYS ON THE SIDE OF THOSE UPHOLDING OR MAKING THE LAWS.
BUT I NEVER DREAMED WE'D ACTUALLY BE AT WAR WITH THEM. I NEVER SAW THIS DAY COMING...

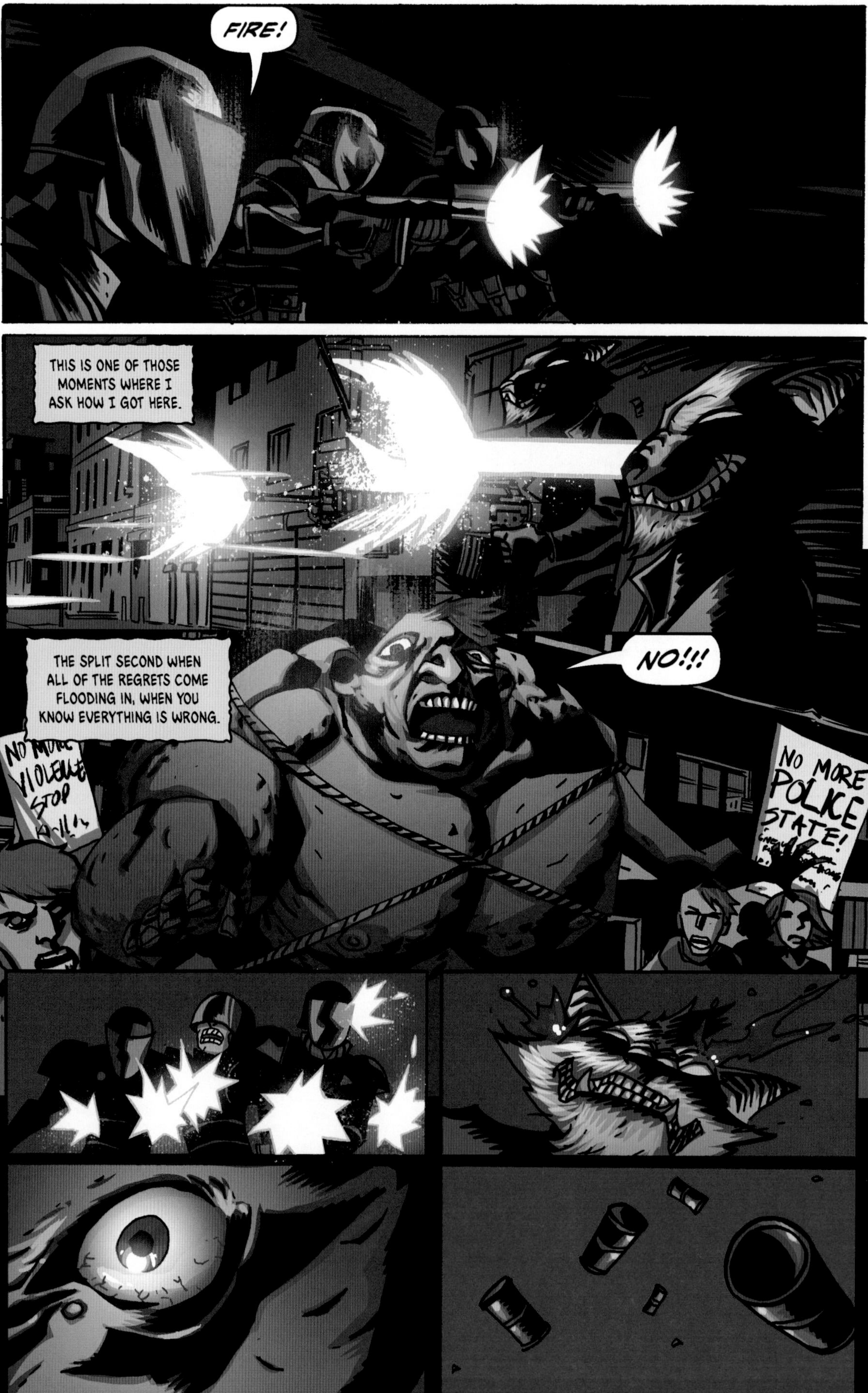
FIRE!
THIS IS ONE OF THOSE MOMENTS WHERE I ASK HOW I GOT HERE.
THE SPLIT SECOND WHEN ALL OF THE REGRETS COME FLOODING IN, WHEN YOU KNOW EVERYTHING IS WRONG.
NO!!!
NO MORE POLICE STATE!

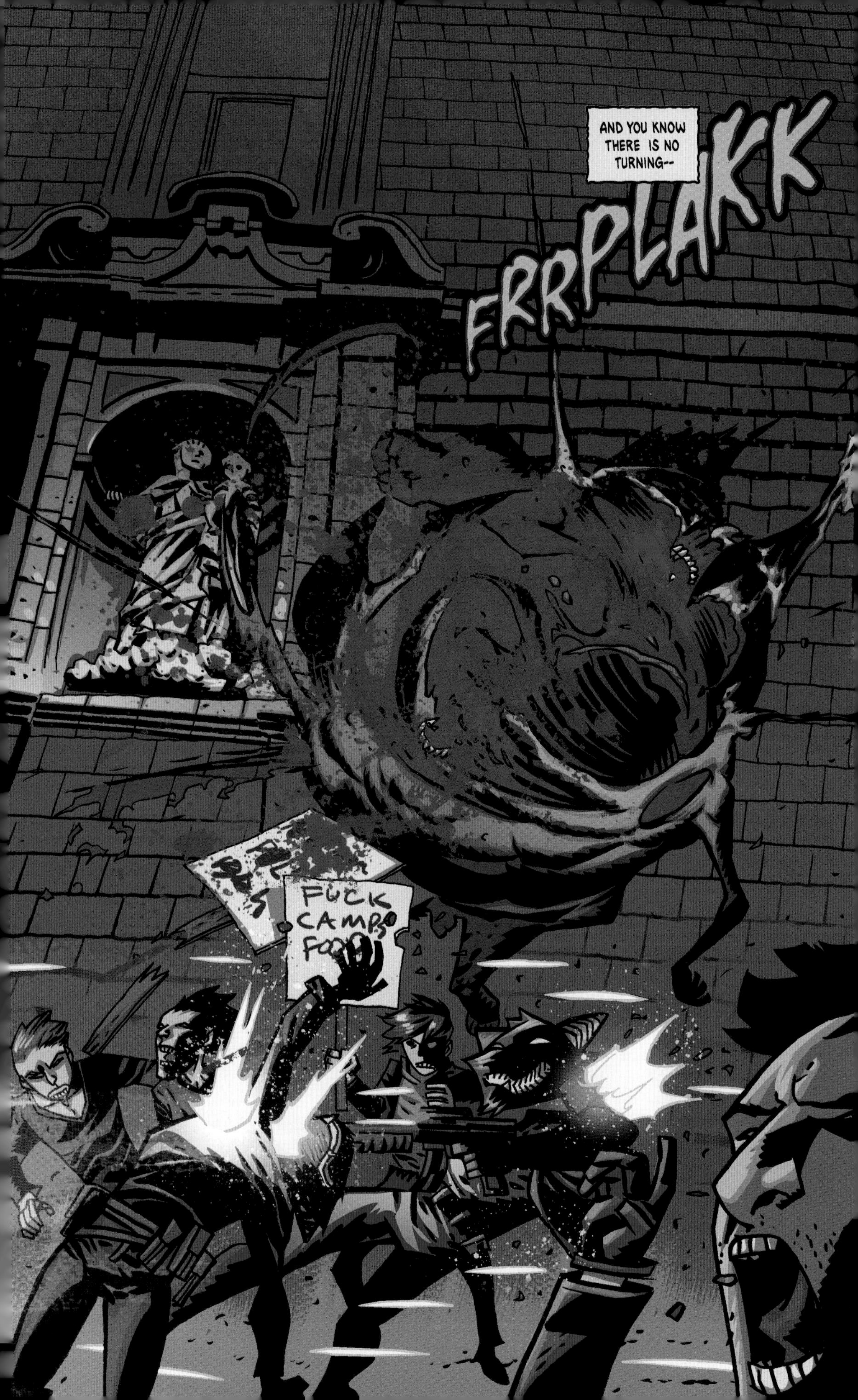
AND YOU KNOW THERE IS NO TURNING--
FRRPLAKK
FUCK CAMP

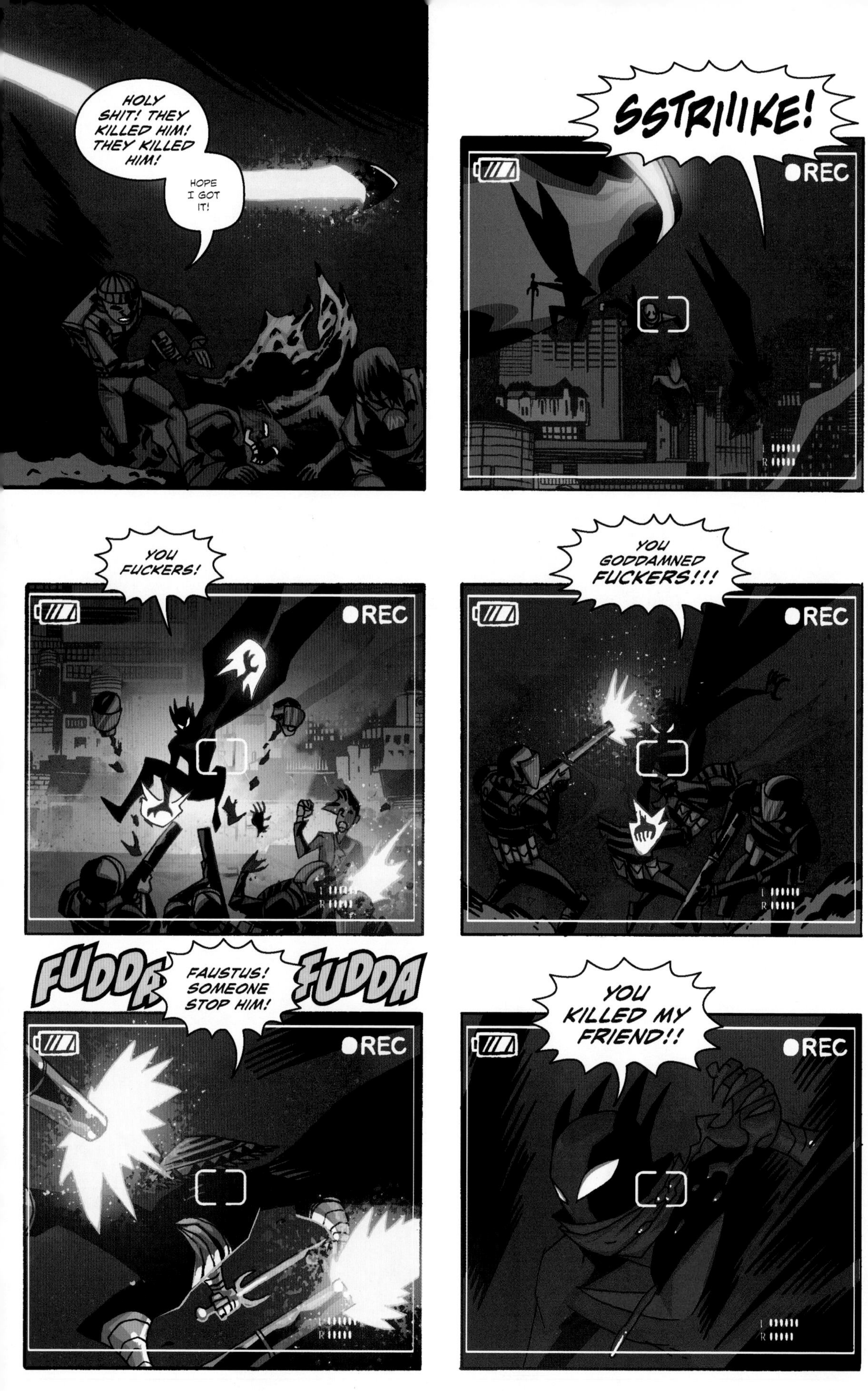
HOLY SHIT! THEY KILLED HIM! THEY KILLED HIM!
HOPE I GOT IT!
SSTRIIIKE!
REC
YOU FUCKERS!
REC
YOU GODDAMNED FUCKERS!!!
REC
FUDDA
FAUSTUS! SOMEONE STOP HIM!
FUDDA
REC
YOU KILLED MY FRIEND!!
REC

STOP IT, MAN!
OREC
WATCH IT, KID--
OREC
OREC
REINFORCE-MENTS, VICTORIES--
OREC
BOOOOOMM
WE HAVE TO RETREAT!
FUCK NO.
OREC
OREC

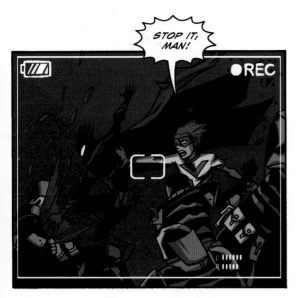

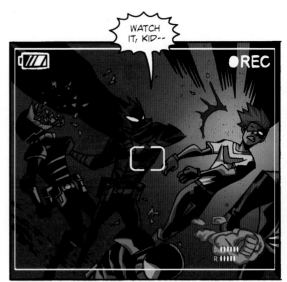

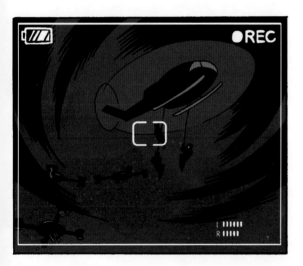

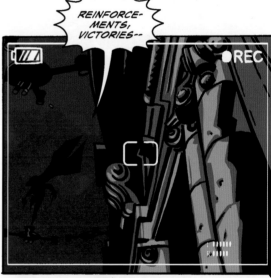

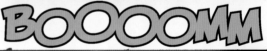

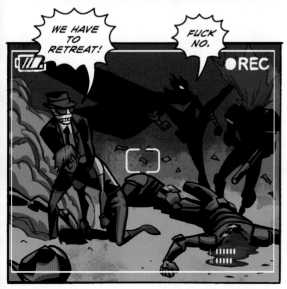

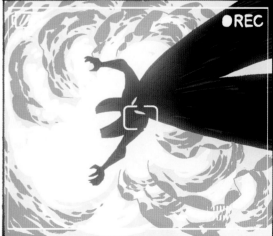

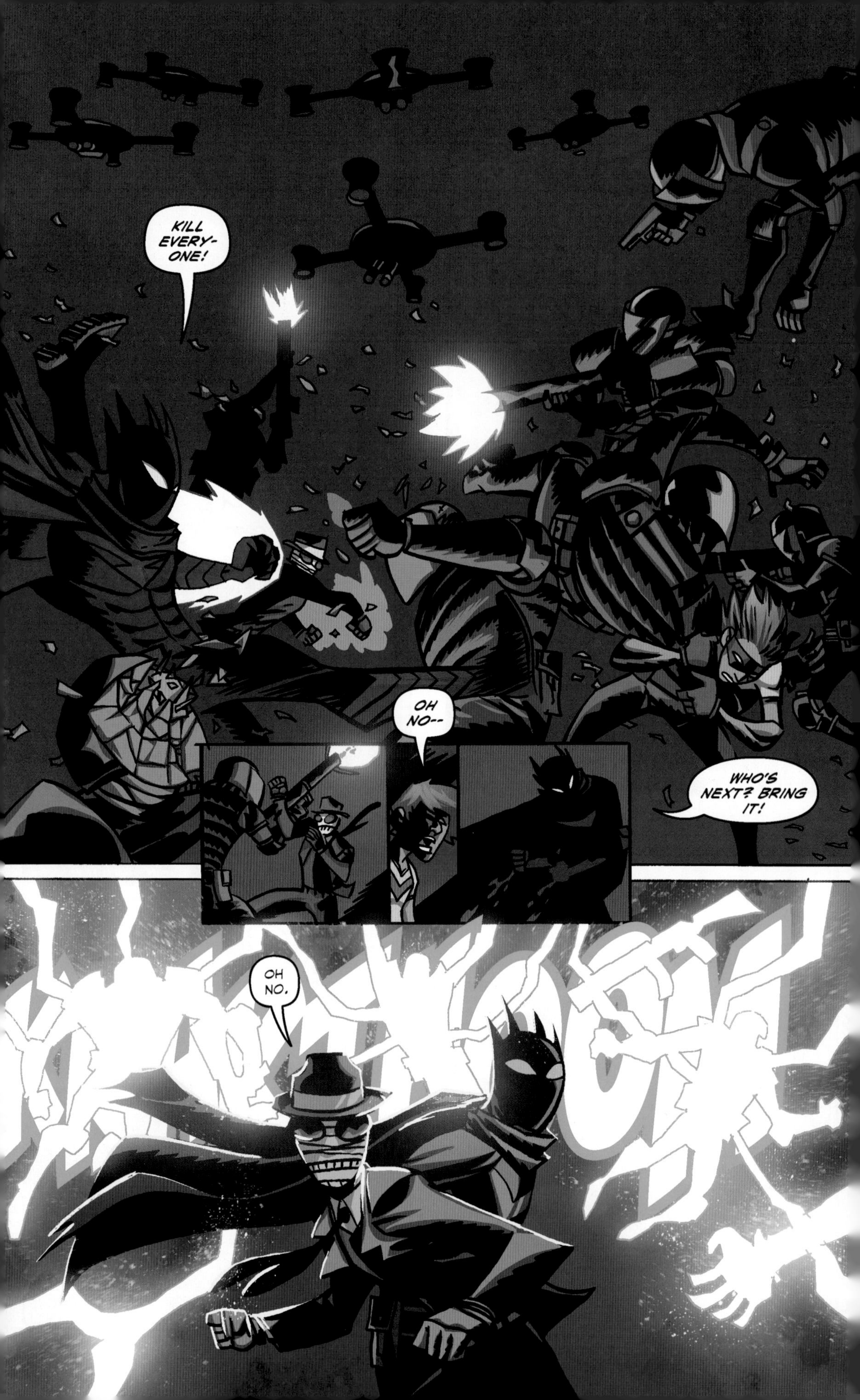
KILL EVERY-ONE!
OH NO--
WHO'S NEXT? BRING IT!
OH NO.

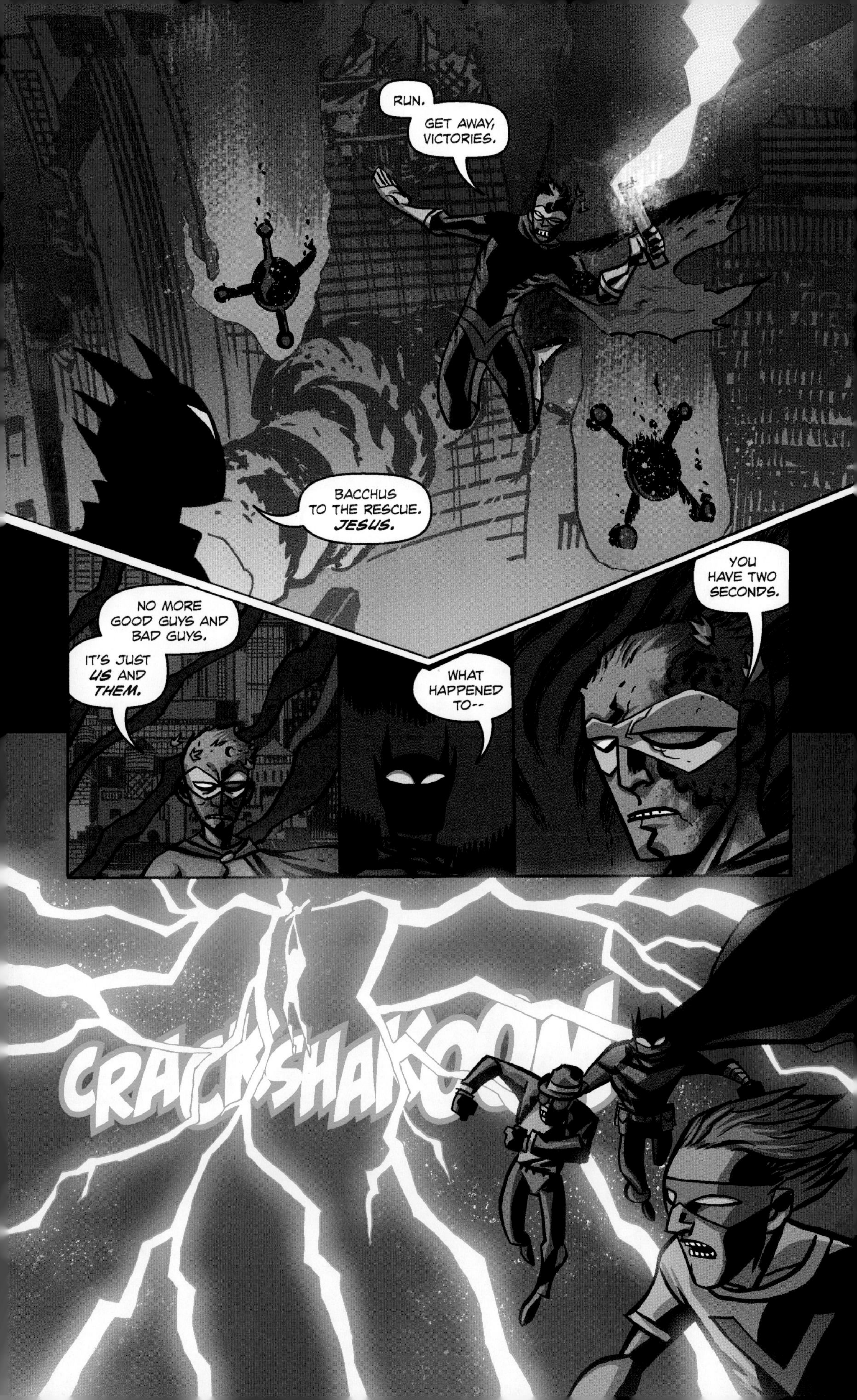
RUN.
GET AWAY, VICTORIES.
BACCHUS TO THE RESCUE. *JESUS.*
NO MORE GOOD GUYS AND BAD GUYS.
IT'S JUST *US* AND *THEM.*
WHAT HAPPENED TO--
YOU HAVE TWO SECONDS.
CRACKSHABOOM

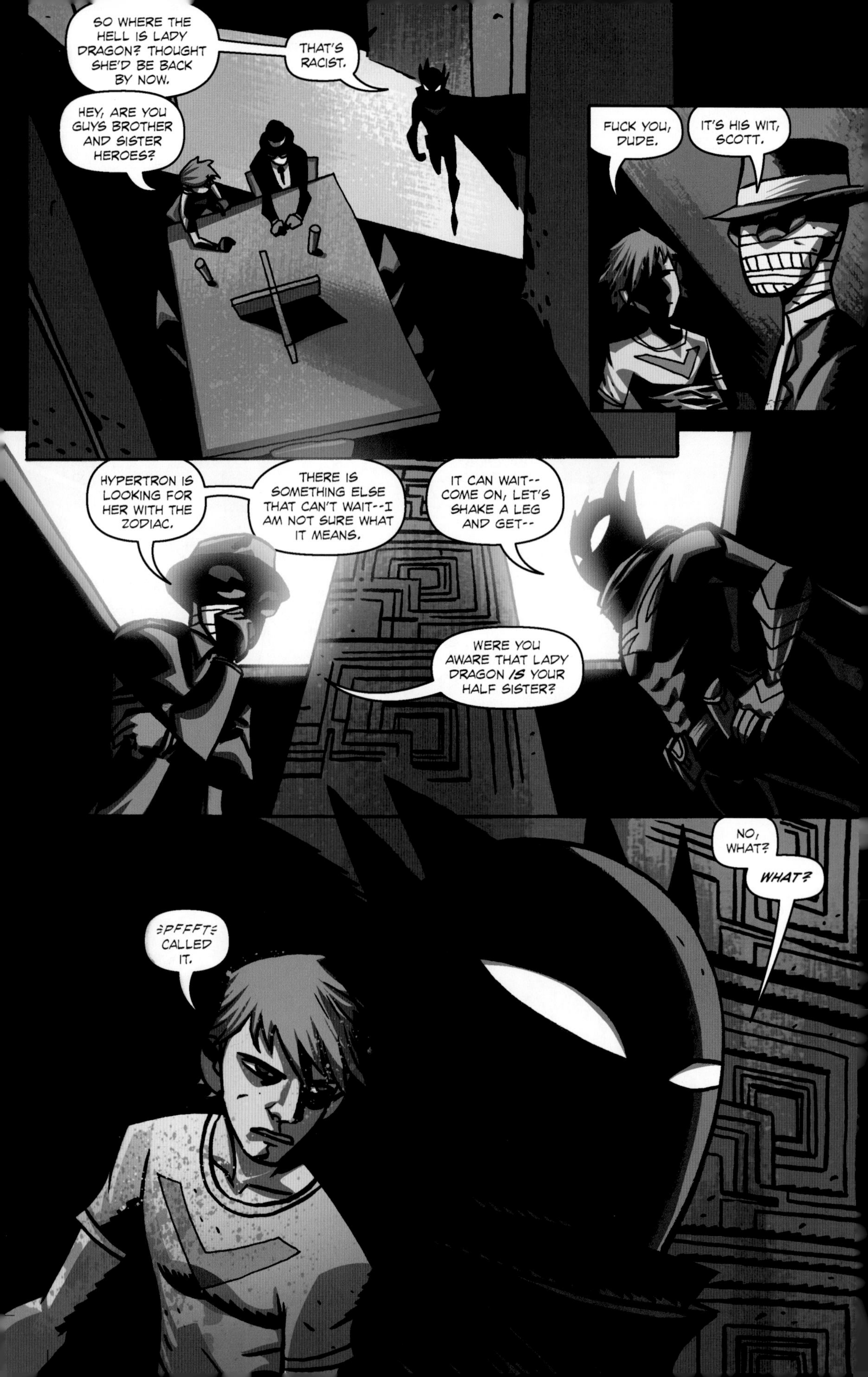
SO WHERE THE HELL IS LADY DRAGON? THOUGHT SHE'D BE BACK BY NOW.
THAT'S RACIST.
HEY, ARE YOU GUYS BROTHER AND SISTER HEROES?
FUCK YOU, DUDE.
IT'S HIS WIT, SCOTT.
HYPERTRON IS LOOKING FOR HER WITH THE ZODIAC.
THERE IS SOMETHING ELSE THAT CAN'T WAIT--I AM NOT SURE WHAT IT MEANS.
IT CAN WAIT--COME ON, LET'S SHAKE A LEG AND GET--
WERE YOU AWARE THAT LADY DRAGON *IS* YOUR HALF SISTER?
NO, WHAT?
WHAT?
PFFFT
CALLED IT.

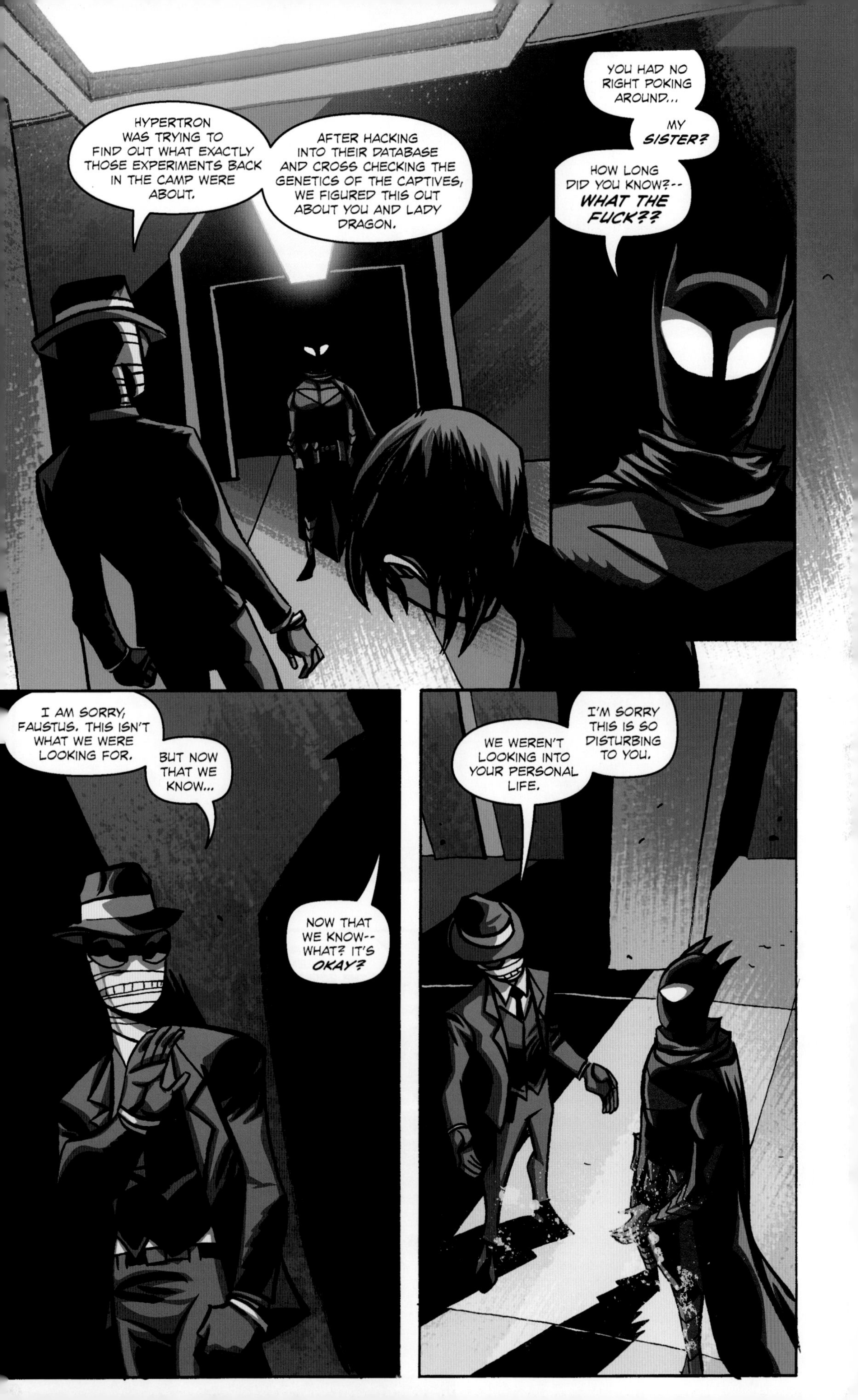
HYPERTRON WAS TRYING TO FIND OUT WHAT EXACTLY THOSE EXPERIMENTS BACK IN THE CAMP WERE ABOUT.
AFTER HACKING INTO THEIR DATABASE AND CROSS CHECKING THE GENETICS OF THE CAPTIVES, WE FIGURED THIS OUT ABOUT YOU AND LADY DRAGON.
YOU HAD NO RIGHT POKING AROUND...
MY SISTER?
HOW LONG DID YOU KNOW?-- WHAT THE FUCK??
I AM SORRY, FAUSTUS. THIS ISN'T WHAT WE WERE LOOKING FOR.
BUT NOW THAT WE KNOW...
NOW THAT WE KNOW-- WHAT? IT'S OKAY?
WE WEREN'T LOOKING INTO YOUR PERSONAL LIFE.
I'M SORRY THIS IS SO DISTURBING TO YOU.

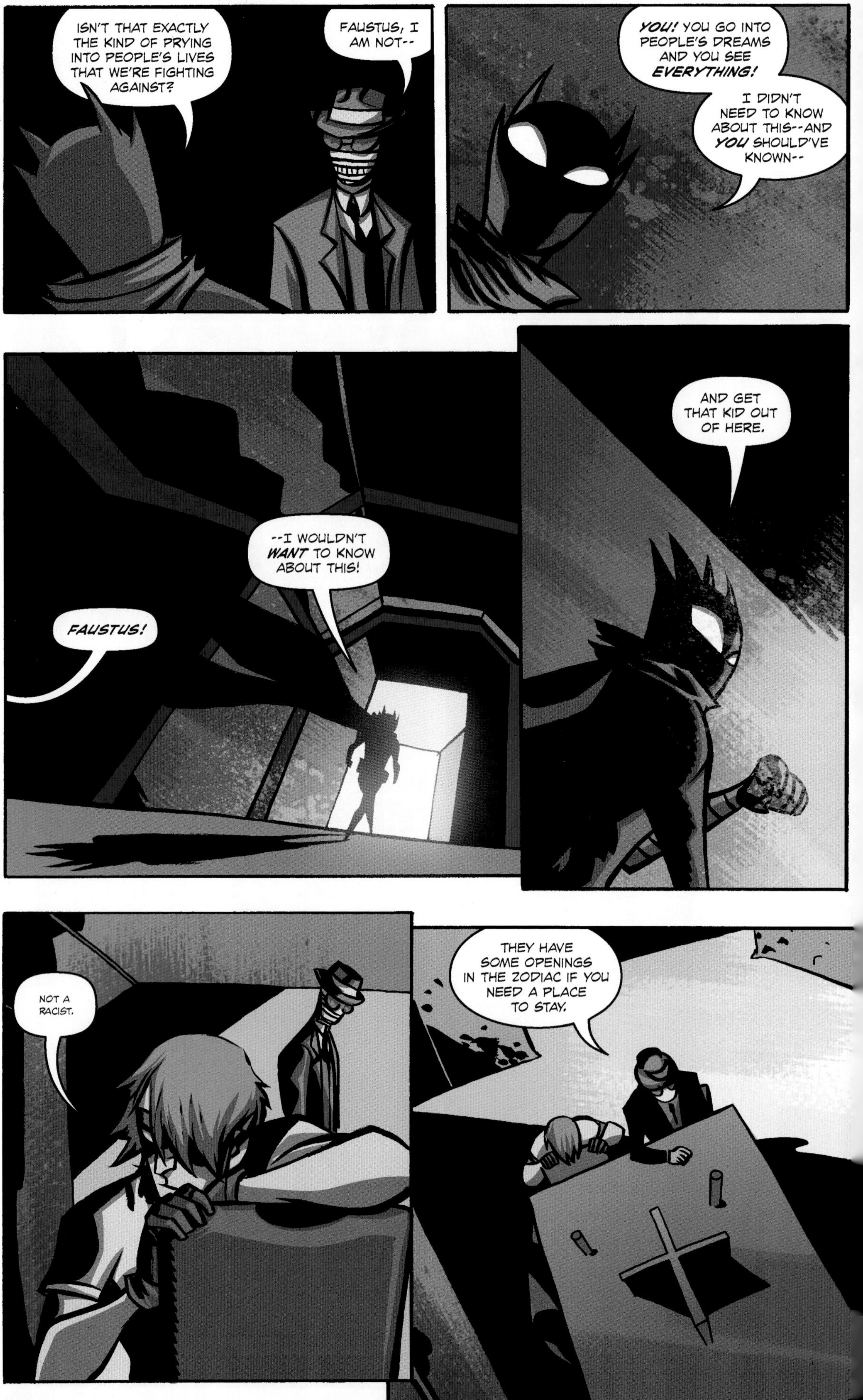
ISN'T THAT EXACTLY THE KIND OF PRYING INTO PEOPLE'S LIVES THAT WE'RE FIGHTING AGAINST?
FAUSTUS, I AM NOT--
YOU! YOU GO INTO PEOPLE'S DREAMS AND YOU SEE EVERYTHING!
I DIDN'T NEED TO KNOW ABOUT THIS--AND YOU SHOULD'VE KNOWN--
--I WOULDN'T WANT TO KNOW ABOUT THIS!
FAUSTUS!
AND GET THAT KID OUT OF HERE.
NOT A RACIST.
THEY HAVE SOME OPENINGS IN THE ZODIAC IF YOU NEED A PLACE TO STAY.

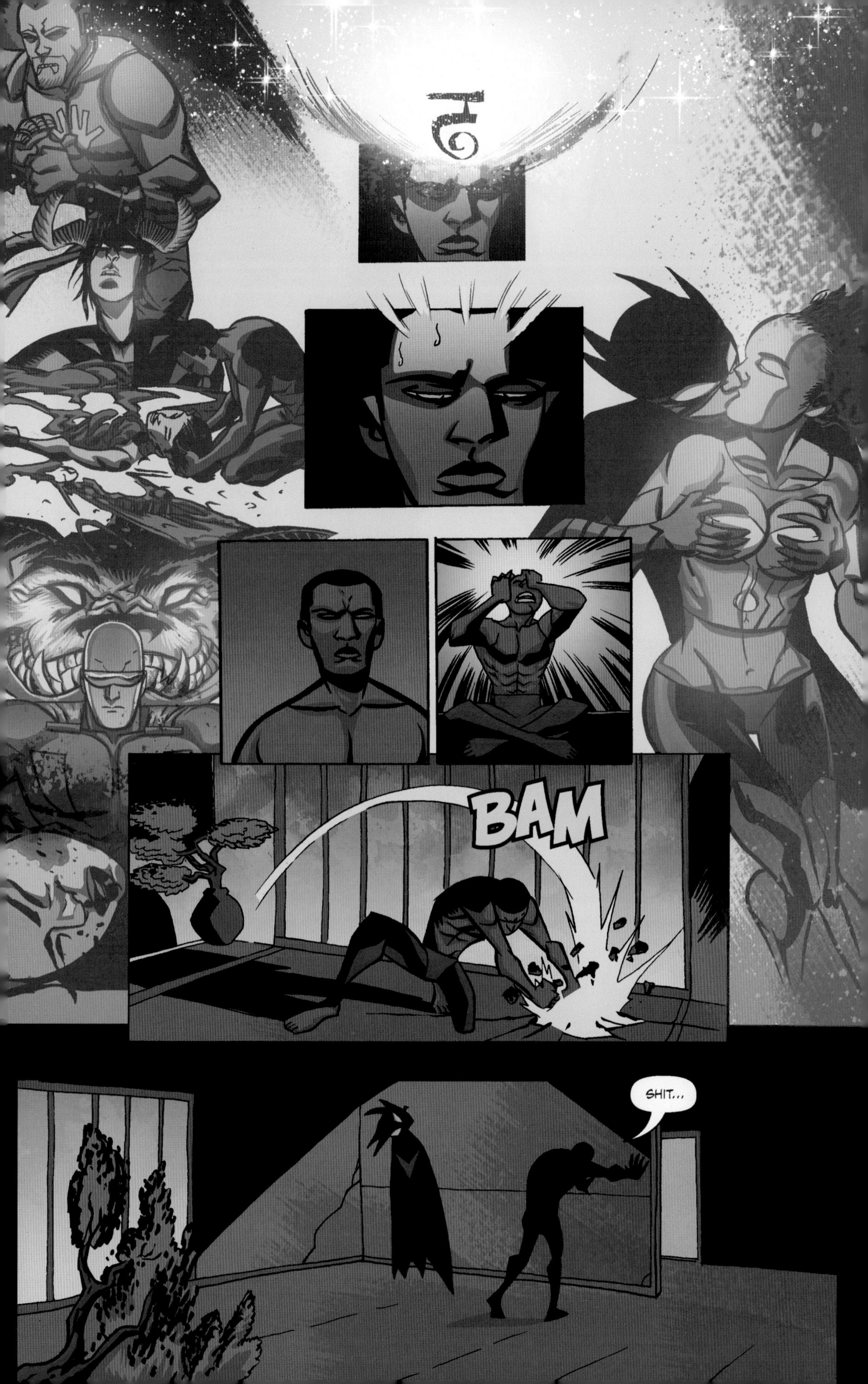
BAM
SHIT...

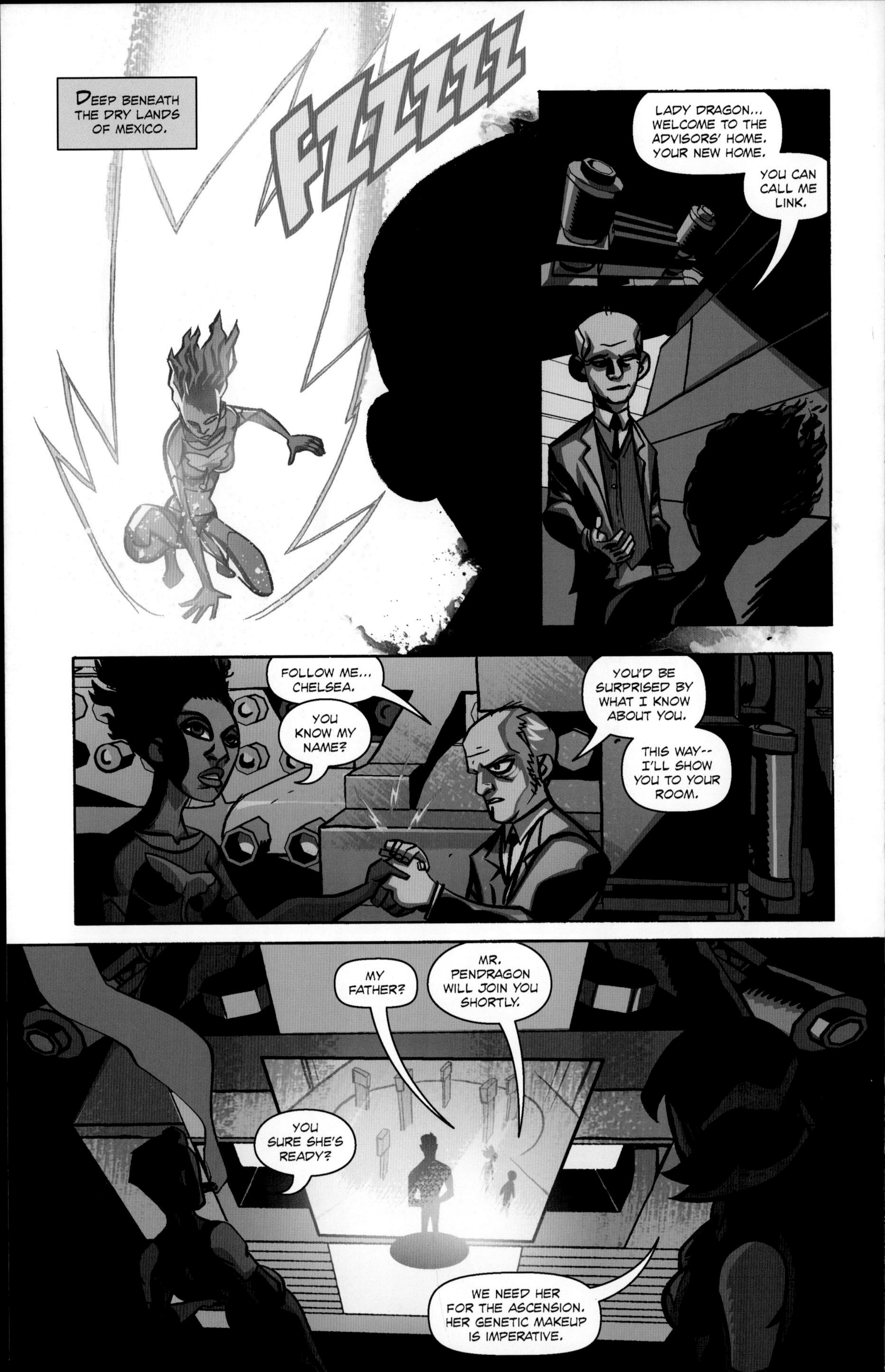
DEEP BENEATH THE DRY LANDS OF MEXICO.
FZZZZZ
LADY DRAGON... WELCOME TO THE ADVISORS' HOME. YOUR NEW HOME.
YOU CAN CALL ME LINK.
FOLLOW ME... CHELSEA.
YOU KNOW MY NAME?
YOU'D BE SURPRISED BY WHAT I KNOW ABOUT YOU.
THIS WAY-- I'LL SHOW YOU TO YOUR ROOM.
MY FATHER?
MR. PENDRAGON WILL JOIN YOU SHORTLY.
YOU SURE SHE'S READY?
WE NEED HER FOR THE ASCENSION. HER GENETIC MAKEUP IS IMPERATIVE.

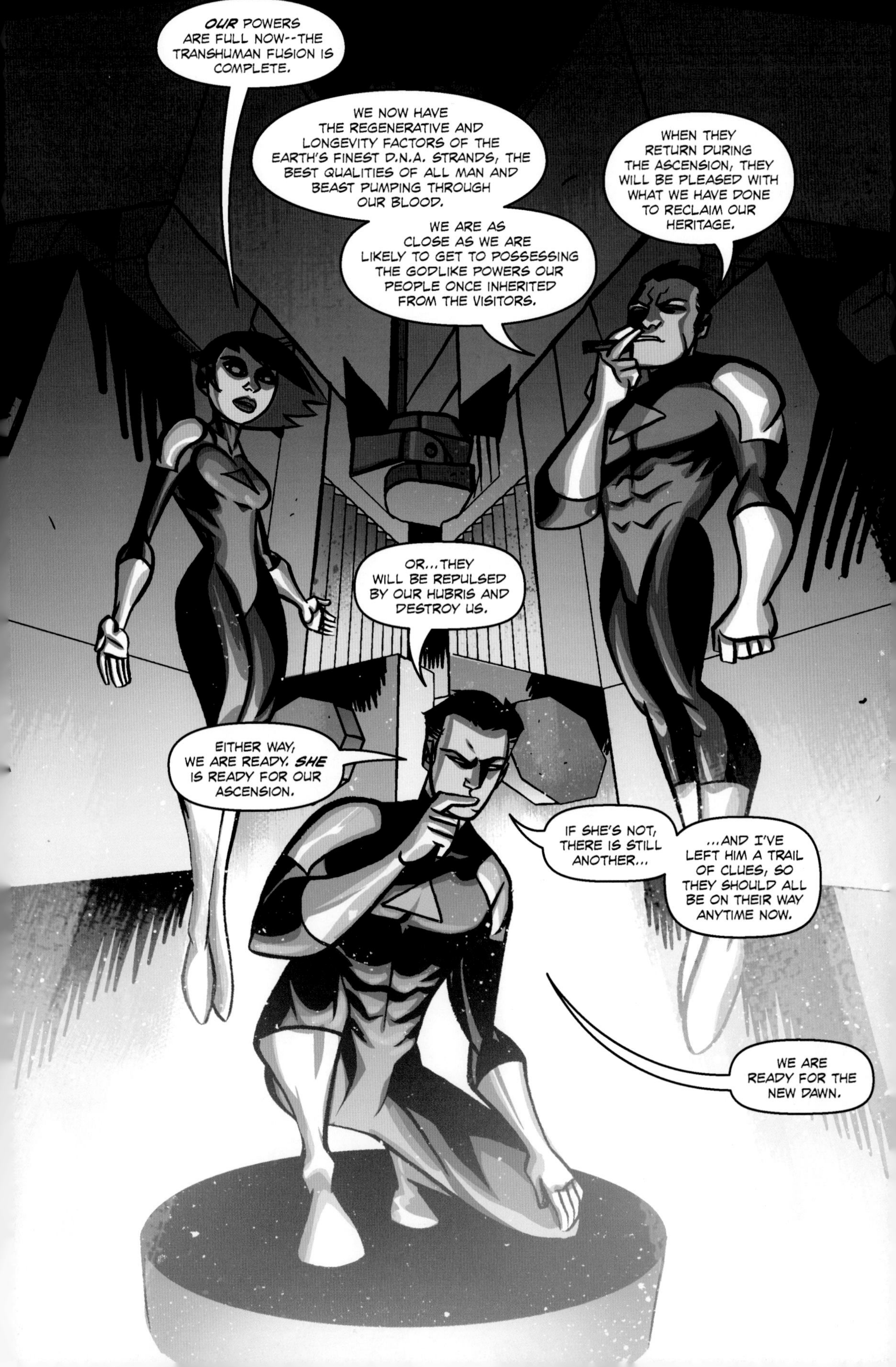
OUR POWERS ARE FULL NOW--THE TRANSHUMAN FUSION IS COMPLETE.
WE NOW HAVE THE REGENERATIVE AND LONGEVITY FACTORS OF THE EARTH'S FINEST D.N.A. STRANDS, THE BEST QUALITIES OF ALL MAN AND BEAST PUMPING THROUGH OUR BLOOD.
WE ARE AS CLOSE AS WE ARE LIKELY TO GET TO POSSESSING THE GODLIKE POWERS OUR PEOPLE ONCE INHERITED FROM THE VISITORS.
WHEN THEY RETURN DURING THE ASCENSION, THEY WILL BE PLEASED WITH WHAT WE HAVE DONE TO RECLAIM OUR HERITAGE.
OR... THEY WILL BE REPULSED BY OUR HUBRIS AND DESTROY US.
EITHER WAY, WE ARE READY. SHE IS READY FOR OUR ASCENSION.
IF SHE'S NOT, THERE IS STILL ANOTHER...
...AND I'VE LEFT HIM A TRAIL OF CLUES, SO THEY SHOULD ALL BE ON THEIR WAY ANYTIME NOW.
WE ARE READY FOR THE NEW DAWN.

CHAPTER TWO

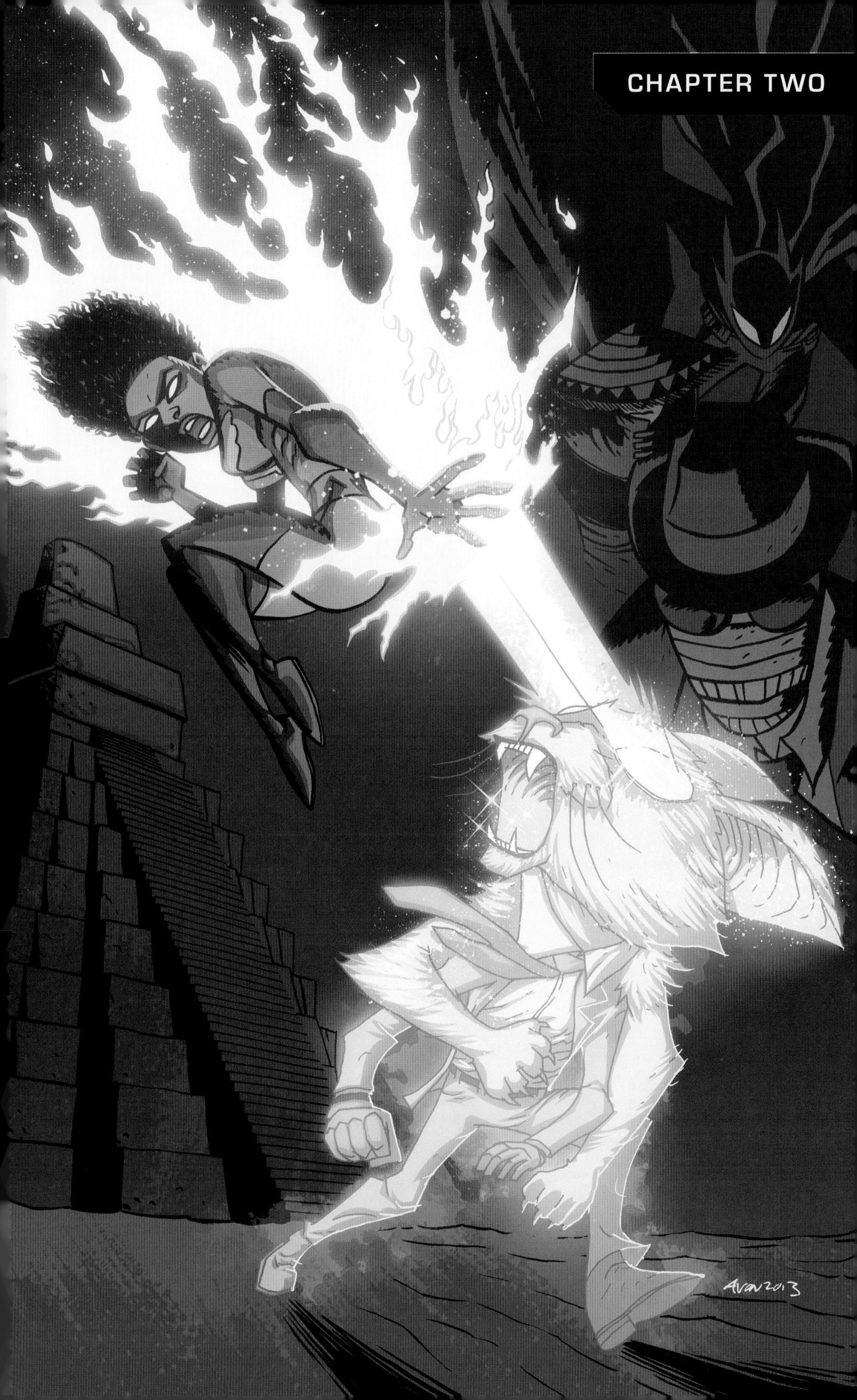

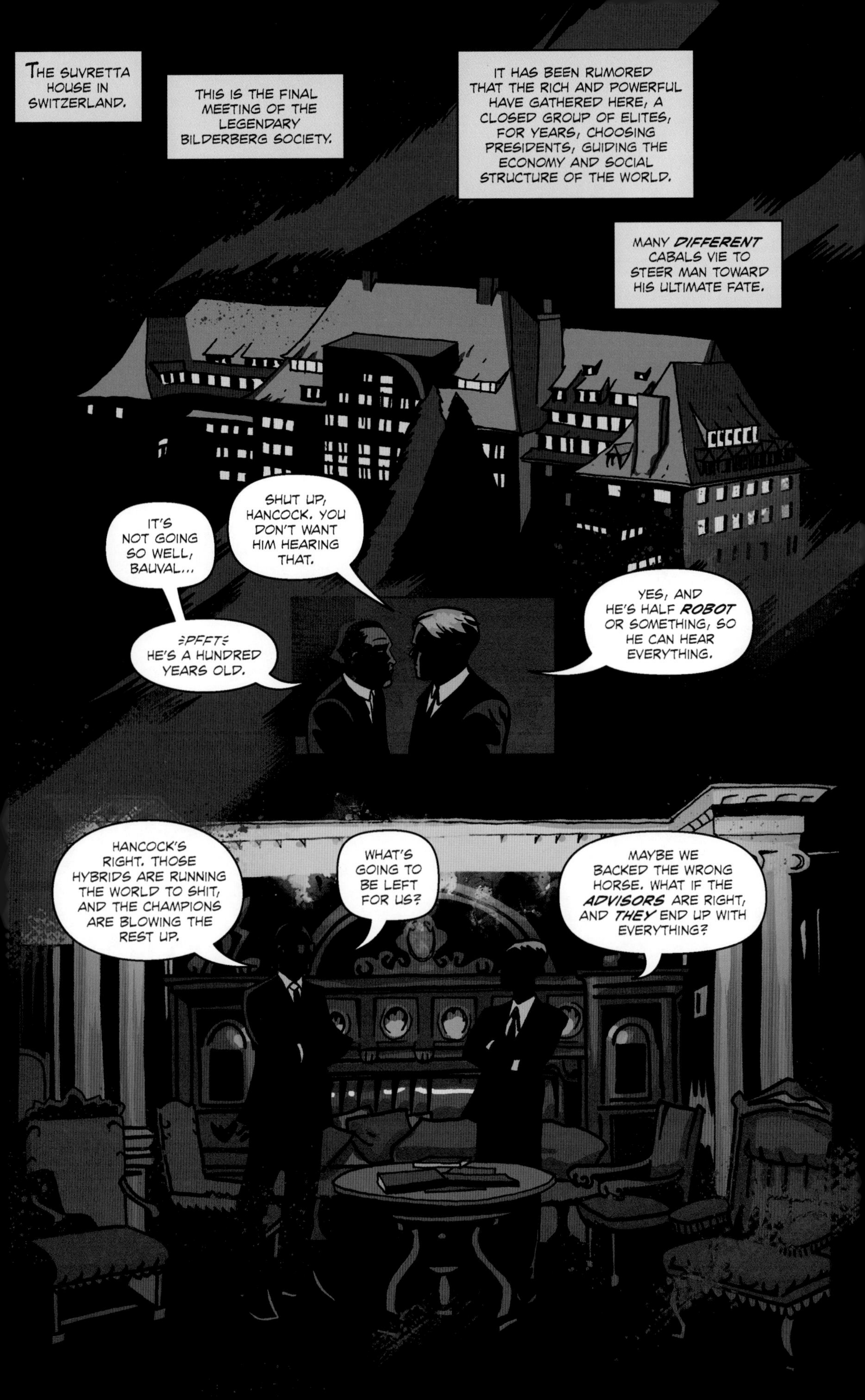
The suvretta house in Switzerland.
This is the final meeting of the legendary Bilderberg Society.
It has been rumored that the rich and powerful have gathered here, a closed group of elites, for years, choosing presidents, guiding the economy and social structure of the world.
Many *different* cabals vie to steer man toward his ultimate fate.
It's not going so well, Bauval...
Shut up, Hancock. You don't want him hearing that.
pfft He's a hundred years old.
Yes, and he's half *robot* or something, so he can hear everything.
Hancock's right. Those hybrids are running the world to shit, and the champions are blowing the rest up.
What's going to be left for us?
Maybe we backed the wrong horse. What if the *advisors* are right, and *they* end up with everything?

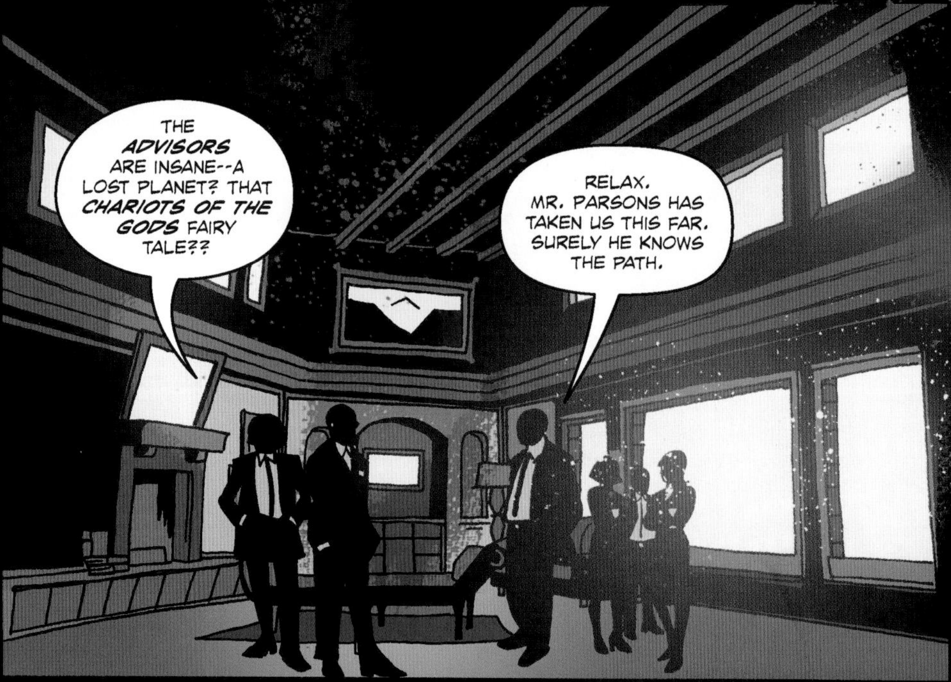
THE *ADVISORS* ARE INSANE--A LOST PLANET? THAT *CHARIOTS OF THE GODS* FAIRY TALE??
RELAX. MR. PARSONS HAS TAKEN US THIS FAR. SURELY HE KNOWS THE PATH.

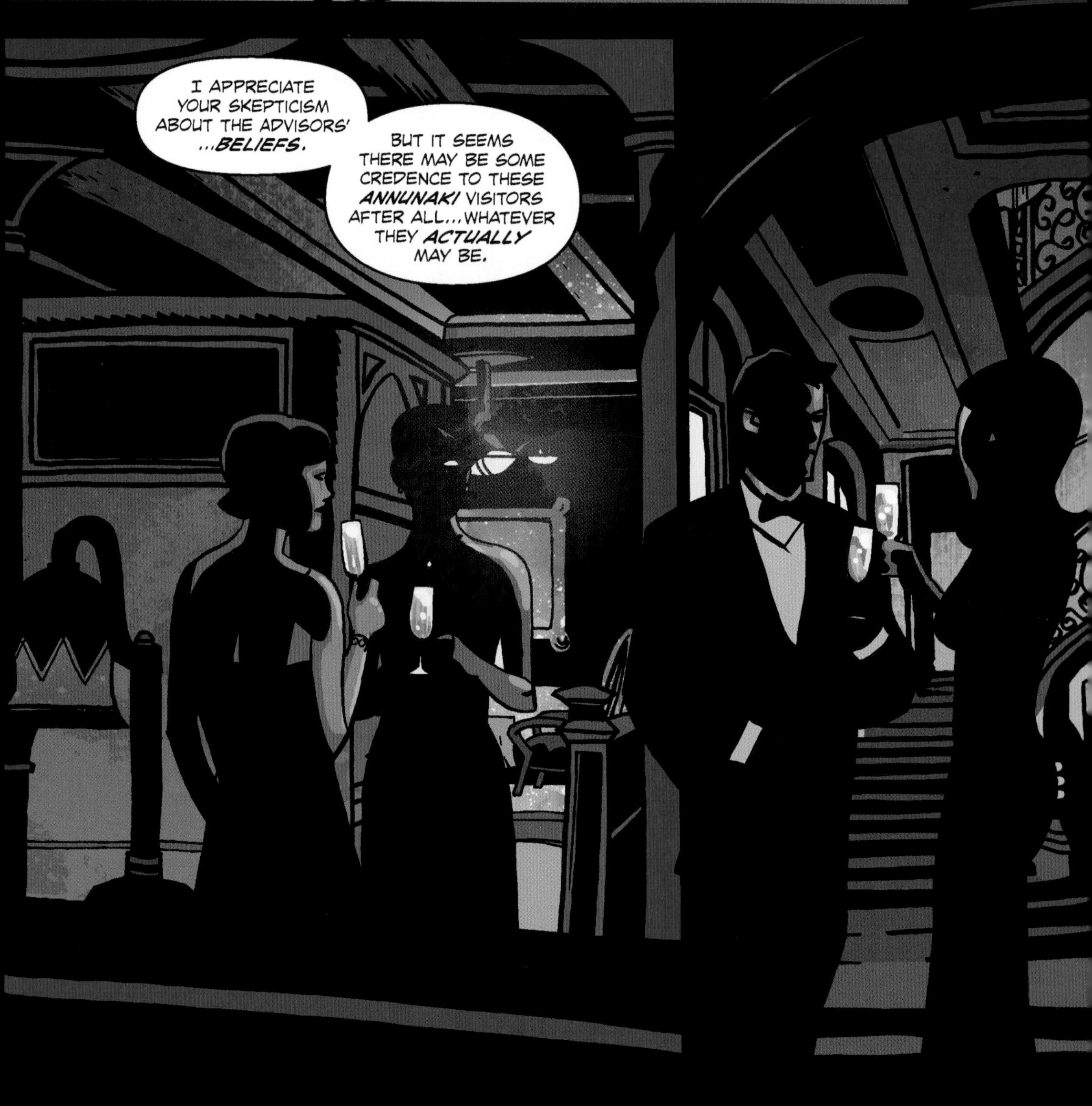
I APPRECIATE YOUR SKEPTICISM ABOUT THE ADVISORS' ...*BELIEFS*.
BUT IT SEEMS THERE MAY BE SOME CREDENCE TO THESE *ANNUNAKI* VISITORS AFTER ALL...WHATEVER THEY *ACTUALLY* MAY BE.

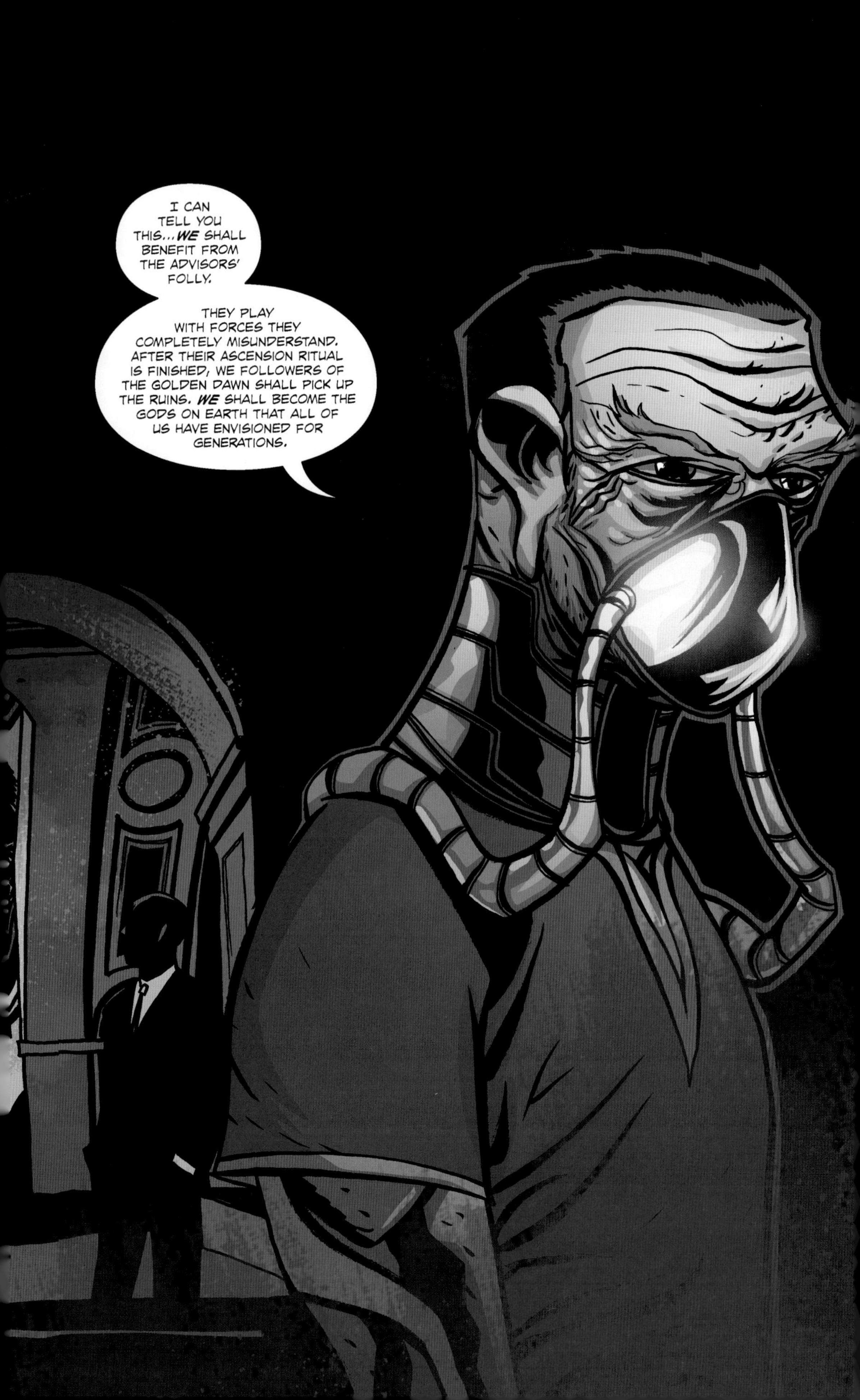
I CAN TELL YOU THIS... *WE* SHALL BENEFIT FROM THE ADVISORS' FOLLY.
THEY PLAY WITH FORCES THEY COMPLETELY MISUNDERSTAND. AFTER THEIR ASCENSION RITUAL IS FINISHED, WE FOLLOWERS OF THE GOLDEN DAWN SHALL PICK UP THE RUINS. *WE* SHALL BECOME THE GODS ON EARTH THAT ALL OF US HAVE ENVISIONED FOR GENERATIONS.

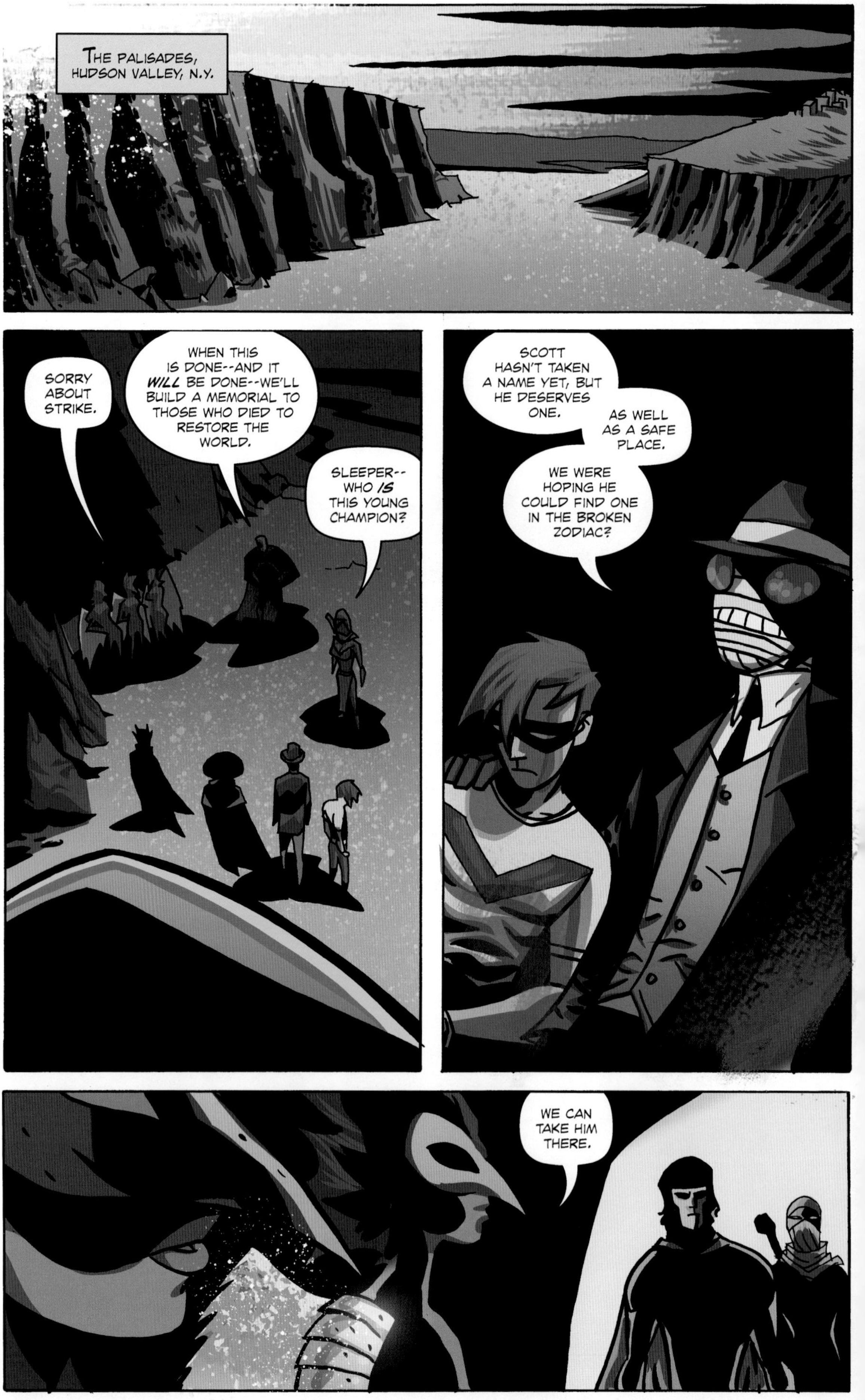
THE PALISADES, HUDSON VALLEY, N.Y.
SORRY ABOUT STRIKE.
WHEN THIS IS DONE--AND IT WILL BE DONE--WE'LL BUILD A MEMORIAL TO THOSE WHO DIED TO RESTORE THE WORLD.
SLEEPER--WHO IS THIS YOUNG CHAMPION?
SCOTT HASN'T TAKEN A NAME YET, BUT HE DESERVES ONE.
AS WELL AS A SAFE PLACE.
WE WERE HOPING HE COULD FIND ONE IN THE BROKEN ZODIAC?
WE CAN TAKE HIM THERE.

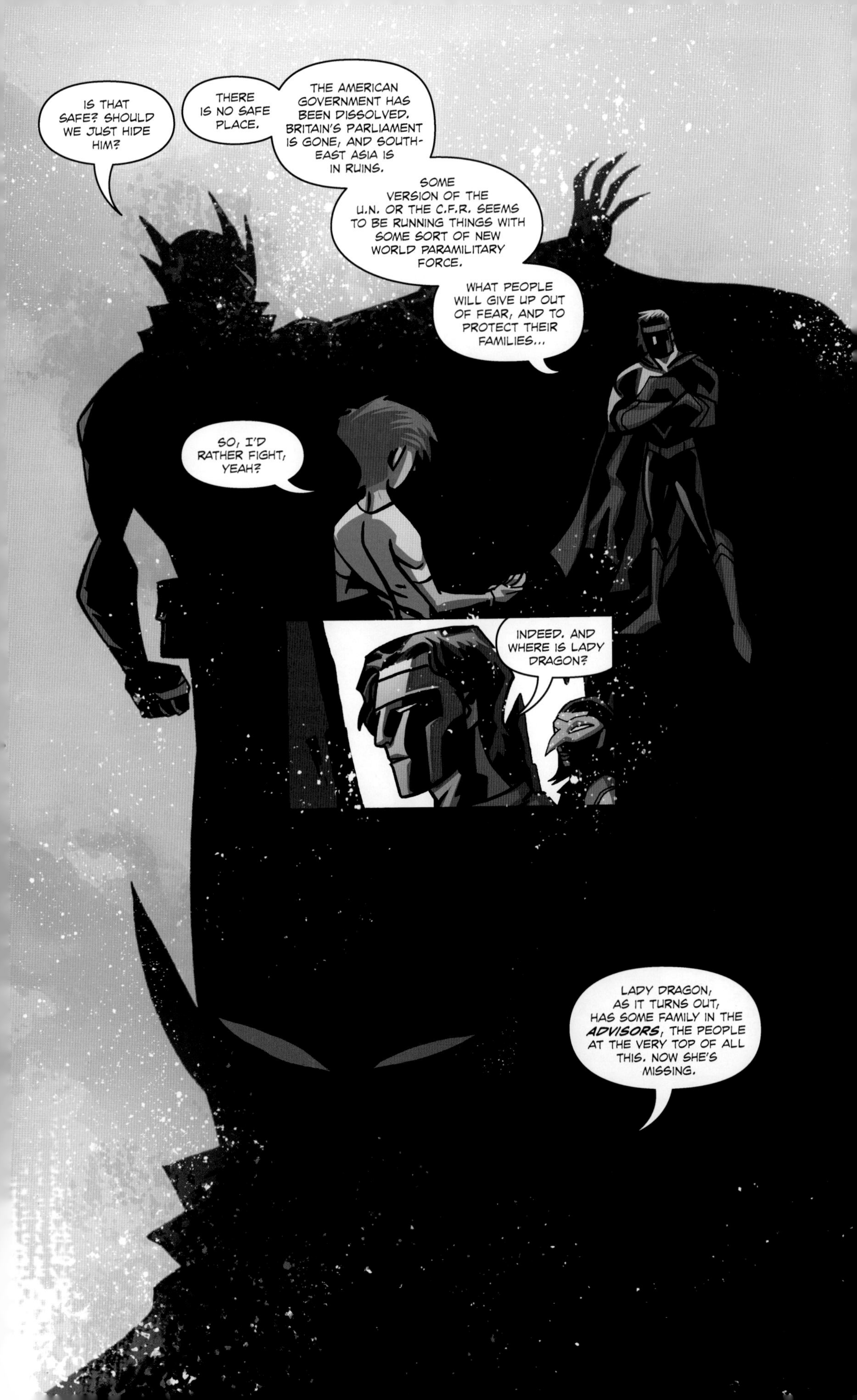
IS THAT SAFE? SHOULD WE JUST HIDE HIM?
THERE IS NO SAFE PLACE.
THE AMERICAN GOVERNMENT HAS BEEN DISSOLVED. BRITAIN'S PARLIAMENT IS GONE, AND SOUTH-EAST ASIA IS IN RUINS.
SOME VERSION OF THE U.N. OR THE C.F.R. SEEMS TO BE RUNNING THINGS WITH SOME SORT OF NEW WORLD PARAMILITARY FORCE.
WHAT PEOPLE WILL GIVE UP OUT OF FEAR, AND TO PROTECT THEIR FAMILIES...
SO, I'D RATHER FIGHT, YEAH?
INDEED. AND WHERE IS LADY DRAGON?
LADY DRAGON, AS IT TURNS OUT, HAS SOME FAMILY IN THE *ADVISORS*, THE PEOPLE AT THE VERY TOP OF ALL THIS. NOW SHE'S MISSING.

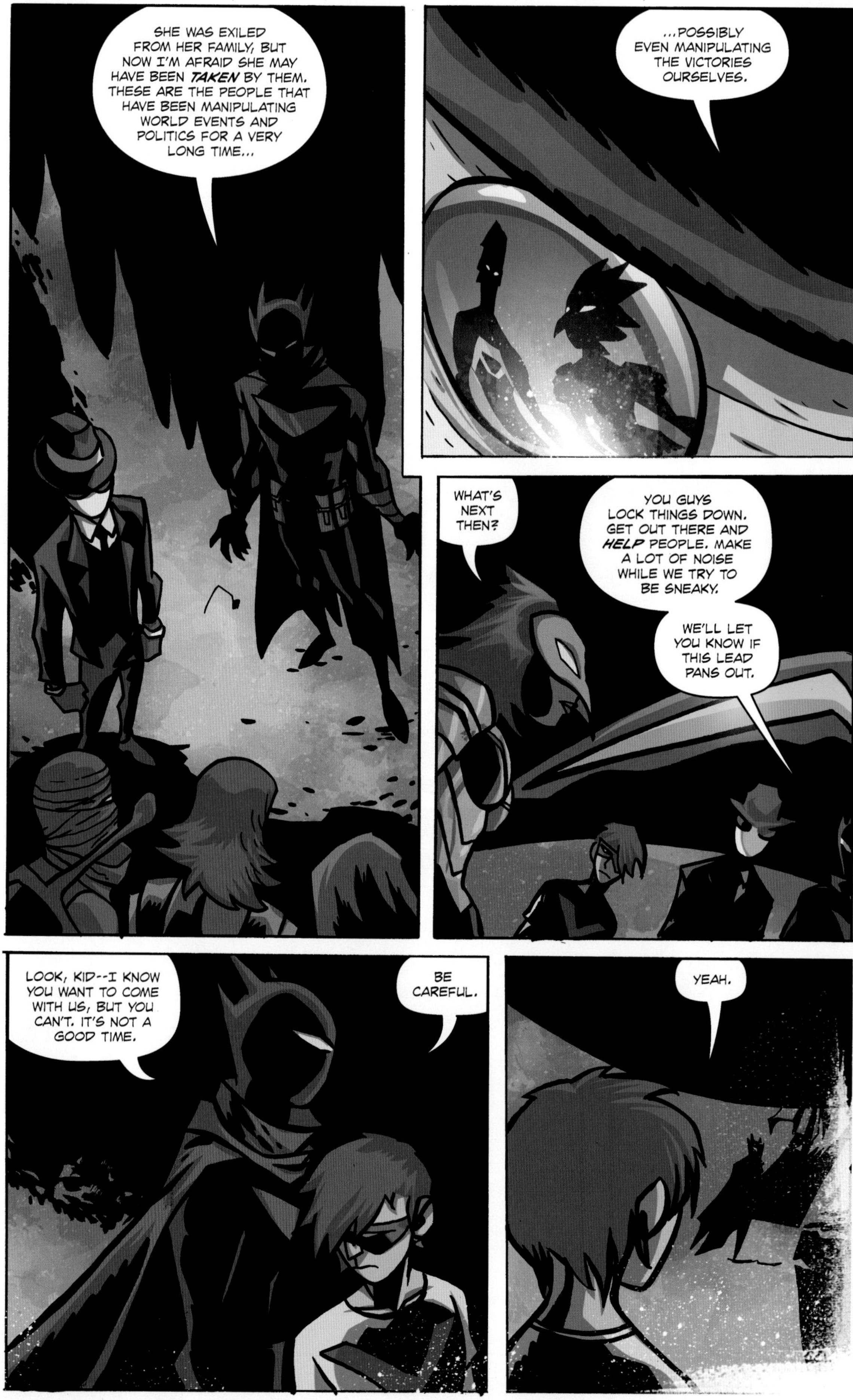
SHE WAS EXILED FROM HER FAMILY, BUT NOW I'M AFRAID SHE MAY HAVE BEEN *TAKEN* BY THEM. THESE ARE THE PEOPLE THAT HAVE BEEN MANIPULATING WORLD EVENTS AND POLITICS FOR A VERY LONG TIME...
...POSSIBLY EVEN MANIPULATING THE VICTORIES OURSELVES.
WHAT'S NEXT THEN?
YOU GUYS LOCK THINGS DOWN. GET OUT THERE AND *HELP* PEOPLE. MAKE A LOT OF NOISE WHILE WE TRY TO BE SNEAKY.
WE'LL LET YOU KNOW IF THIS LEAD PANS OUT.
LOOK, KID--I KNOW YOU WANT TO COME WITH US, BUT YOU CAN'T. IT'S NOT A GOOD TIME.
BE CAREFUL.
YEAH.

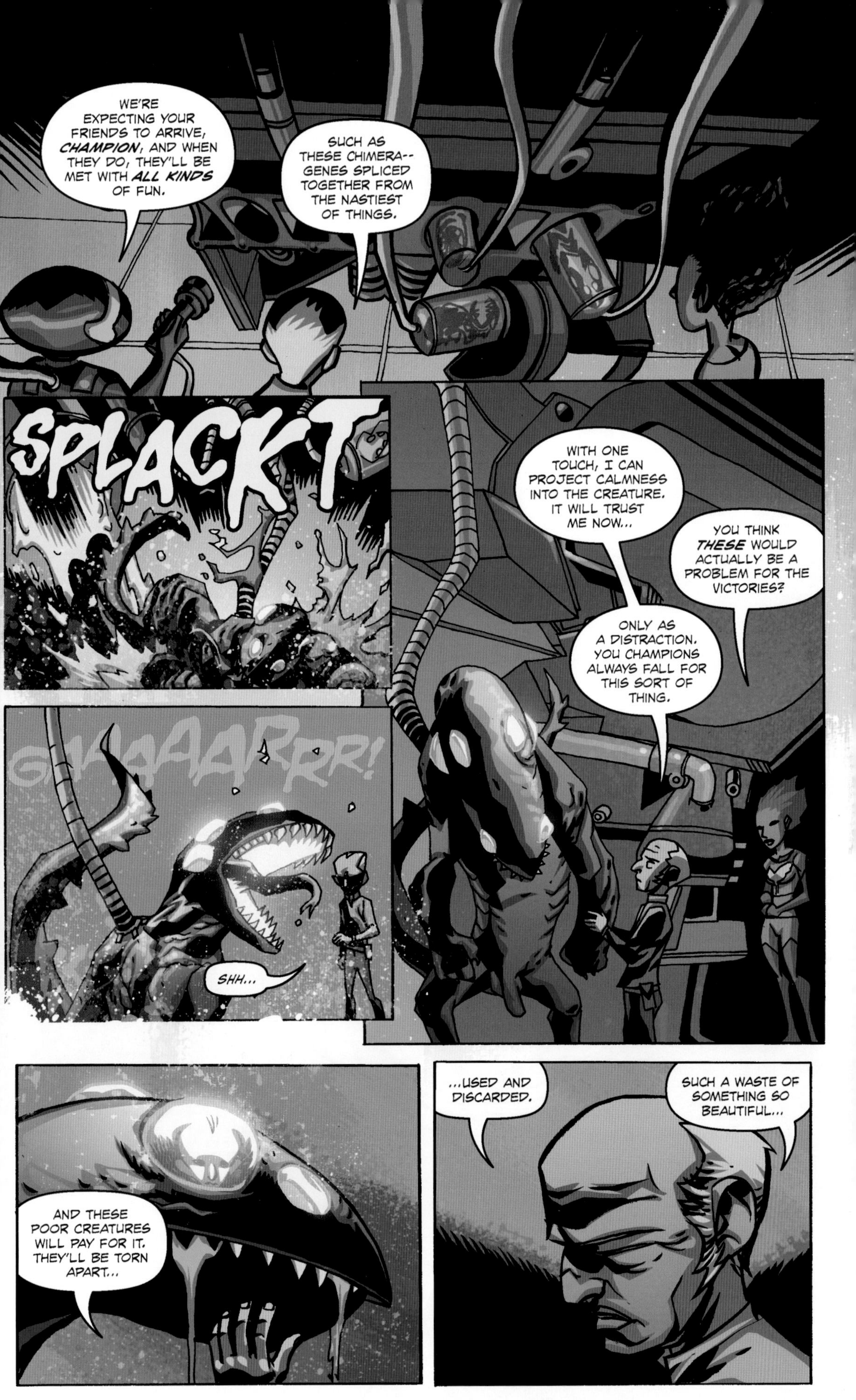

WE'RE EXPECTING YOUR FRIENDS TO ARRIVE, CHAMPION, AND WHEN THEY DO, THEY'LL BE MET WITH ALL KINDS OF FUN.
SUCH AS THESE CHIMERA-- GENES SPLICED TOGETHER FROM THE NASTIEST OF THINGS.
SPLACKT
GAAAAARRR!
SHH...
WITH ONE TOUCH, I CAN PROJECT CALMNESS INTO THE CREATURE. IT WILL TRUST ME NOW...
YOU THINK THESE WOULD ACTUALLY BE A PROBLEM FOR THE VICTORIES?
ONLY AS A DISTRACTION. YOU CHAMPIONS ALWAYS FALL FOR THIS SORT OF THING.
AND THESE POOR CREATURES WILL PAY FOR IT. THEY'LL BE TORN APART...
...USED AND DISCARDED.
SUCH A WASTE OF SOMETHING SO BEAUTIFUL...

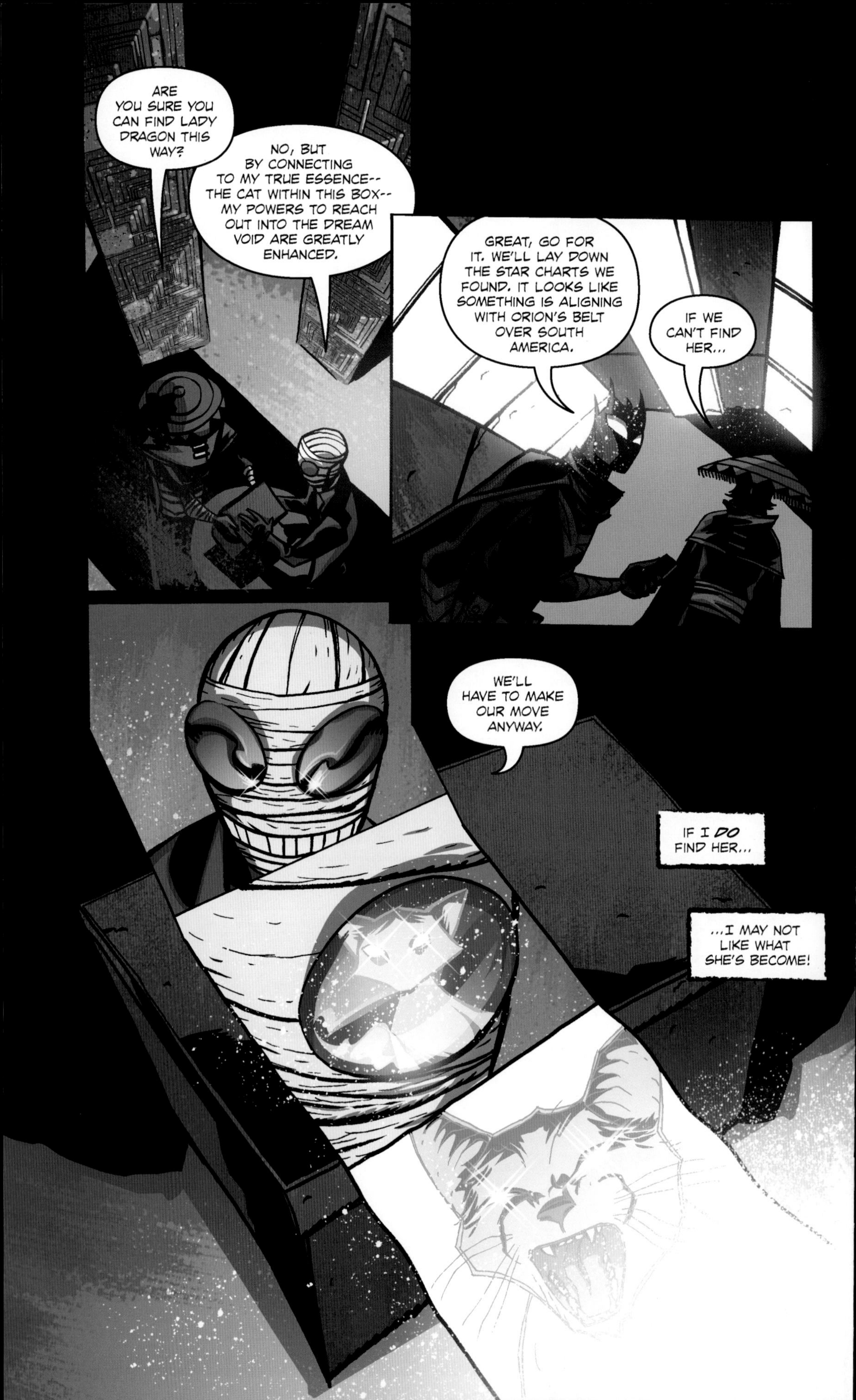
ARE YOU SURE YOU CAN FIND LADY DRAGON THIS WAY?
NO, BUT BY CONNECTING TO MY TRUE ESSENCE-- THE CAT WITHIN THIS BOX-- MY POWERS TO REACH OUT INTO THE DREAM VOID ARE GREATLY ENHANCED.
GREAT, GO FOR IT. WE'LL LAY DOWN THE STAR CHARTS WE FOUND. IT LOOKS LIKE SOMETHING IS ALIGNING WITH ORION'S BELT OVER SOUTH AMERICA.
IF WE CAN'T FIND HER...
WE'LL HAVE TO MAKE OUR MOVE ANYWAY.
IF I *DO* FIND HER...
...I MAY NOT LIKE WHAT SHE'S BECOME!

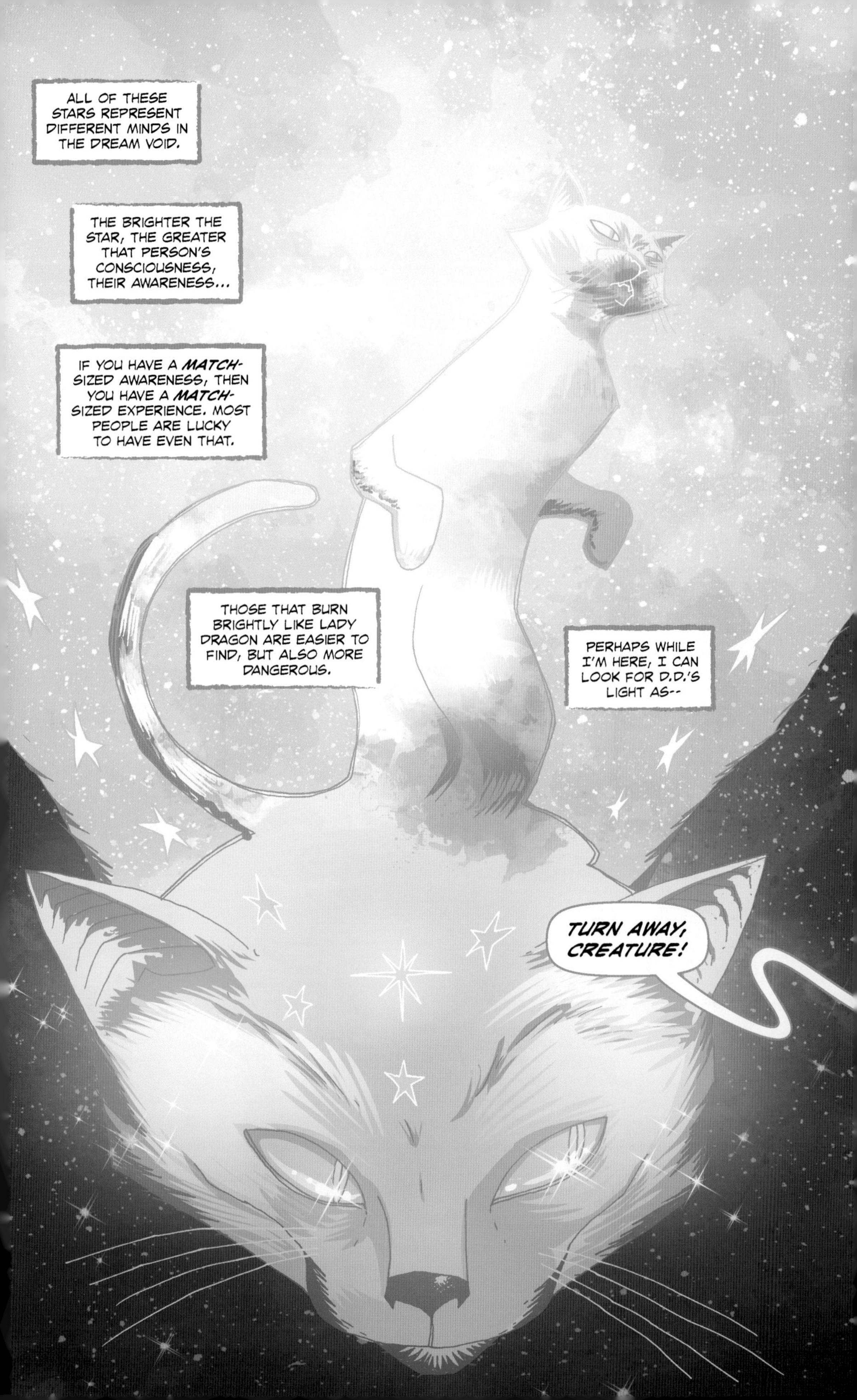
ALL OF THESE STARS REPRESENT DIFFERENT MINDS IN THE DREAM VOID.
THE BRIGHTER THE STAR, THE GREATER THAT PERSON'S CONSCIOUSNESS, THEIR AWARENESS...
IF YOU HAVE A *MATCH*-SIZED AWARENESS, THEN YOU HAVE A *MATCH*-SIZED EXPERIENCE. MOST PEOPLE ARE LUCKY TO HAVE EVEN THAT.
THOSE THAT BURN BRIGHTLY LIKE LADY DRAGON ARE EASIER TO FIND, BUT ALSO MORE DANGEROUS.
PERHAPS WHILE I'M HERE, I CAN LOOK FOR D.D.'S LIGHT AS--
TURN AWAY, CREATURE!

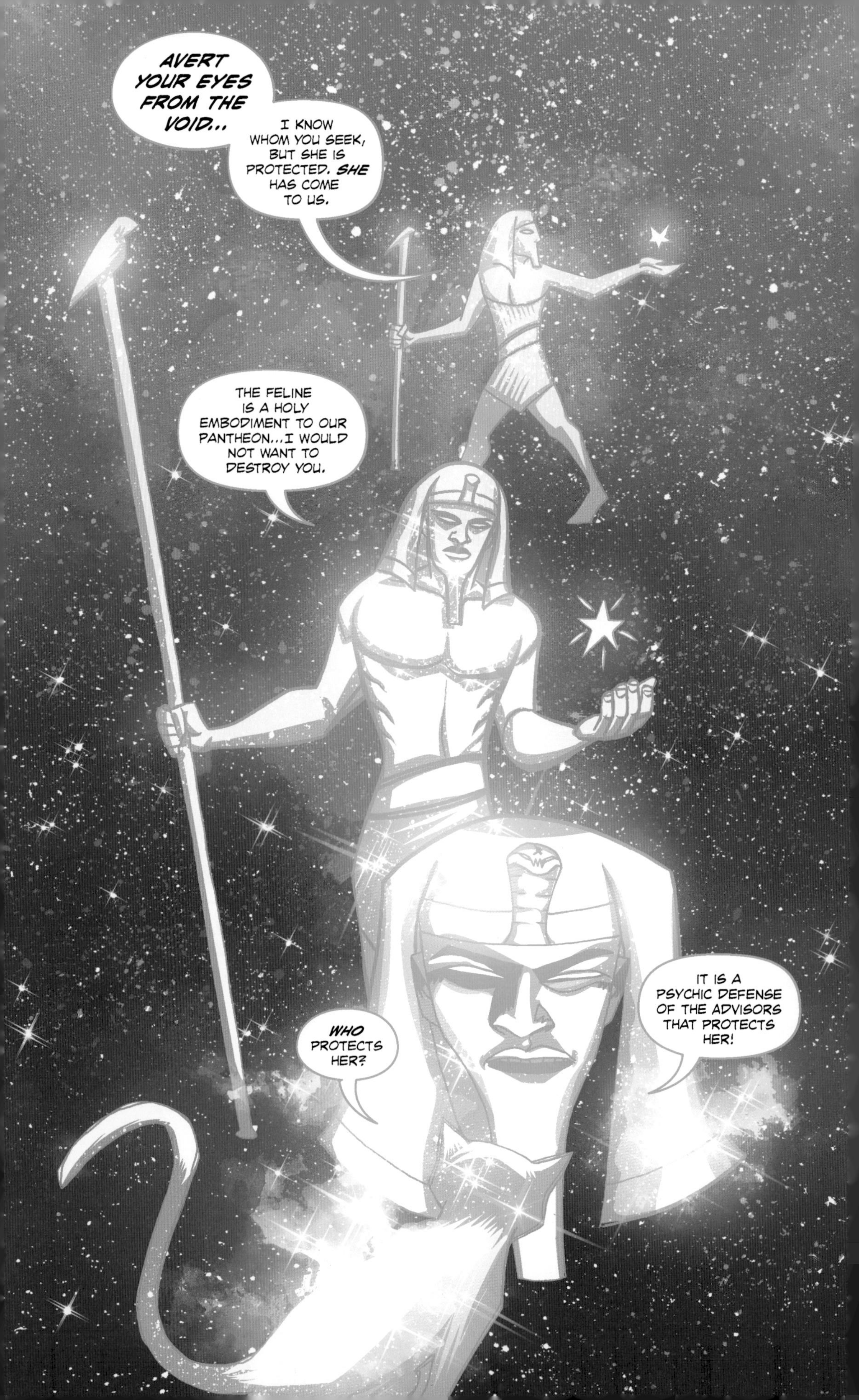
AVERT YOUR EYES FROM THE VOID...
I KNOW WHOM YOU SEEK, BUT SHE IS PROTECTED. SHE HAS COME TO US.
THE FELINE IS A HOLY EMBODIMENT TO OUR PANTHEON...I WOULD NOT WANT TO DESTROY YOU.
WHO PROTECTS HER?
IT IS A PSYCHIC DEFENSE OF THE ADVISORS THAT PROTECTS HER!

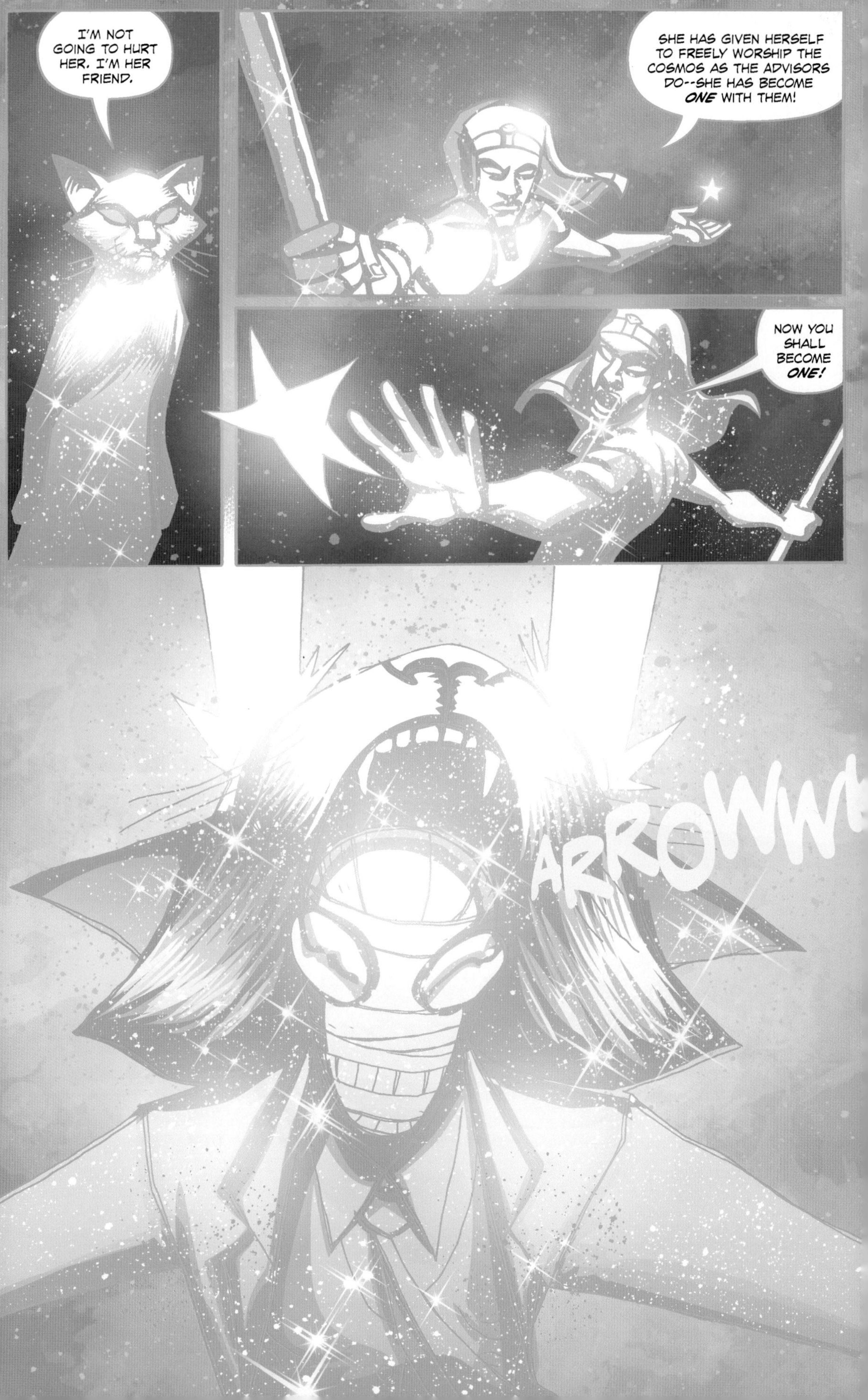
I'M NOT GOING TO HURT HER. I'M HER FRIEND.
SHE HAS GIVEN HERSELF TO FREELY WORSHIP THE COSMOS AS THE ADVISORS DO--SHE HAS BECOME *ONE* WITH THEM!
NOW YOU SHALL BECOME *ONE!*
ARROWW

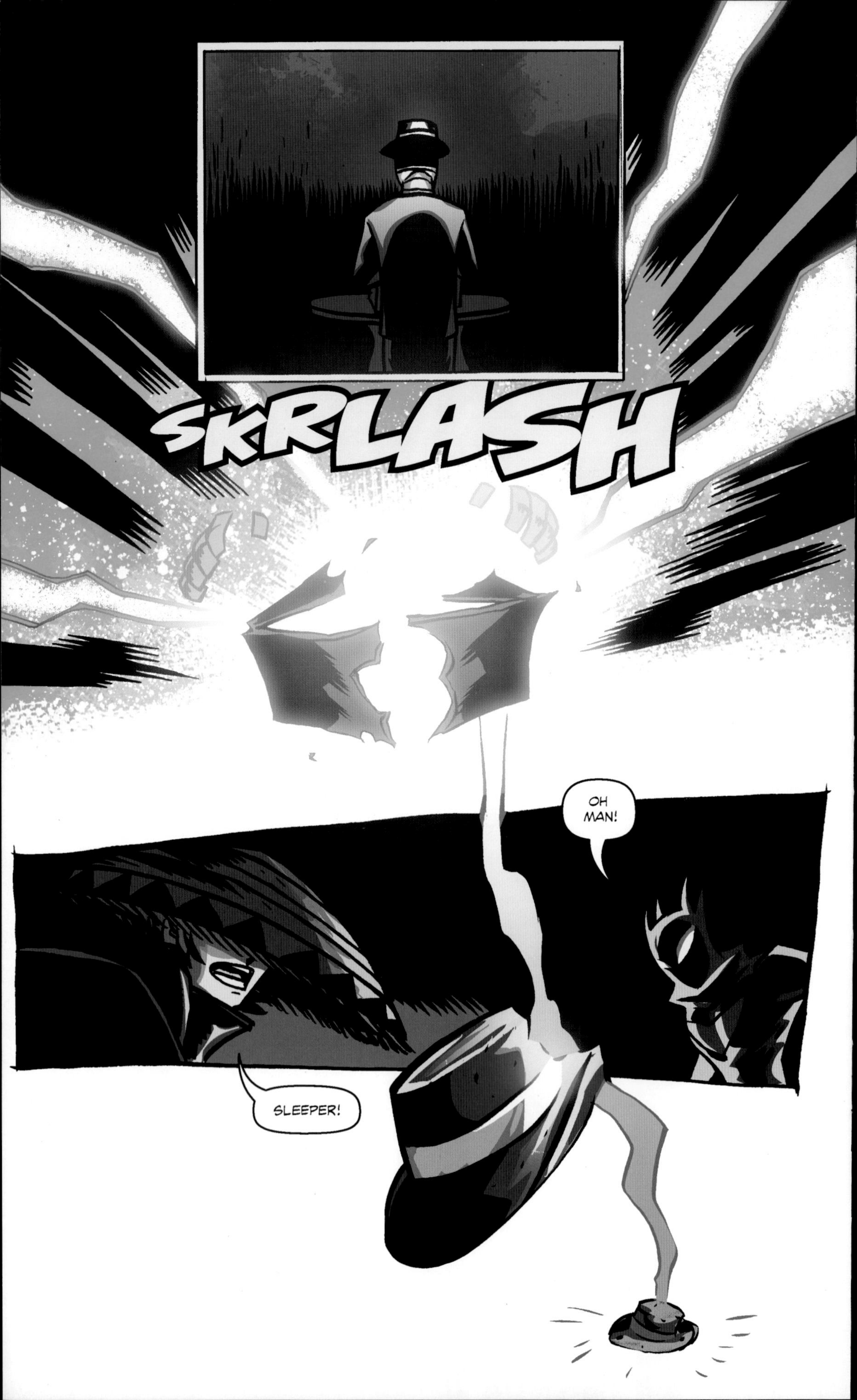
SKRLASH
OH MAN!
SLEEPER!

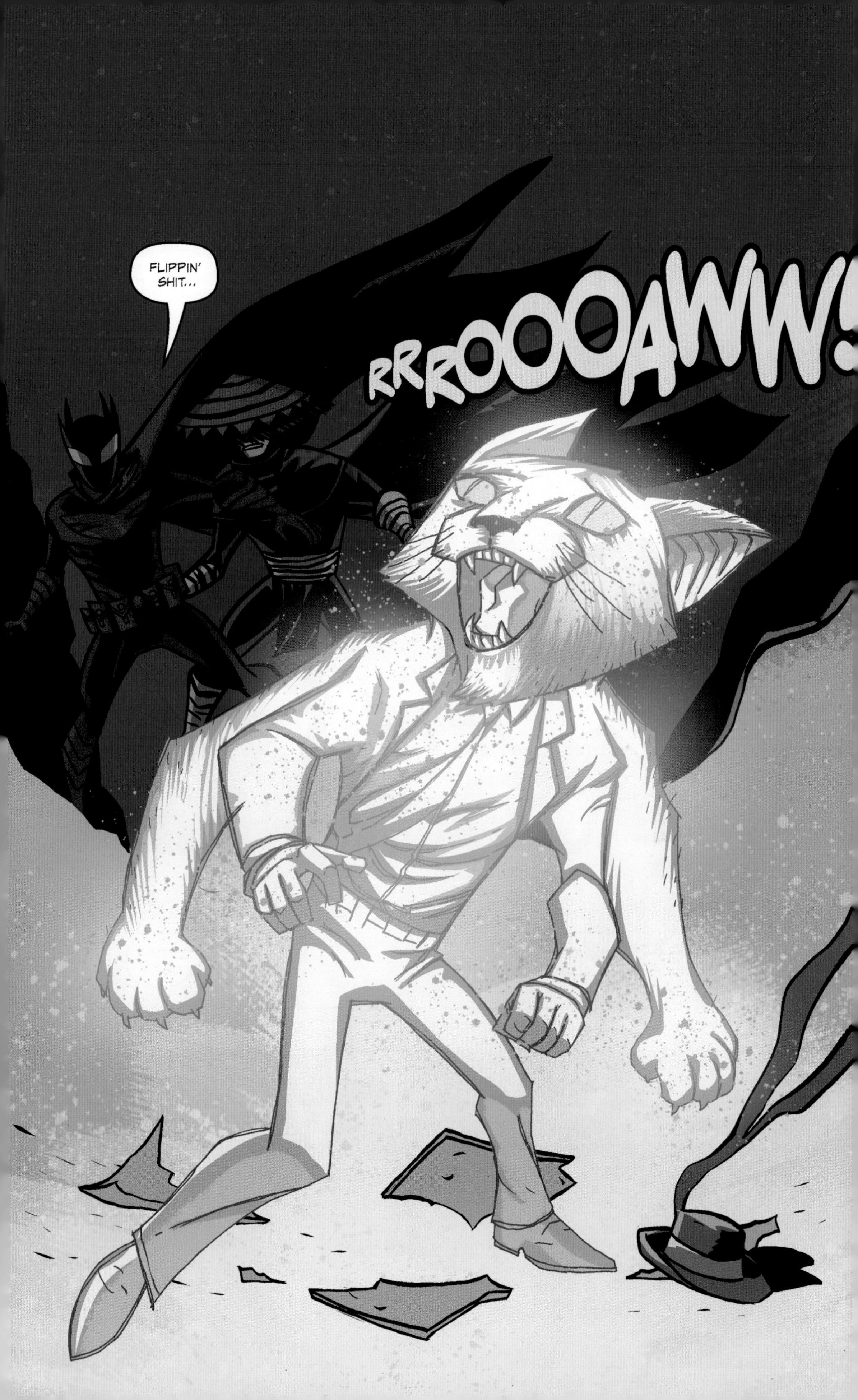
FLIPPIN' SHIT...
RRROOOAWW!

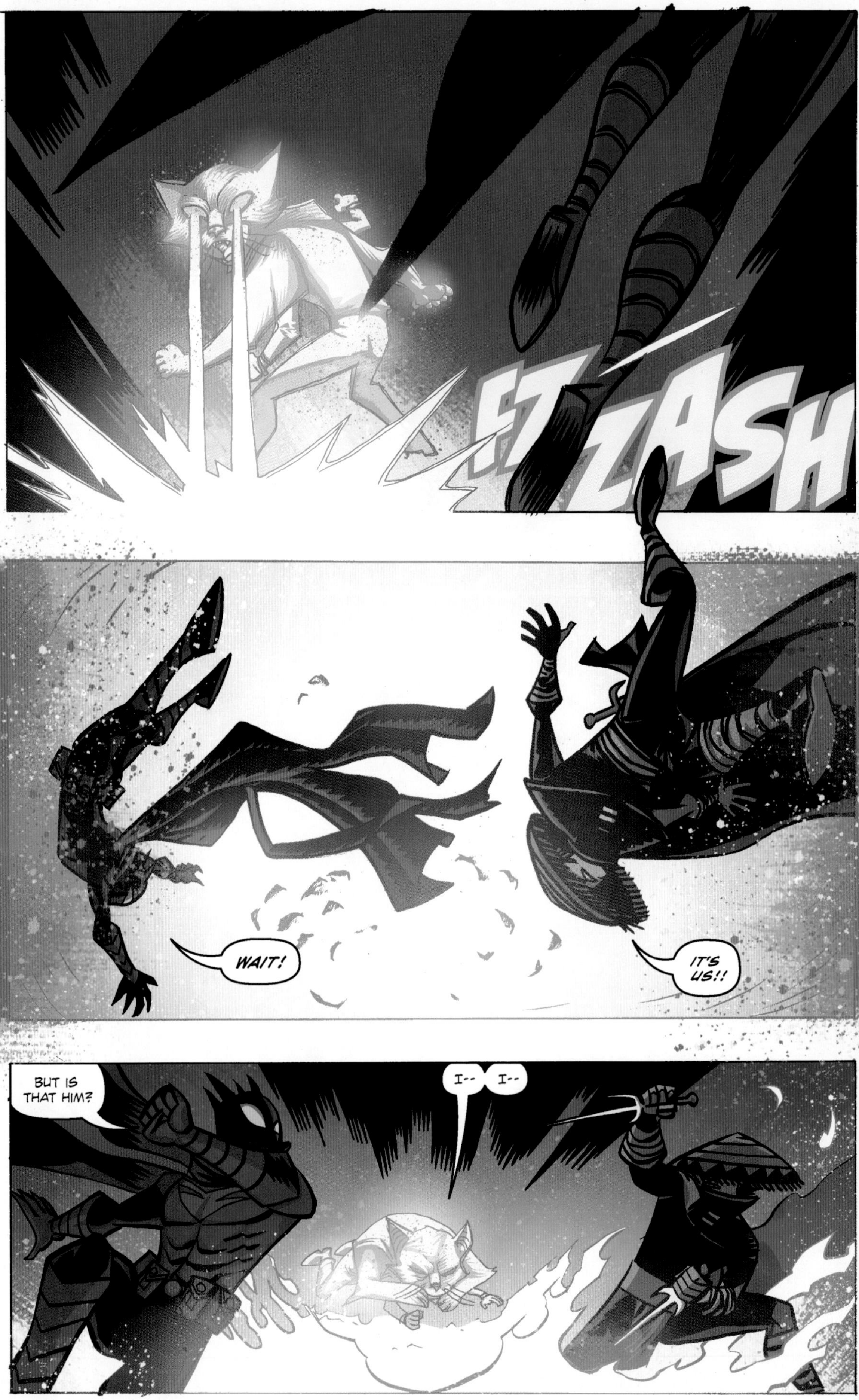
FT ZASH
WAIT!
IT'S US!!
BUT IS THAT HIM?
I-- I--

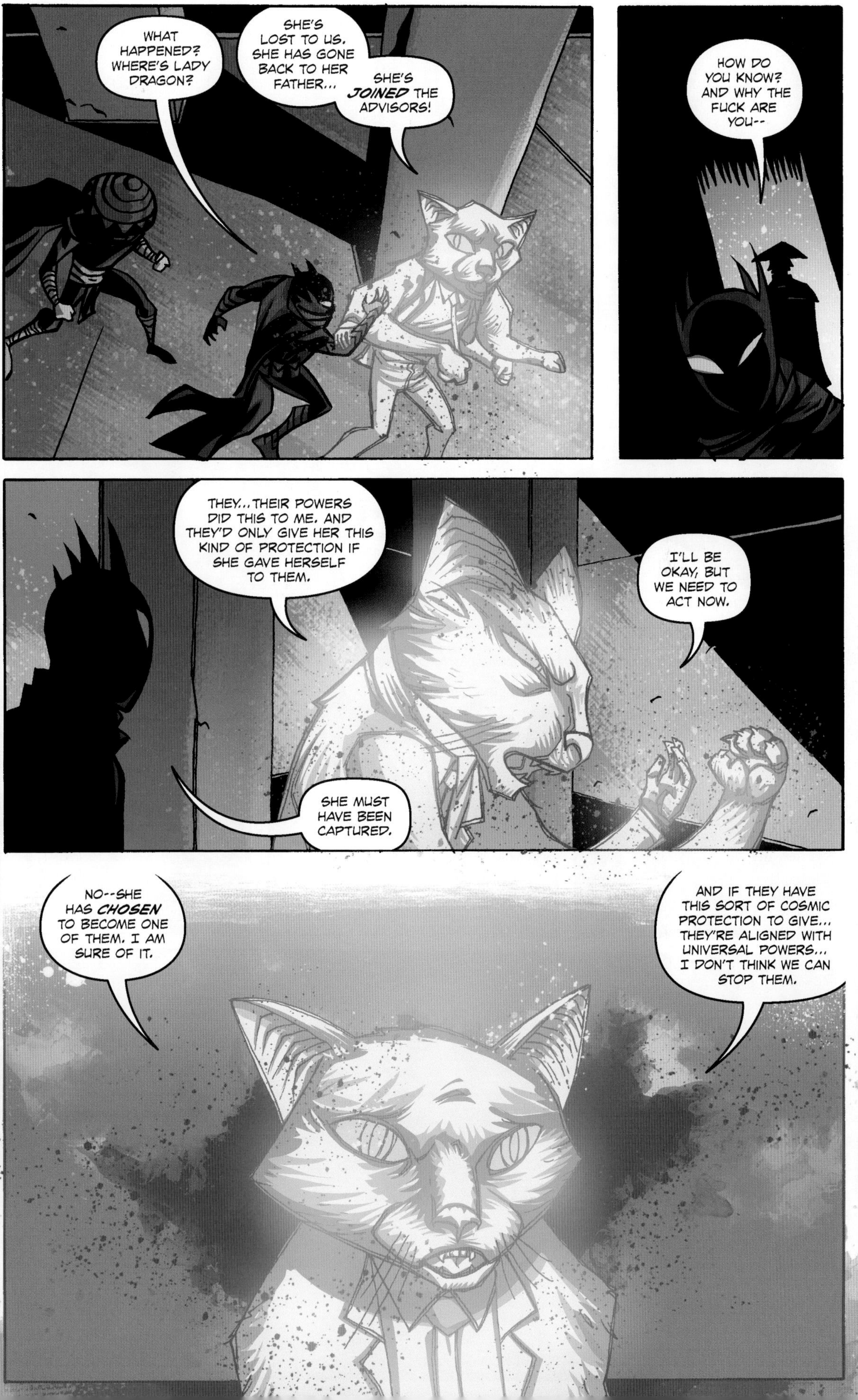
WHAT HAPPENED? WHERE'S LADY DRAGON?
SHE'S LOST TO US. SHE HAS GONE BACK TO HER FATHER...
SHE'S JOINED THE ADVISORS!
HOW DO YOU KNOW? AND WHY THE FUCK ARE YOU--
THEY...THEIR POWERS DID THIS TO ME. AND THEY'D ONLY GIVE HER THIS KIND OF PROTECTION IF SHE GAVE HERSELF TO THEM.
I'LL BE OKAY, BUT WE NEED TO ACT NOW.
SHE MUST HAVE BEEN CAPTURED.
NO--SHE HAS CHOSEN TO BECOME ONE OF THEM. I AM SURE OF IT.
AND IF THEY HAVE THIS SORT OF COSMIC PROTECTION TO GIVE... THEY'RE ALIGNED WITH UNIVERSAL POWERS... I DON'T THINK WE CAN STOP THEM.

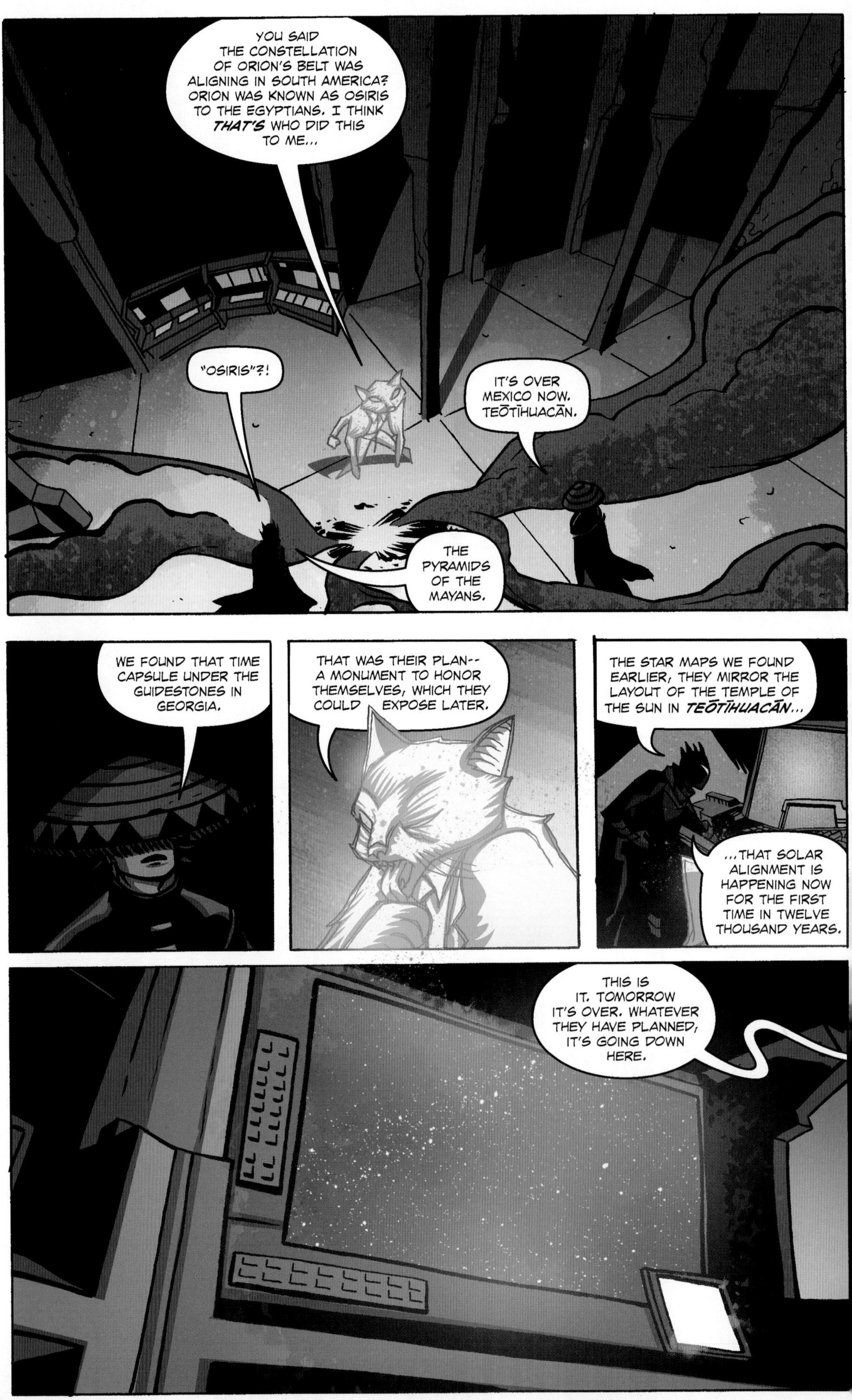
YOU SAID THE CONSTELLATION OF ORION'S BELT WAS ALIGNING IN SOUTH AMERICA? ORION WAS KNOWN AS OSIRIS TO THE EGYPTIANS. I THINK *THAT'S* WHO DID THIS TO ME...
"OSIRIS"?!
IT'S OVER MEXICO NOW. TEŌTĪHUACĀN.
THE PYRAMIDS OF THE MAYANS.
WE FOUND THAT TIME CAPSULE UNDER THE GUIDESTONES IN GEORGIA.
THAT WAS THEIR PLAN-- A MONUMENT TO HONOR THEMSELVES, WHICH THEY COULD EXPOSE LATER.
THE STAR MAPS WE FOUND EARLIER, THEY MIRROR THE LAYOUT OF THE TEMPLE OF THE SUN IN *TEŌTĪHUACĀN*...
...THAT SOLAR ALIGNMENT IS HAPPENING NOW FOR THE FIRST TIME IN TWELVE THOUSAND YEARS.
THIS IS IT. TOMORROW IT'S OVER. WHATEVER THEY HAVE PLANNED, IT'S GOING DOWN HERE.

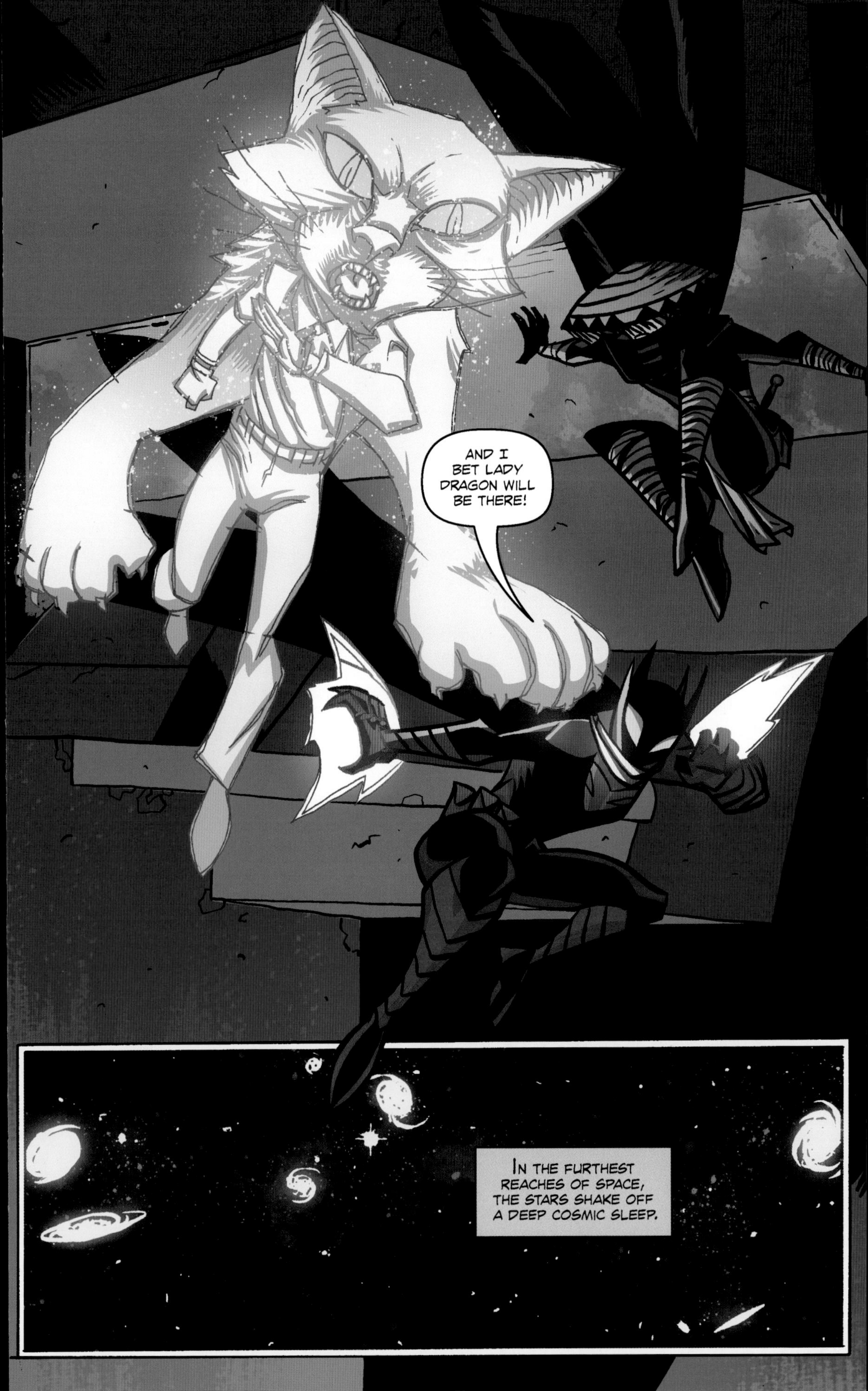
AND I BET LADY DRAGON WILL BE THERE!
IN THE FURTHEST REACHES OF SPACE, THE STARS SHAKE OFF A DEEP COSMIC SLEEP.

CHAPTER THREE

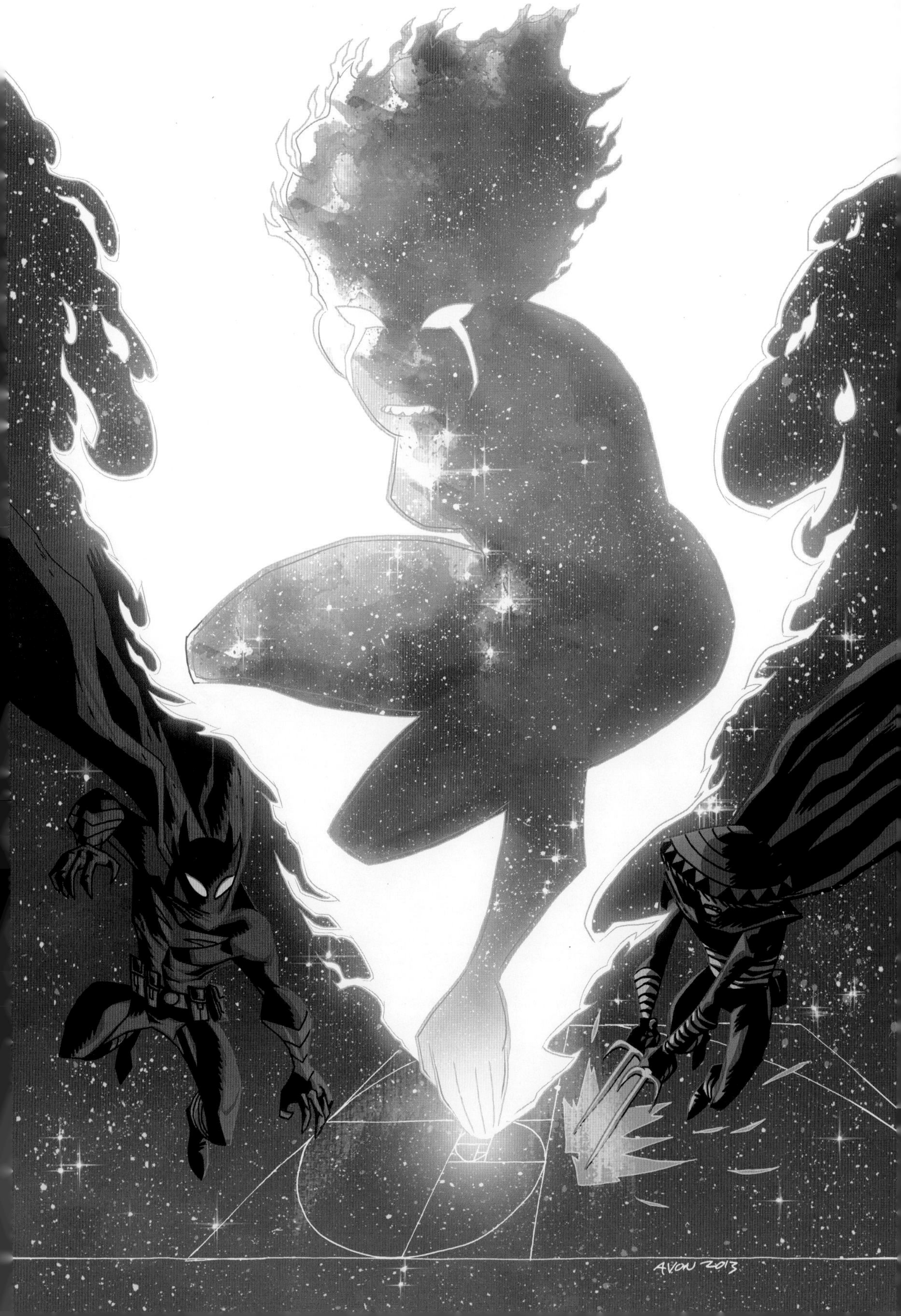
AVON 2013

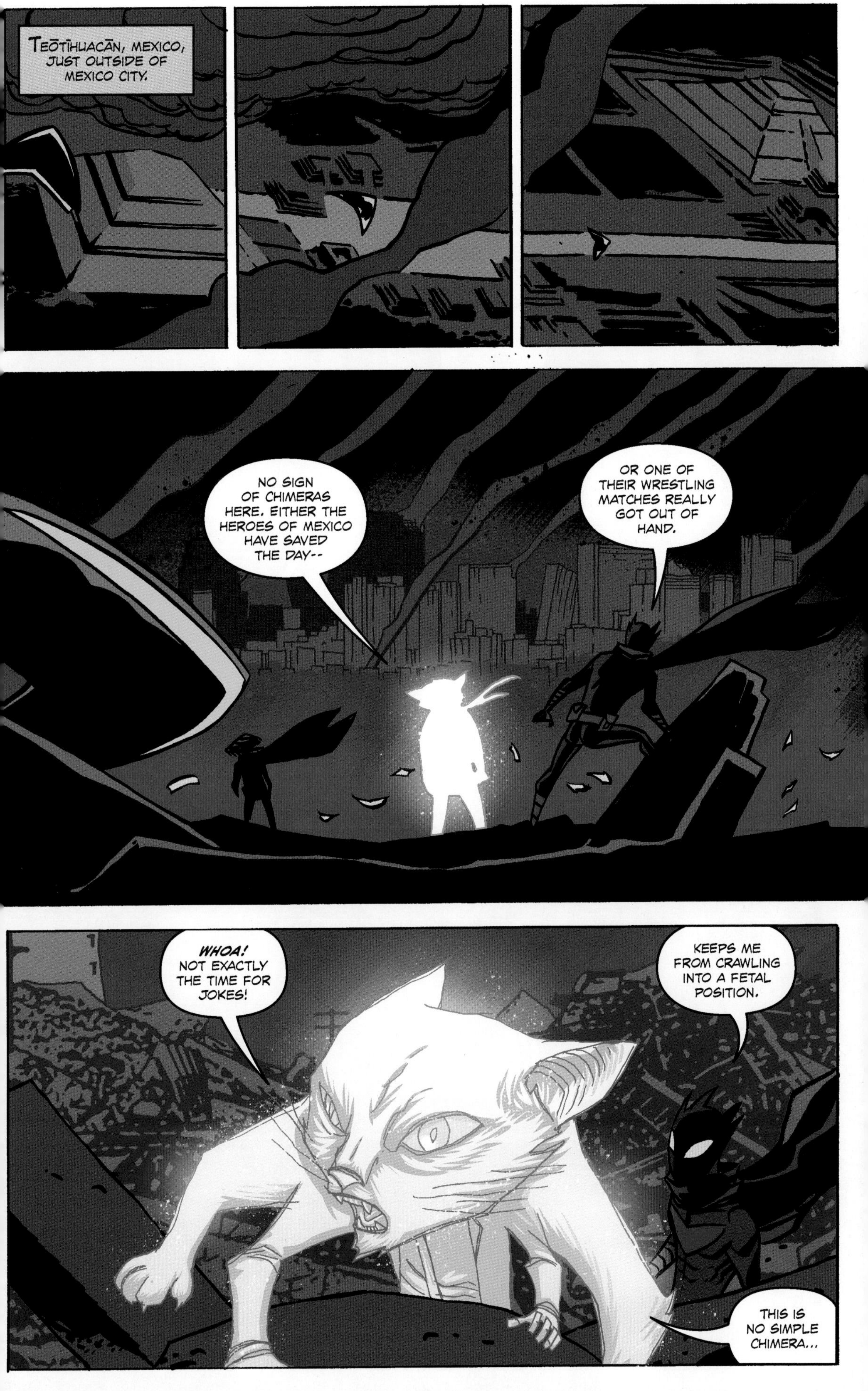
TEŌTĪHUACĀN, MEXICO, JUST OUTSIDE OF MEXICO CITY.
NO SIGN OF CHIMERAS HERE. EITHER THE HEROES OF MEXICO HAVE SAVED THE DAY--
OR ONE OF THEIR WRESTLING MATCHES REALLY GOT OUT OF HAND.
WHOA! NOT EXACTLY THE TIME FOR JOKES!
KEEPS ME FROM CRAWLING INTO A FETAL POSITION.
THIS IS NO SIMPLE CHIMERA...

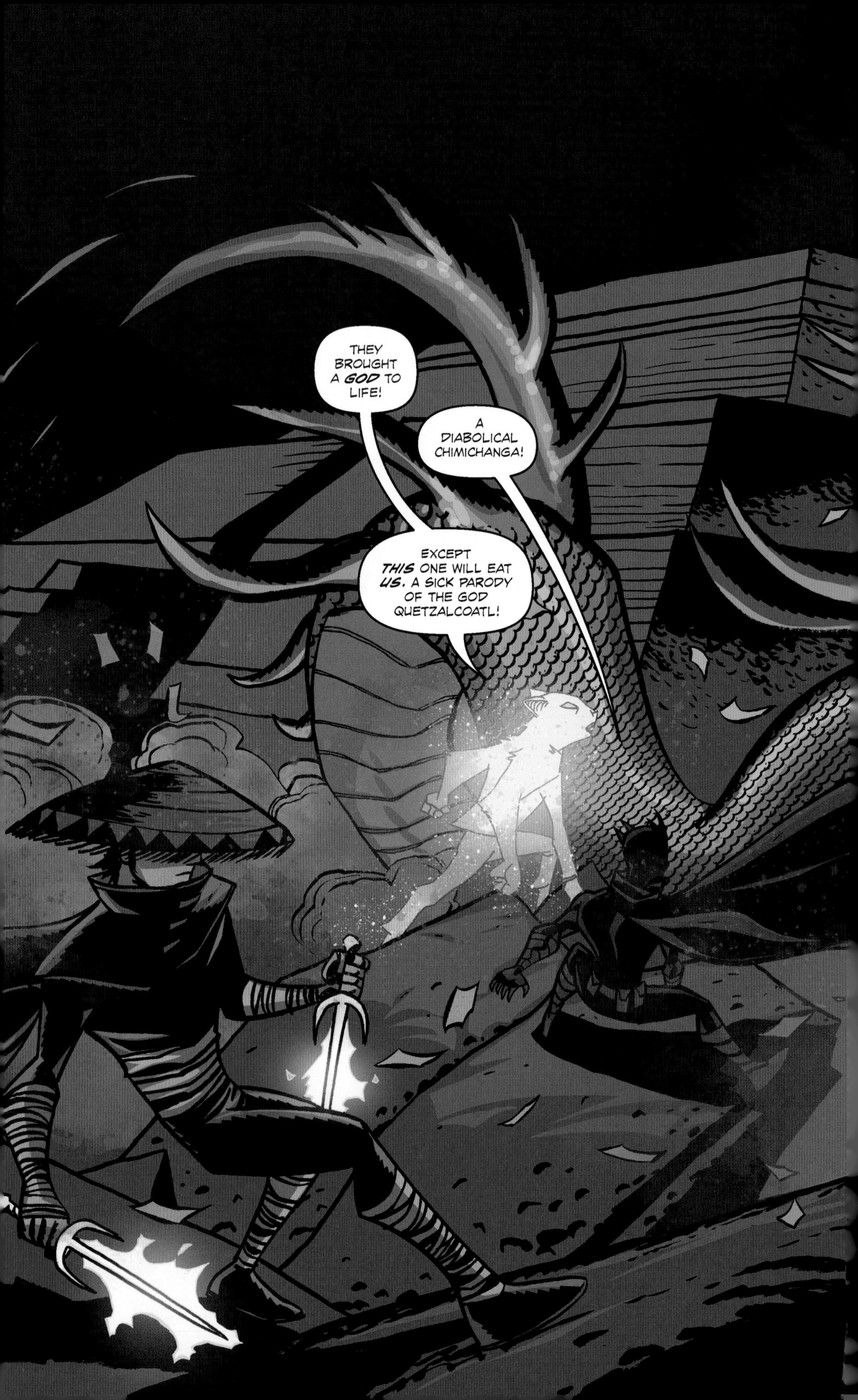
THEY BROUGHT A *GOD* TO LIFE!
A DIABOLICAL CHIMICHANGA!
EXCEPT *THIS* ONE WILL EAT *US*. A SICK PARODY OF THE GOD QUETZALCOATL!

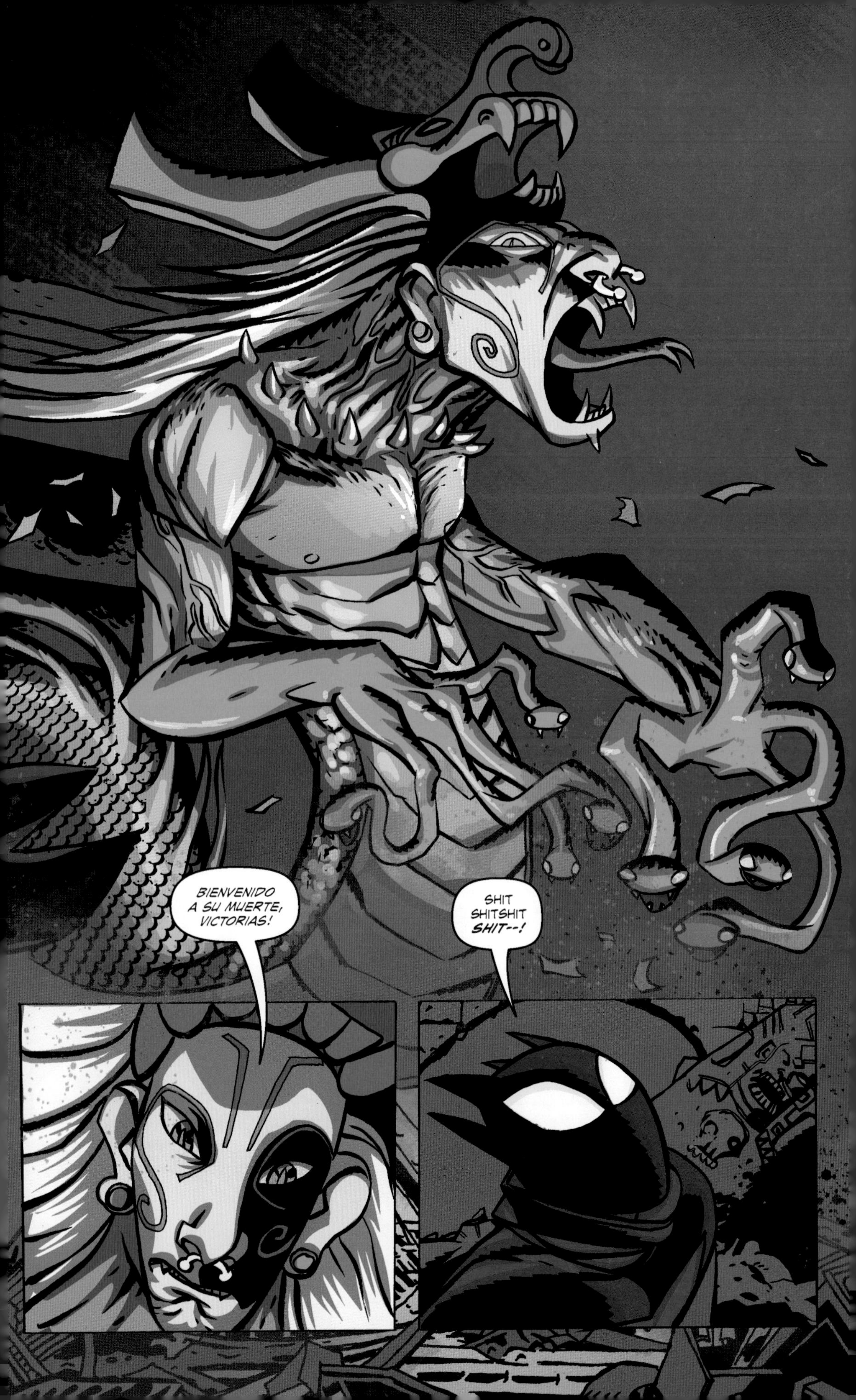
BIENVENIDO A SU MUERTE, VICTORIAS!
SHIT SHITSHIT SHIT--!

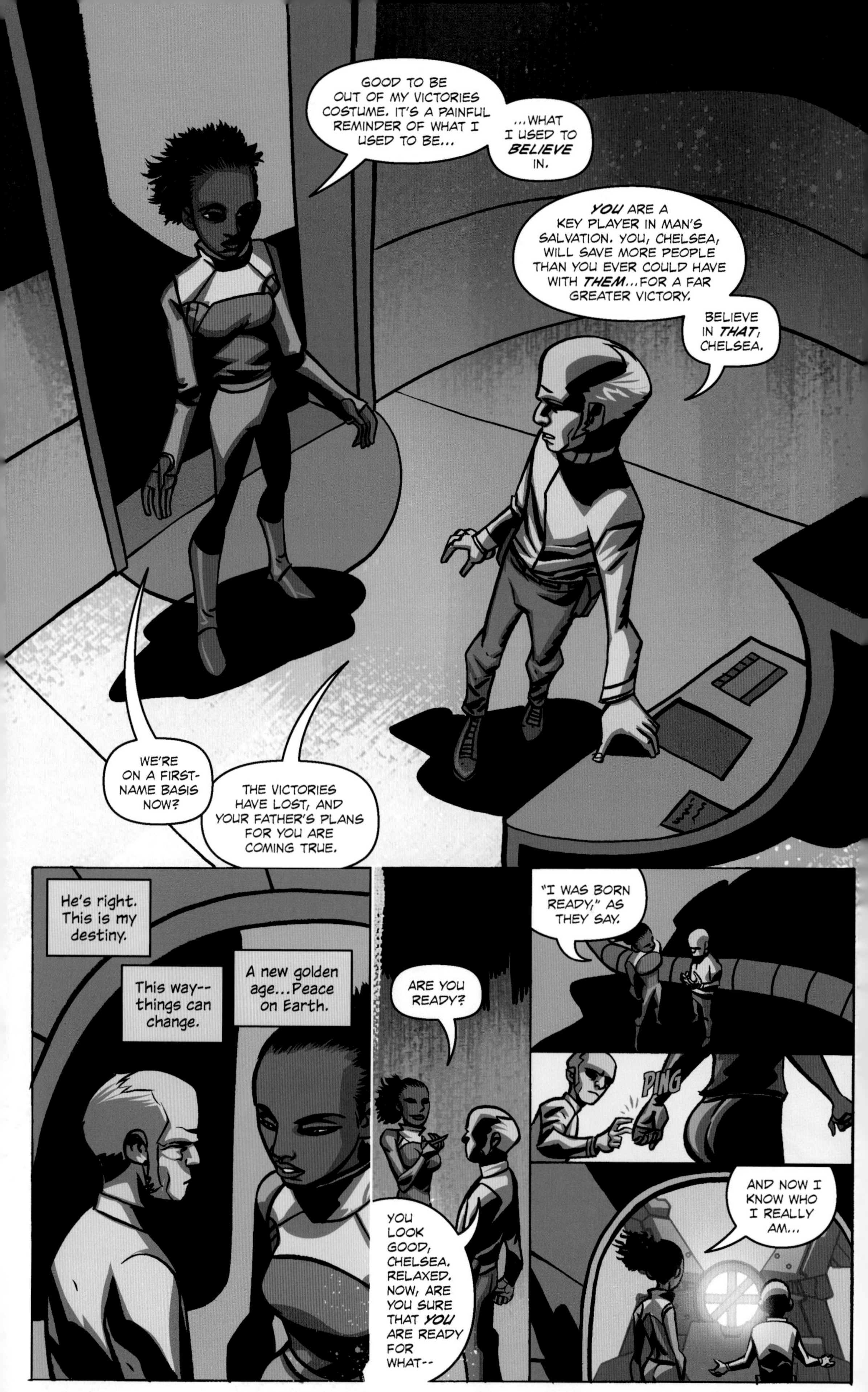
GOOD TO BE OUT OF MY VICTORIES COSTUME. IT'S A PAINFUL REMINDER OF WHAT I USED TO BE...
...WHAT I USED TO BELIEVE IN.
YOU ARE A KEY PLAYER IN MAN'S SALVATION. YOU, CHELSEA, WILL SAVE MORE PEOPLE THAN YOU EVER COULD HAVE WITH THEM...FOR A FAR GREATER VICTORY.
BELIEVE IN THAT, CHELSEA.
WE'RE ON A FIRST-NAME BASIS NOW?
THE VICTORIES HAVE LOST, AND YOUR FATHER'S PLANS FOR YOU ARE COMING TRUE.
He's right. This is my destiny.
This way--things can change.
A new golden age...Peace on Earth.
ARE YOU READY?
YOU LOOK GOOD, CHELSEA. RELAXED. NOW, ARE YOU SURE THAT YOU ARE READY FOR WHAT--
"I WAS BORN READY," AS THEY SAY.
PING
AND NOW I KNOW WHO I REALLY AM...

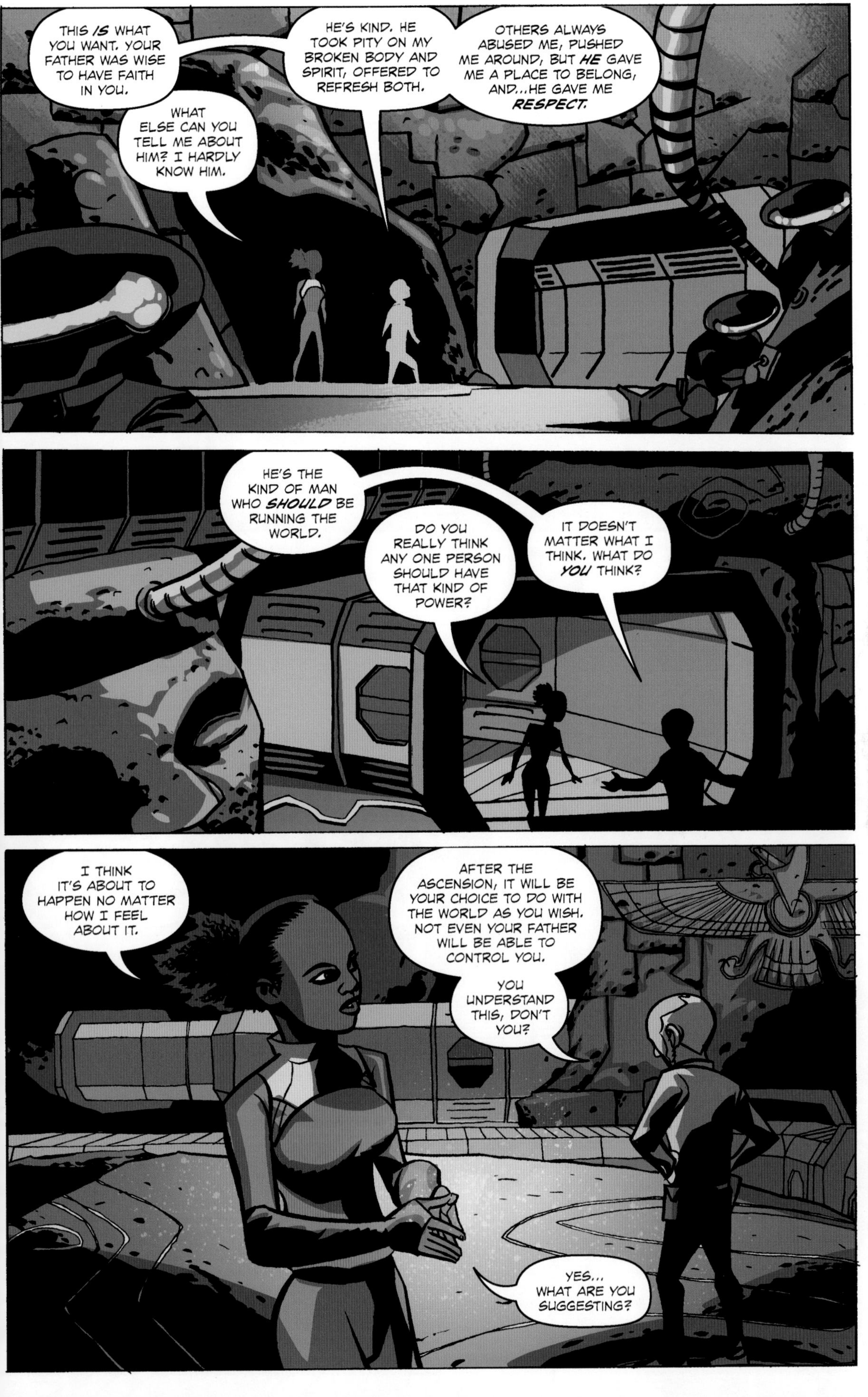
THIS *IS* WHAT YOU WANT. YOUR FATHER WAS WISE TO HAVE FAITH IN YOU.
WHAT ELSE CAN YOU TELL ME ABOUT HIM? I HARDLY KNOW HIM.
HE'S KIND. HE TOOK PITY ON MY BROKEN BODY AND SPIRIT, OFFERED TO REFRESH BOTH.
OTHERS ALWAYS ABUSED ME, PUSHED ME AROUND, BUT *HE* GAVE ME A PLACE TO BELONG, AND...HE GAVE ME *RESPECT.*
HE'S THE KIND OF MAN WHO *SHOULD* BE RUNNING THE WORLD.
DO YOU REALLY THINK ANY ONE PERSON SHOULD HAVE THAT KIND OF POWER?
IT DOESN'T MATTER WHAT I THINK. WHAT DO *YOU* THINK?
I THINK IT'S ABOUT TO HAPPEN NO MATTER HOW I FEEL ABOUT IT.
AFTER THE ASCENSION, IT WILL BE YOUR CHOICE TO DO WITH THE WORLD AS YOU WISH. NOT EVEN YOUR FATHER WILL BE ABLE TO CONTROL YOU.
YOU UNDERSTAND THIS, DON'T YOU?
YES... WHAT ARE YOU SUGGESTING?

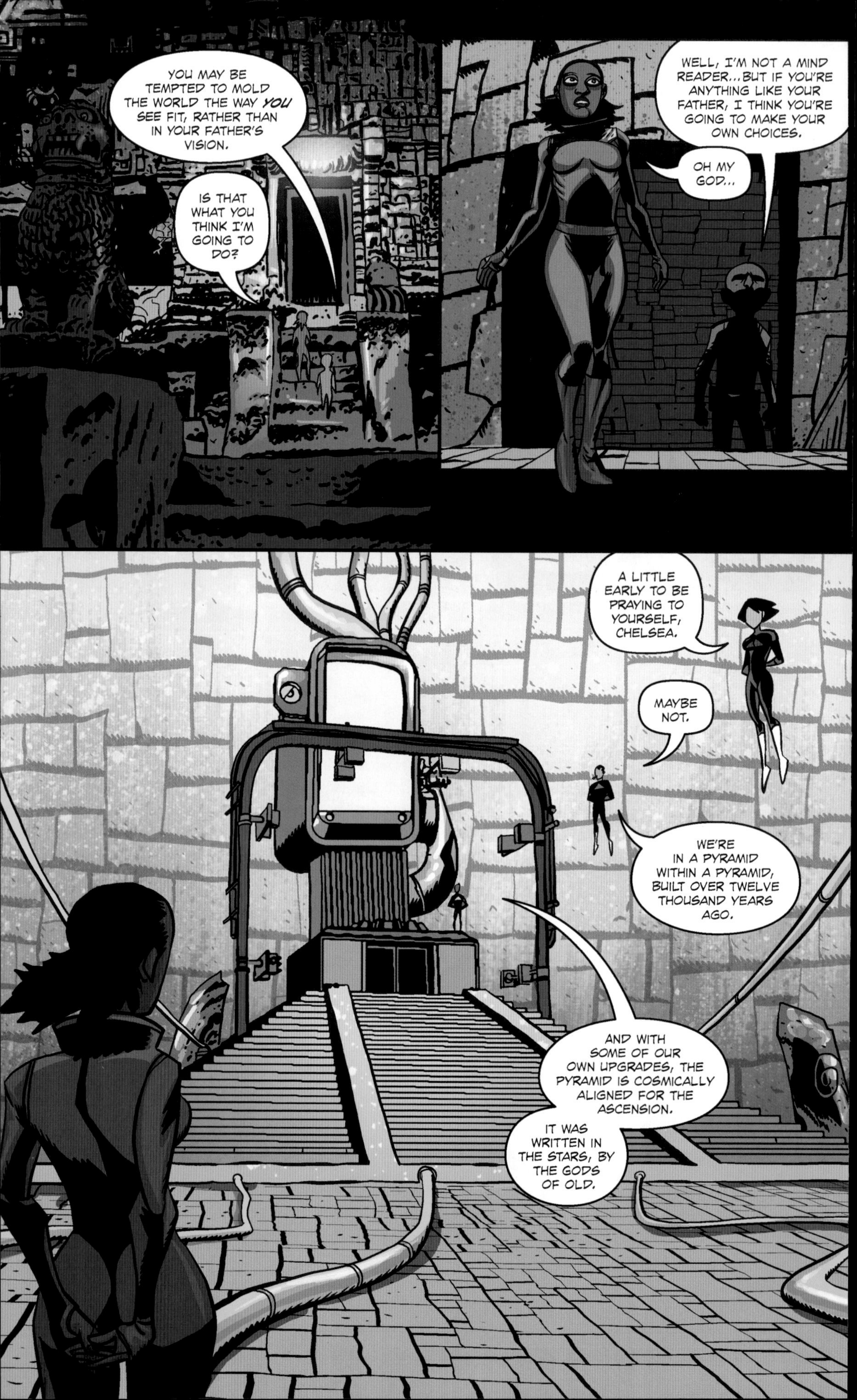

YOU MAY BE TEMPTED TO MOLD THE WORLD THE WAY *YOU* SEE FIT, RATHER THAN IN YOUR FATHER'S VISION.
IS THAT WHAT YOU THINK I'M GOING TO DO?
WELL, I'M NOT A MIND READER...BUT IF YOU'RE ANYTHING LIKE YOUR FATHER, I THINK YOU'RE GOING TO MAKE YOUR OWN CHOICES.
OH MY GOD...
A LITTLE EARLY TO BE PRAYING TO YOURSELF, CHELSEA.
MAYBE NOT.
WE'RE IN A PYRAMID WITHIN A PYRAMID, BUILT OVER TWELVE THOUSAND YEARS AGO.
AND WITH SOME OF OUR OWN UPGRADES, THE PYRAMID IS COSMICALLY ALIGNED FOR THE ASCENSION.
IT WAS WRITTEN IN THE STARS, BY THE GODS OF OLD.

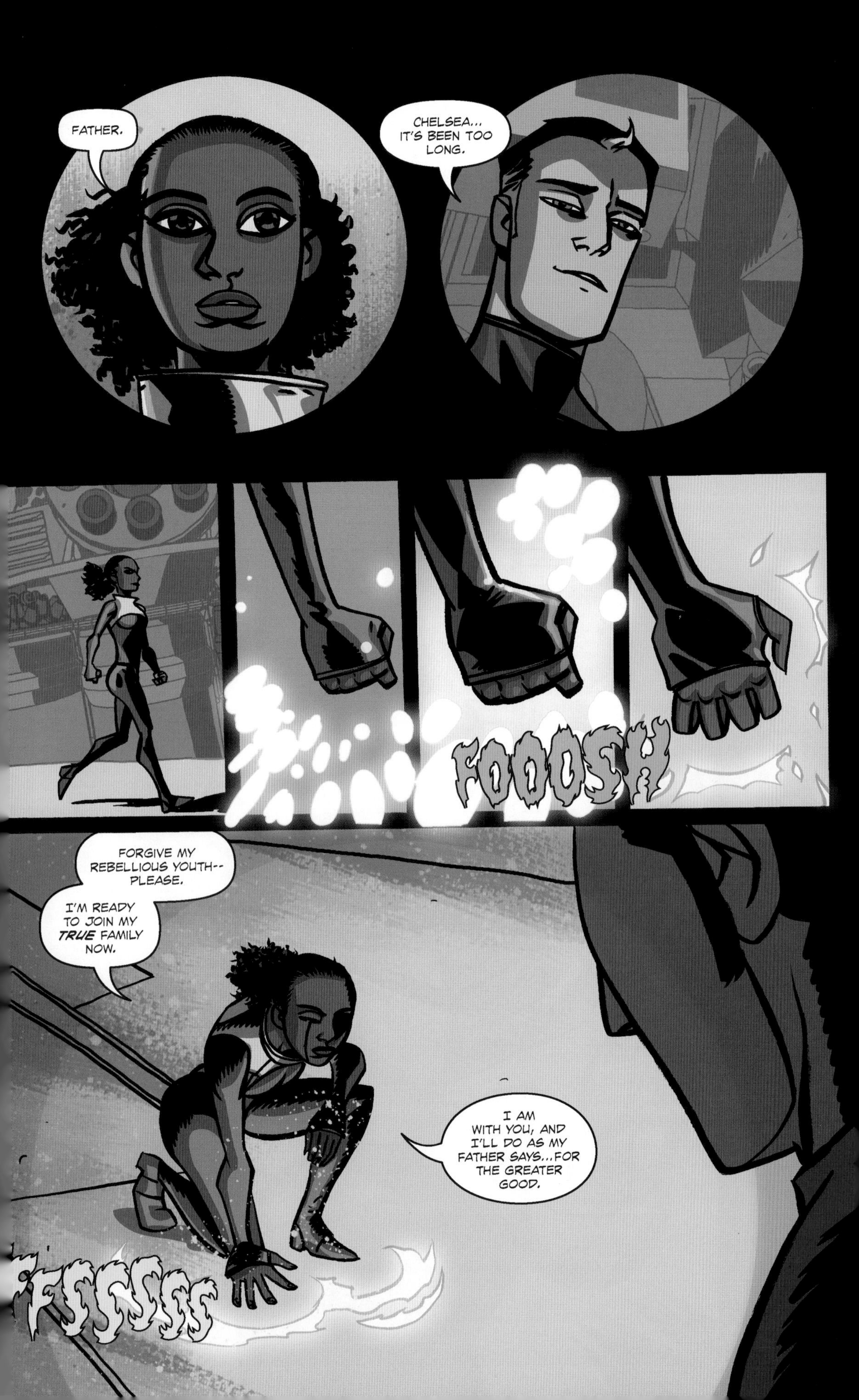
FATHER.
CHELSEA... IT'S BEEN TOO LONG.
FOOOSH
FORGIVE MY REBELLIOUS YOUTH-- PLEASE.
I'M READY TO JOIN MY *TRUE* FAMILY NOW.
I AM WITH YOU, AND I'LL DO AS MY FATHER SAYS...FOR THE GREATER GOOD.
FSSSSS

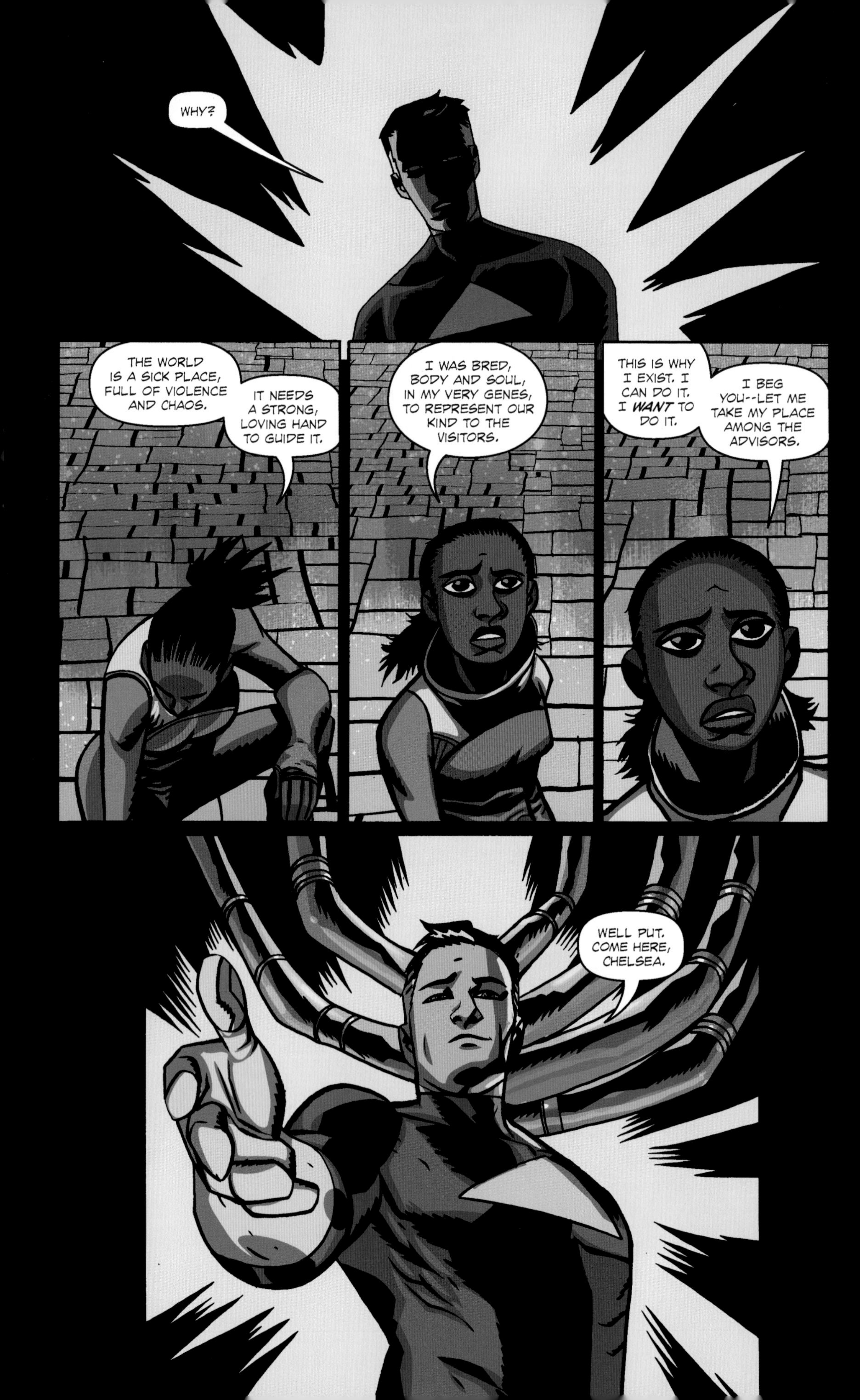
WHY?
THE WORLD IS A SICK PLACE, FULL OF VIOLENCE AND CHAOS.
IT NEEDS A STRONG, LOVING HAND TO GUIDE IT.
I WAS BRED, BODY AND SOUL, IN MY VERY GENES, TO REPRESENT OUR KIND TO THE VISITORS.
THIS IS WHY I EXIST. I CAN DO IT. I *WANT* TO DO IT.
I BEG YOU--LET ME TAKE MY PLACE AMONG THE ADVISORS.
WELL PUT. COME HERE, CHELSEA.

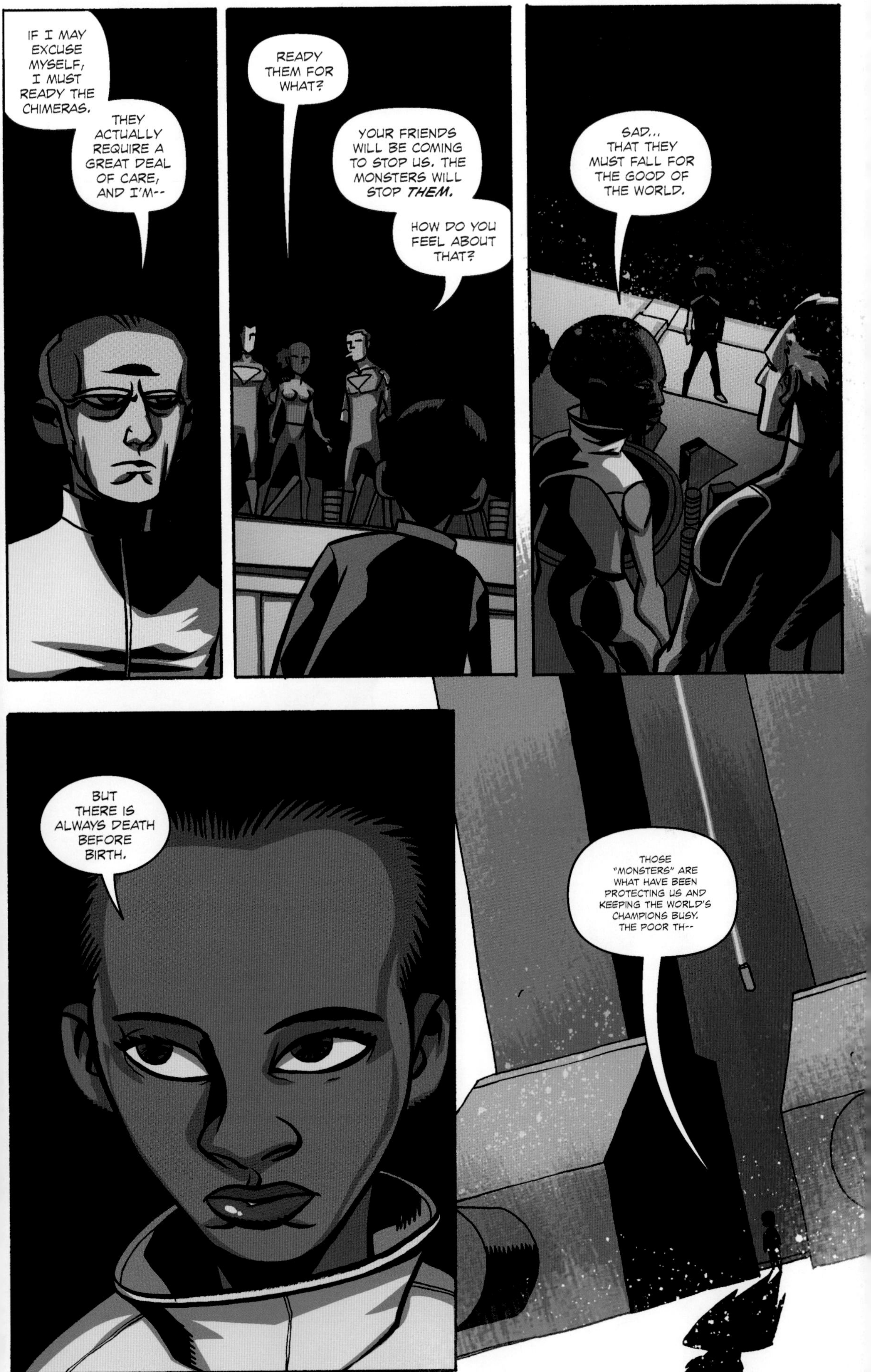
IF I MAY EXCUSE MYSELF, I MUST READY THE CHIMERAS.
THEY ACTUALLY REQUIRE A GREAT DEAL OF CARE, AND I'M--
READY THEM FOR WHAT?
YOUR FRIENDS WILL BE COMING TO STOP US. THE MONSTERS WILL STOP *THEM.*
HOW DO YOU FEEL ABOUT THAT?
SAD... THAT THEY MUST FALL FOR THE GOOD OF THE WORLD.
BUT THERE IS ALWAYS DEATH BEFORE BIRTH.
THOSE "MONSTERS" ARE WHAT HAVE BEEN PROTECTING US AND KEEPING THE WORLD'S CHAMPIONS BUSY. THE POOR TH--

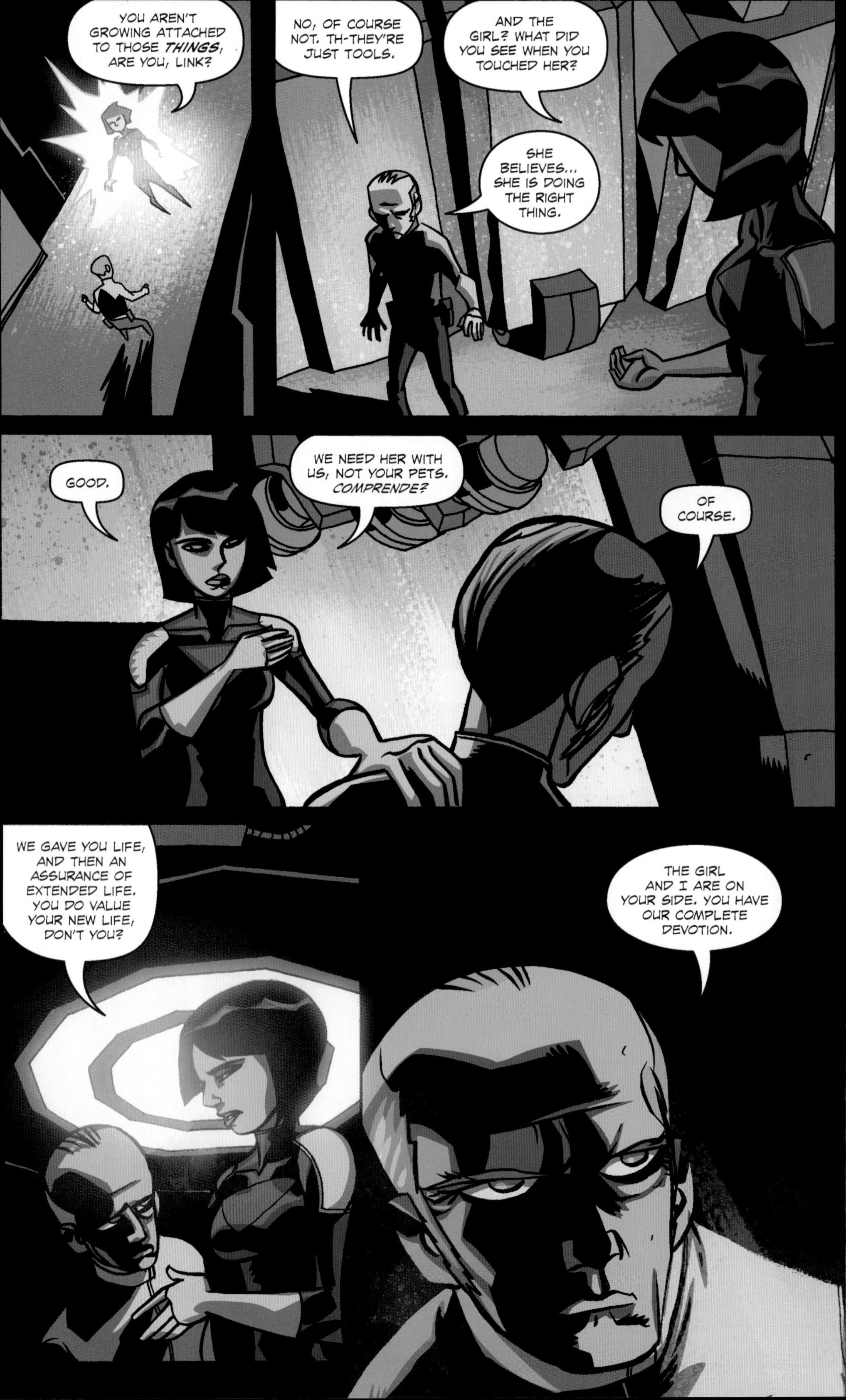
YOU AREN'T GROWING ATTACHED TO THOSE *THINGS*, ARE YOU, LINK?
NO, OF COURSE NOT. TH-THEY'RE JUST TOOLS.
AND THE GIRL? WHAT DID YOU SEE WHEN YOU TOUCHED HER?
SHE BELIEVES... SHE IS DOING THE RIGHT THING.
GOOD.
WE NEED HER WITH US, NOT YOUR PETS. *COMPRENDE?*
OF COURSE.
WE GAVE YOU LIFE, AND THEN AN ASSURANCE OF EXTENDED LIFE. YOU DO VALUE YOUR NEW LIFE, DON'T YOU?
THE GIRL AND I ARE ON YOUR SIDE. YOU HAVE OUR COMPLETE DEVOTION.

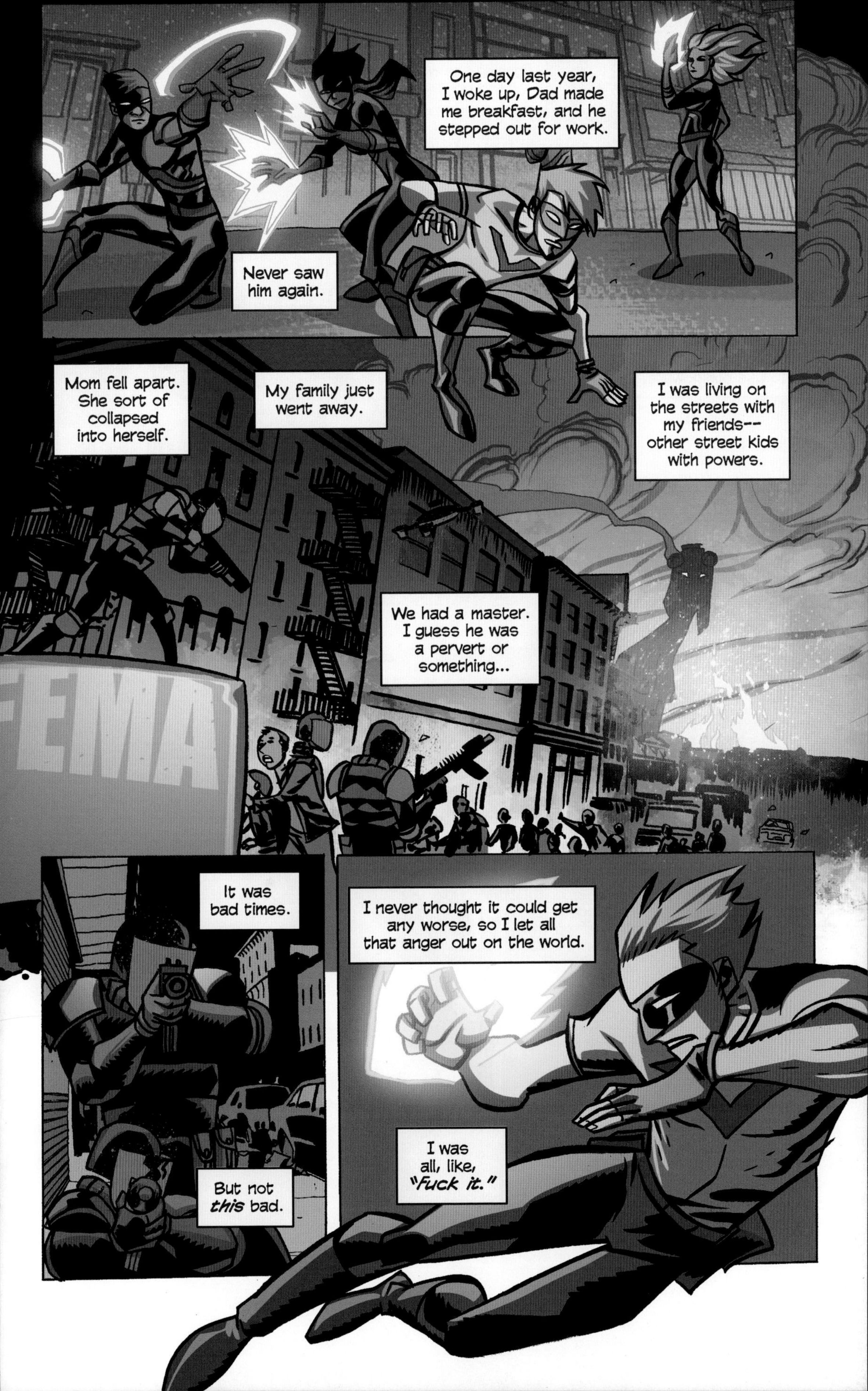
One day last year, I woke up, Dad made me breakfast, and he stepped out for work.
Never saw him again.
Mom fell apart. She sort of collapsed into herself.
My family just went away.
I was living on the streets with my friends-- other street kids with powers.
FEMA
We had a master. I guess he was a pervert or something...
It was bad times.
But not *this* bad.
I never thought it could get any worse, so I let all that anger out on the world.
I was all, like, *"Fuck it."*

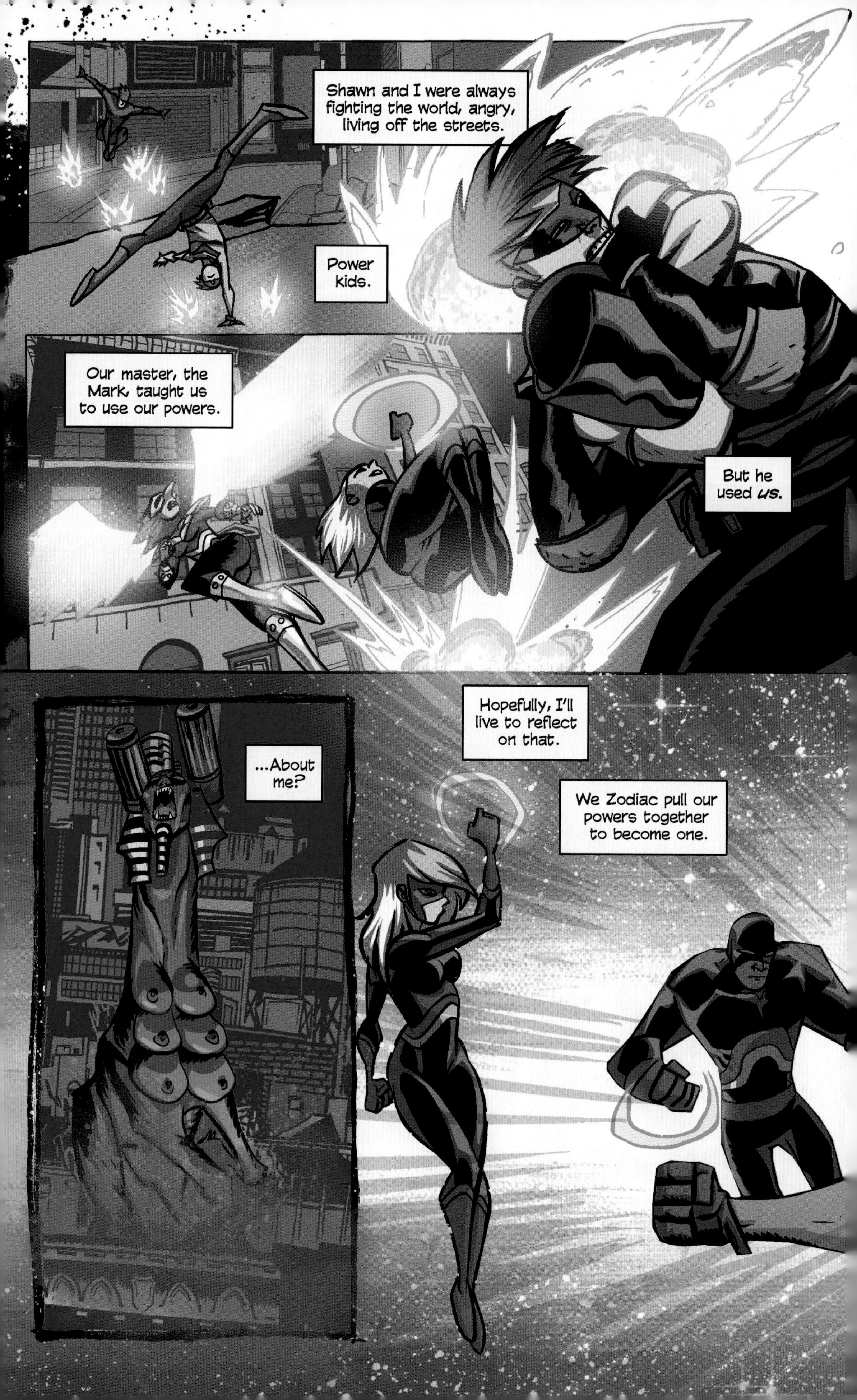

Shawn and I were always fighting the world, angry, living off the streets.
Power kids.
Our master, the Mark, taught us to use our powers.
But he used *us*.
...About me?
Hopefully, I'll live to reflect on that.
We Zodiac pull our powers together to become one.

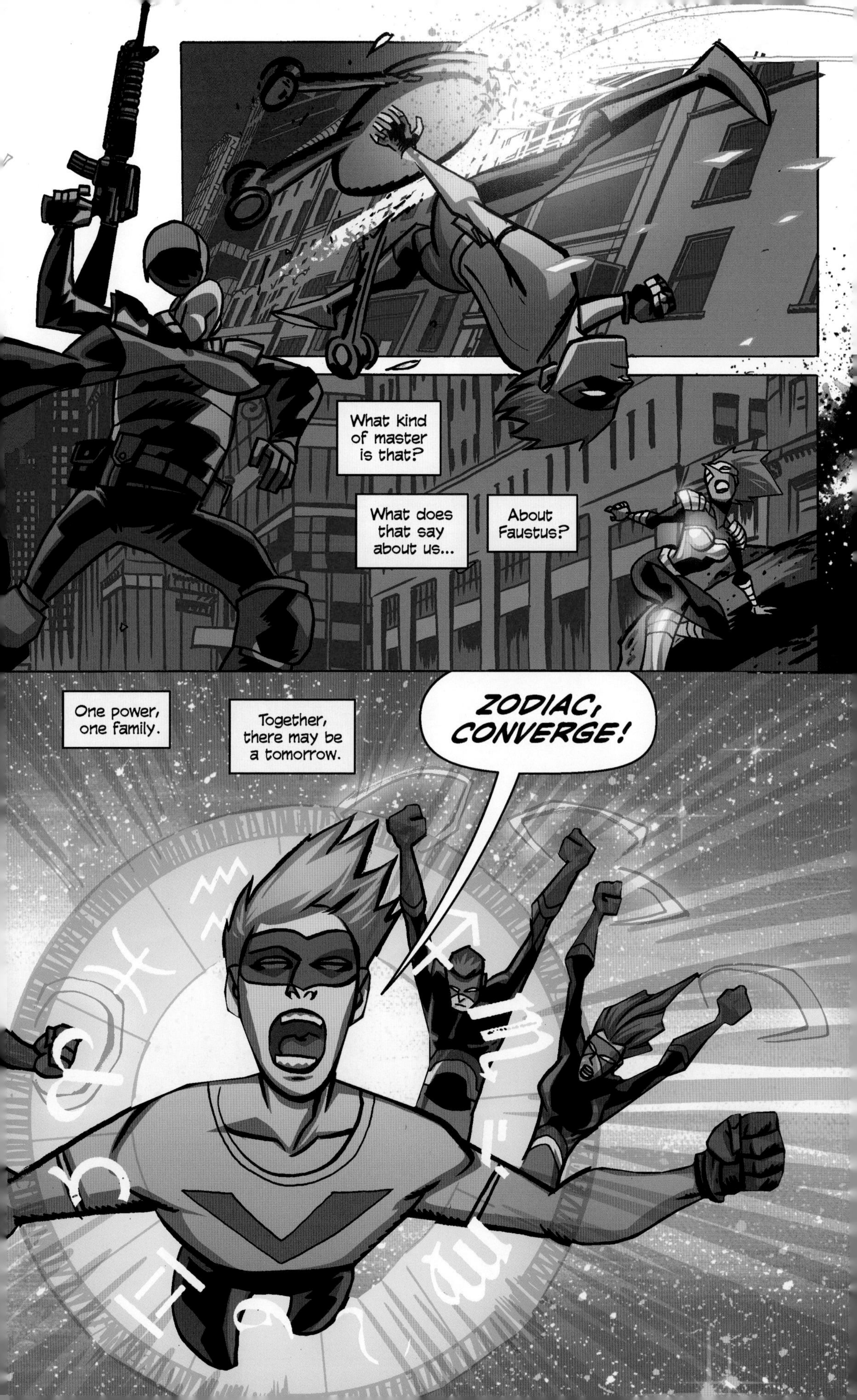
What kind of master is that?
What does that say about us...
About Faustus?
One power, one family.
Together, there may be a tomorrow.
ZODIAC, CONVERGE!

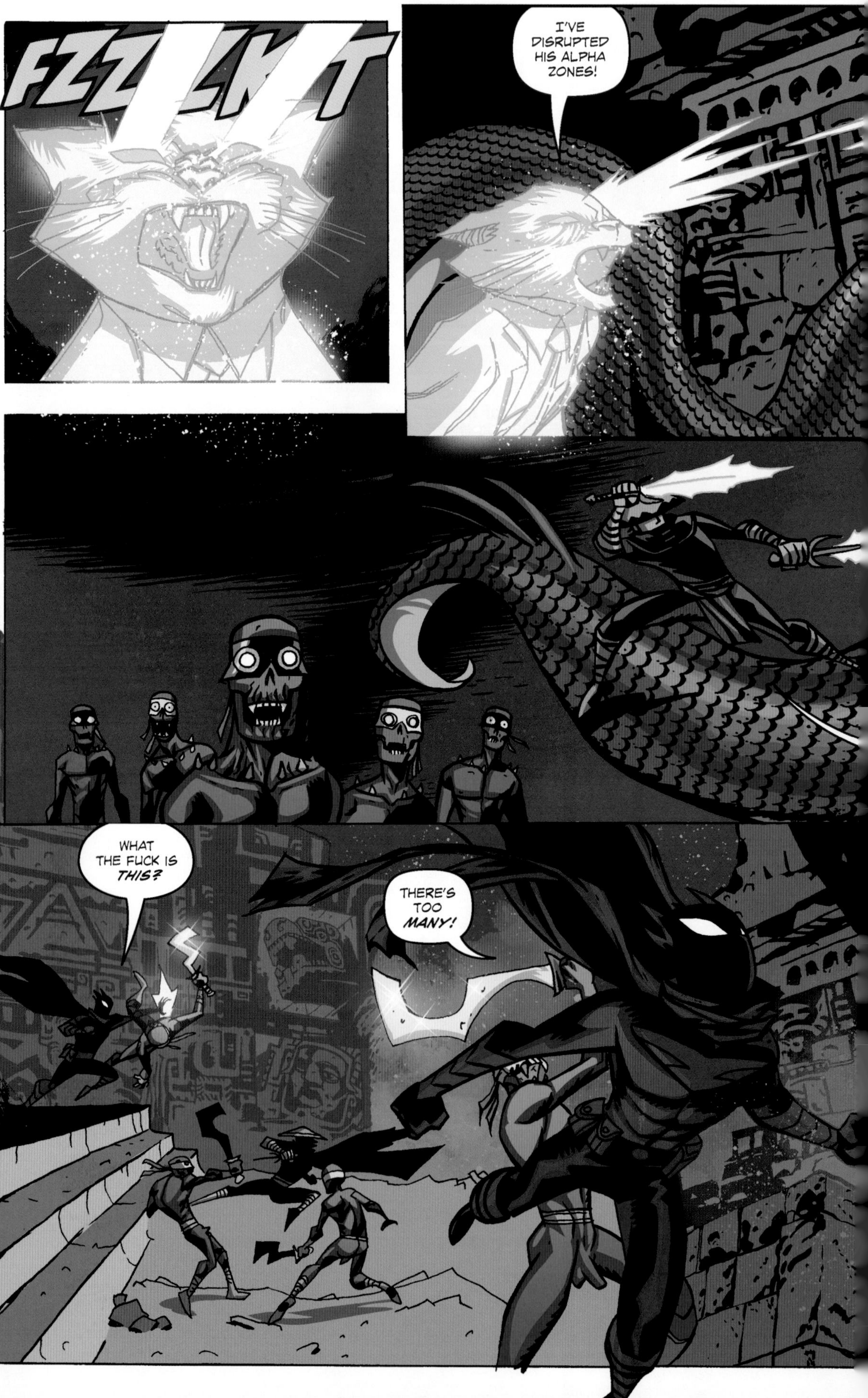
FZZLKT
I'VE DISRUPTED HIS ALPHA ZONES!
WHAT THE FUCK IS *THIS?*
THERE'S TOO *MANY!*

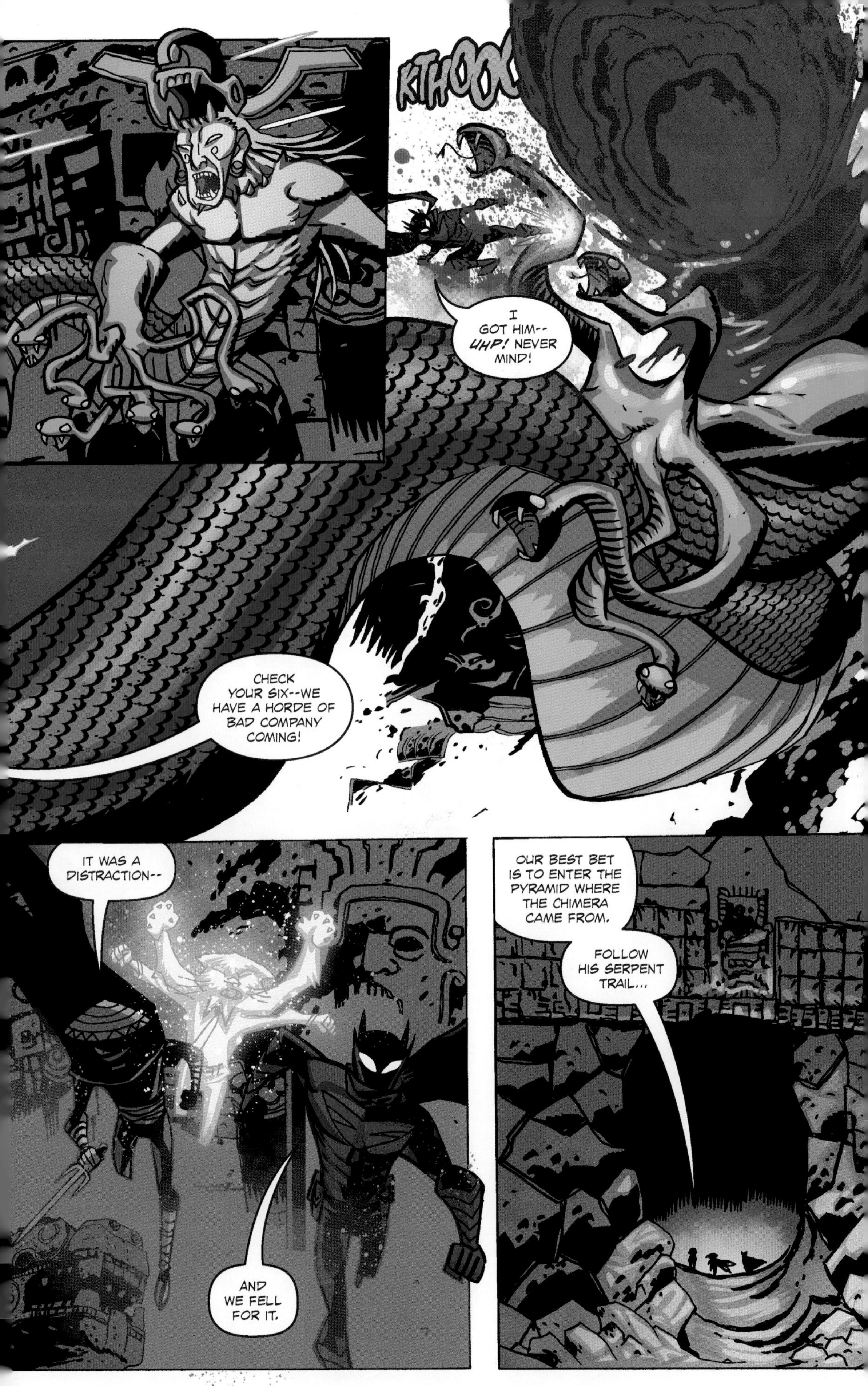
KTHOOO
I GOT HIM-- UHP! NEVER MIND!
CHECK YOUR SIX--WE HAVE A HORDE OF BAD COMPANY COMING!
IT WAS A DISTRACTION--
AND WE FELL FOR IT.
OUR BEST BET IS TO ENTER THE PYRAMID WHERE THE CHIMERA CAME FROM.
FOLLOW HIS SERPENT TRAIL...

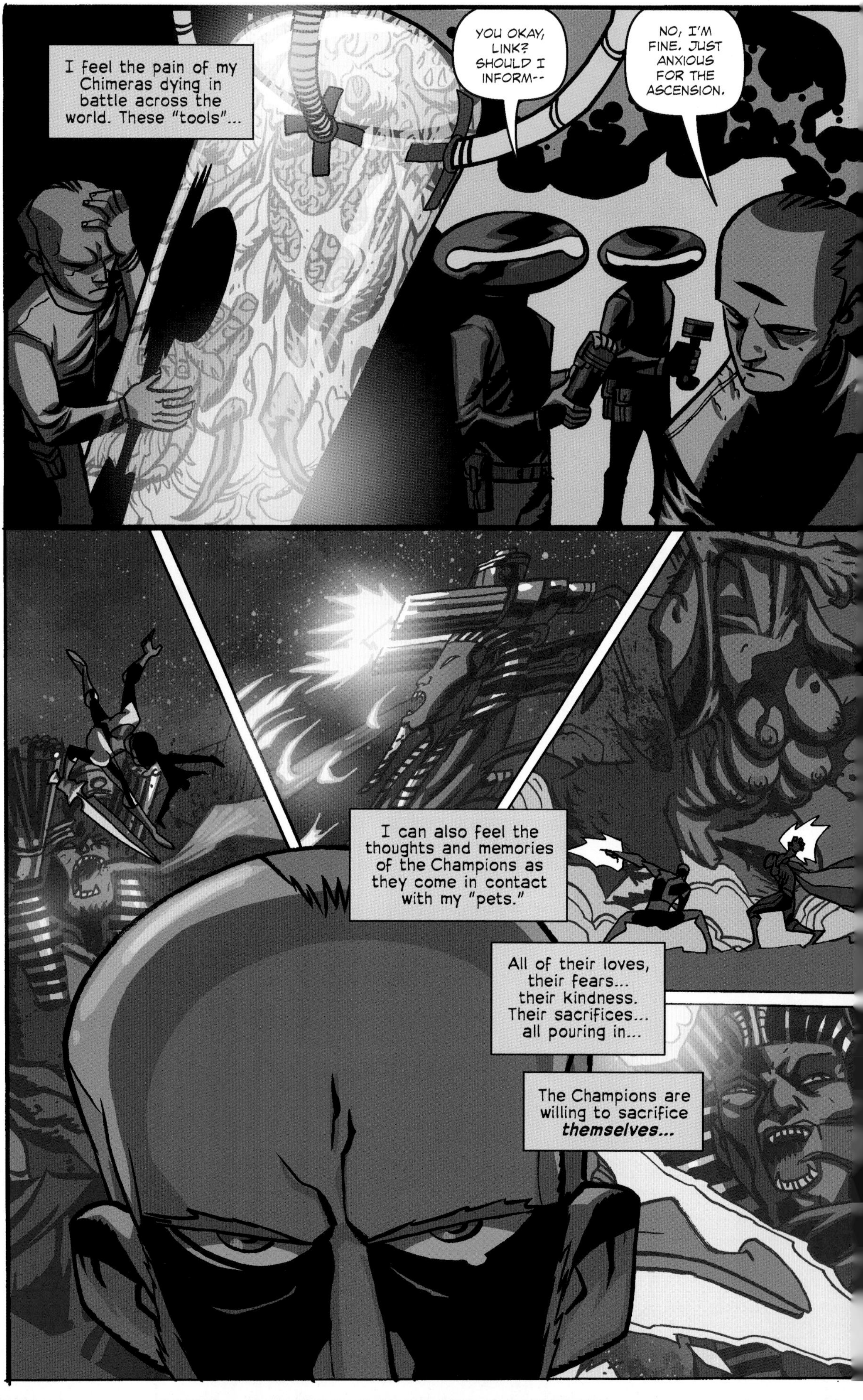
I feel the pain of my Chimeras dying in battle across the world. These "tools"...
YOU OKAY, LINK? SHOULD I INFORM--
NO, I'M FINE. JUST ANXIOUS FOR THE ASCENSION.
I can also feel the thoughts and memories of the Champions as they come in contact with my "pets."
All of their loves, their fears... their kindness. Their sacrifices... all pouring in...
The Champions are willing to sacrifice *themselves...*

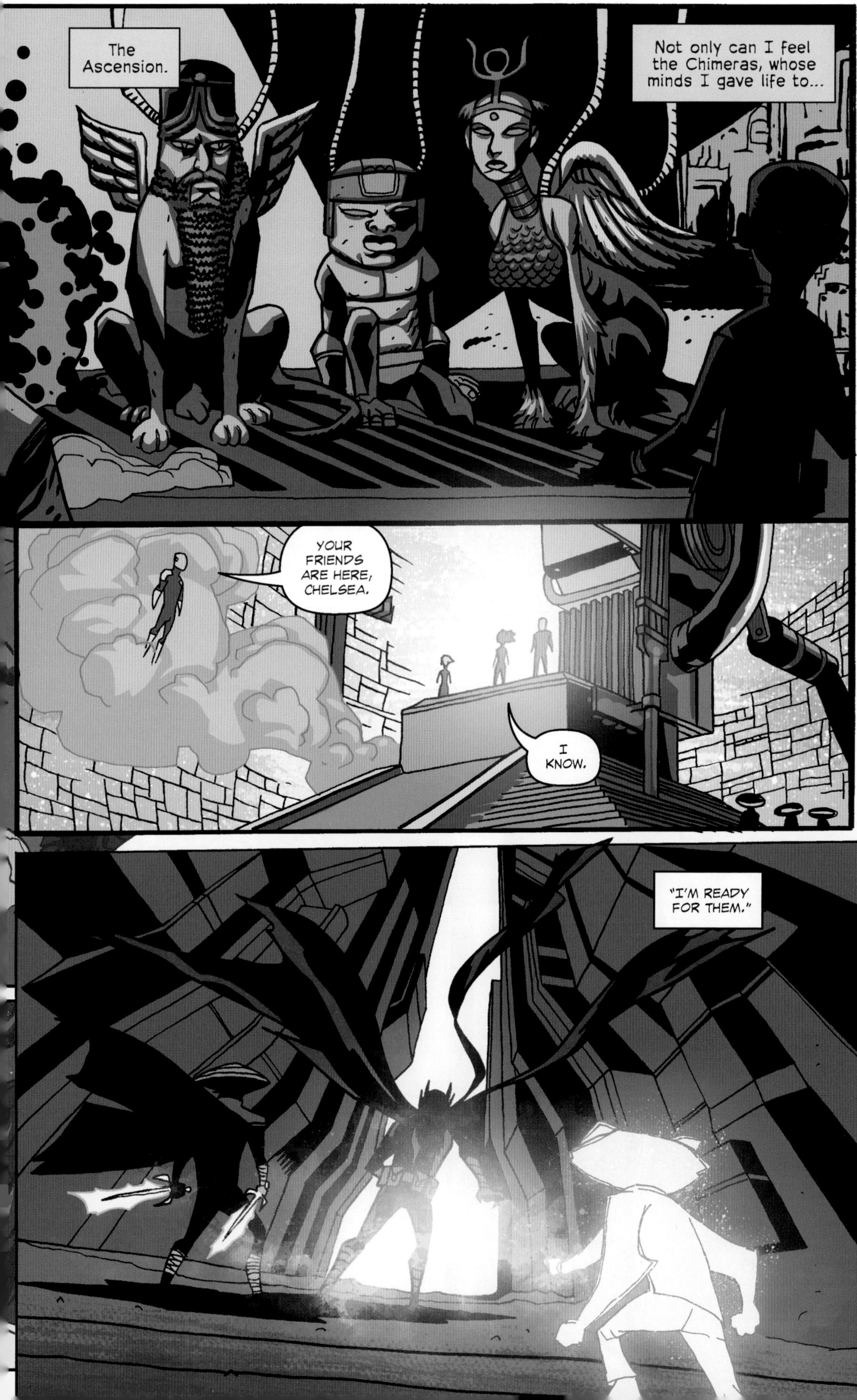
The Ascension.
Not only can I feel the Chimeras, whose minds I gave life to...
YOUR FRIENDS ARE HERE, CHELSEA.
I KNOW.
"I'M READY FOR THEM."

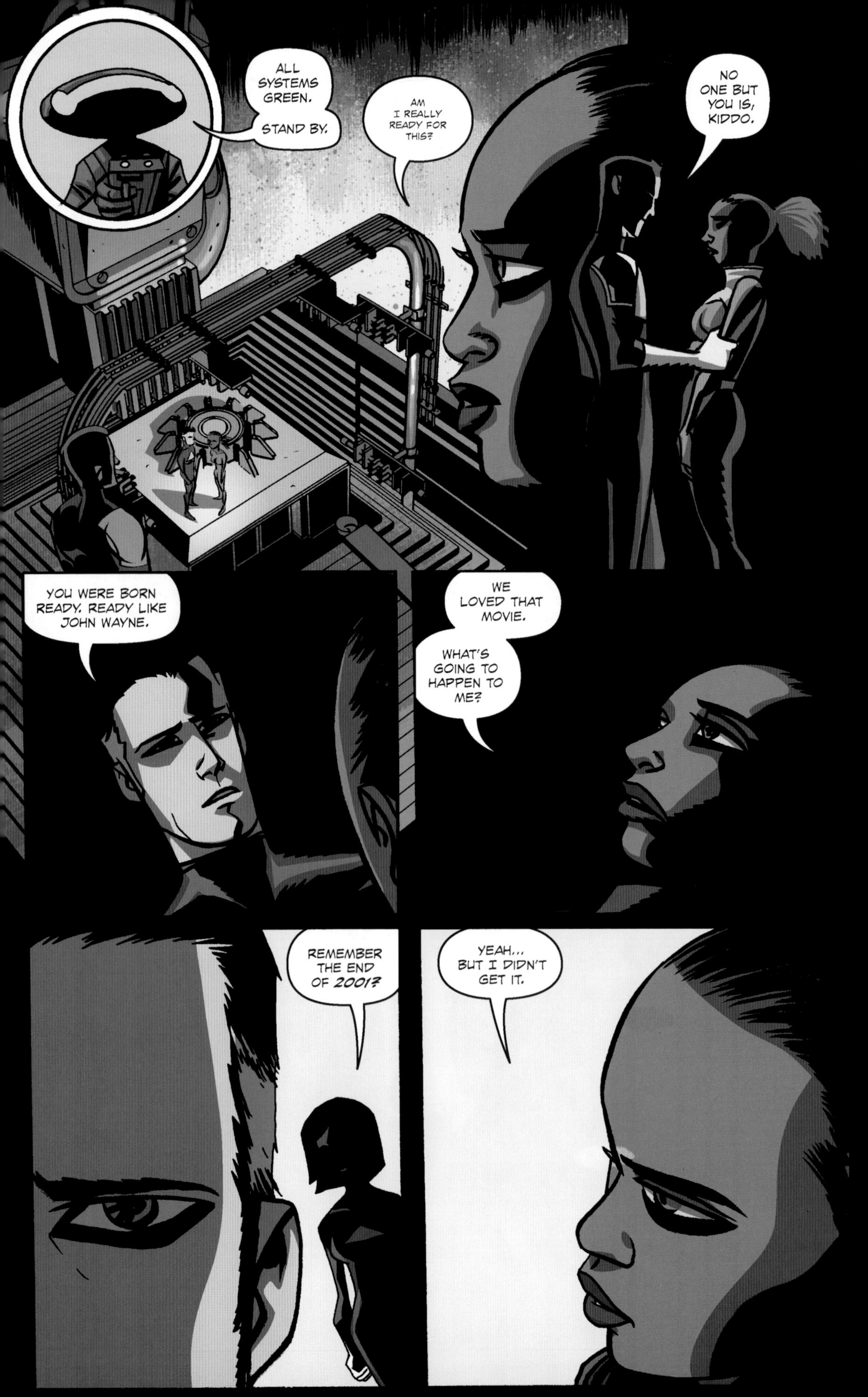
ALL SYSTEMS GREEN.
STAND BY.
AM I REALLY READY FOR THIS?
NO ONE BUT YOU IS, KIDDO.
YOU WERE BORN READY. READY LIKE JOHN WAYNE.
WE LOVED THAT MOVIE.
WHAT'S GOING TO HAPPEN TO ME?
REMEMBER THE END OF *2001*?
YEAH... BUT I DIDN'T GET IT.

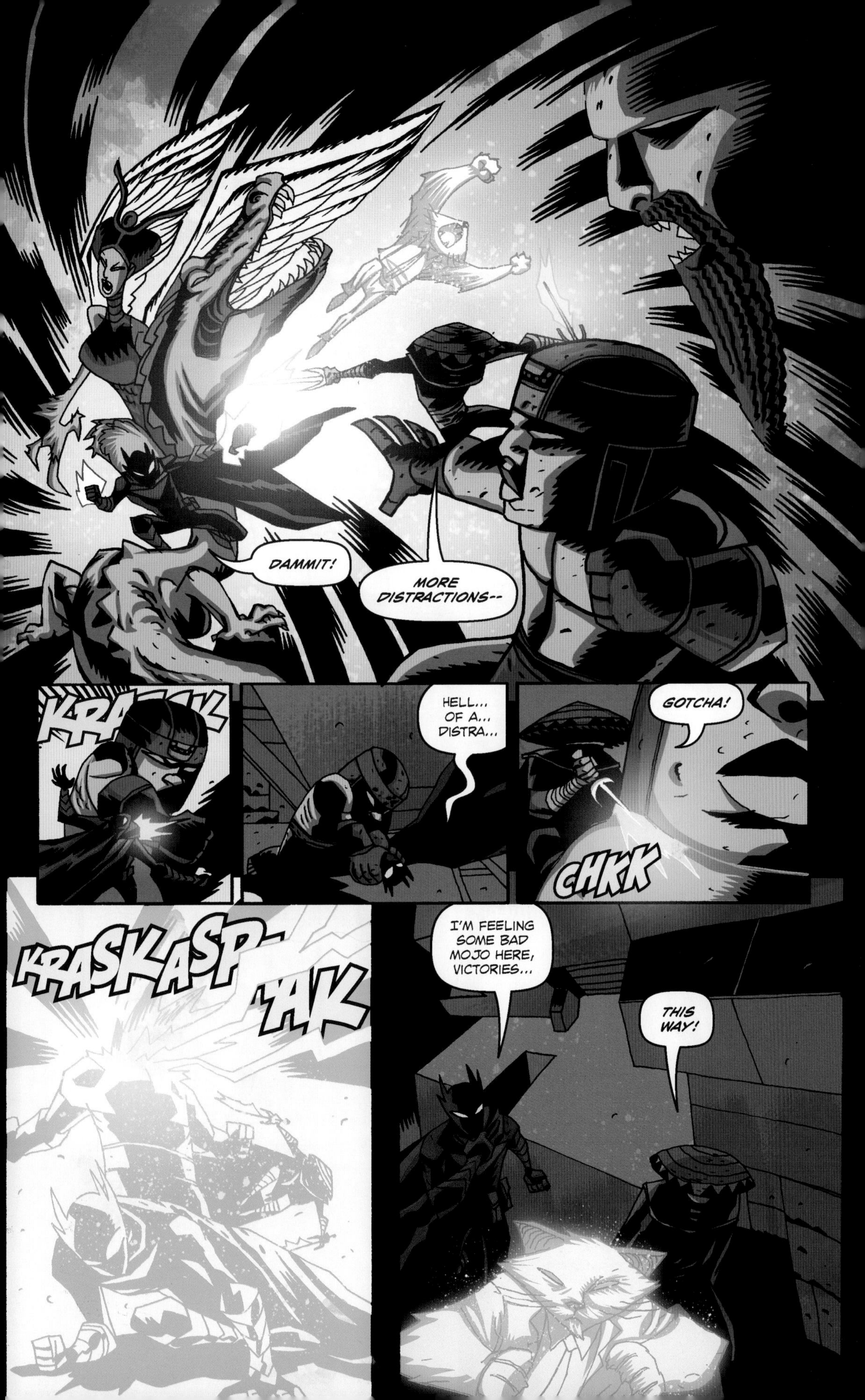
DAMMIT!
MORE DISTRACTIONS--
KRAKAK
HELL... OF A... DISTRA...
GOTCHA!
CHKK
KRASKASP-TAK
I'M FEELING SOME BAD MOJO HERE, VICTORIES...
THIS WAY!

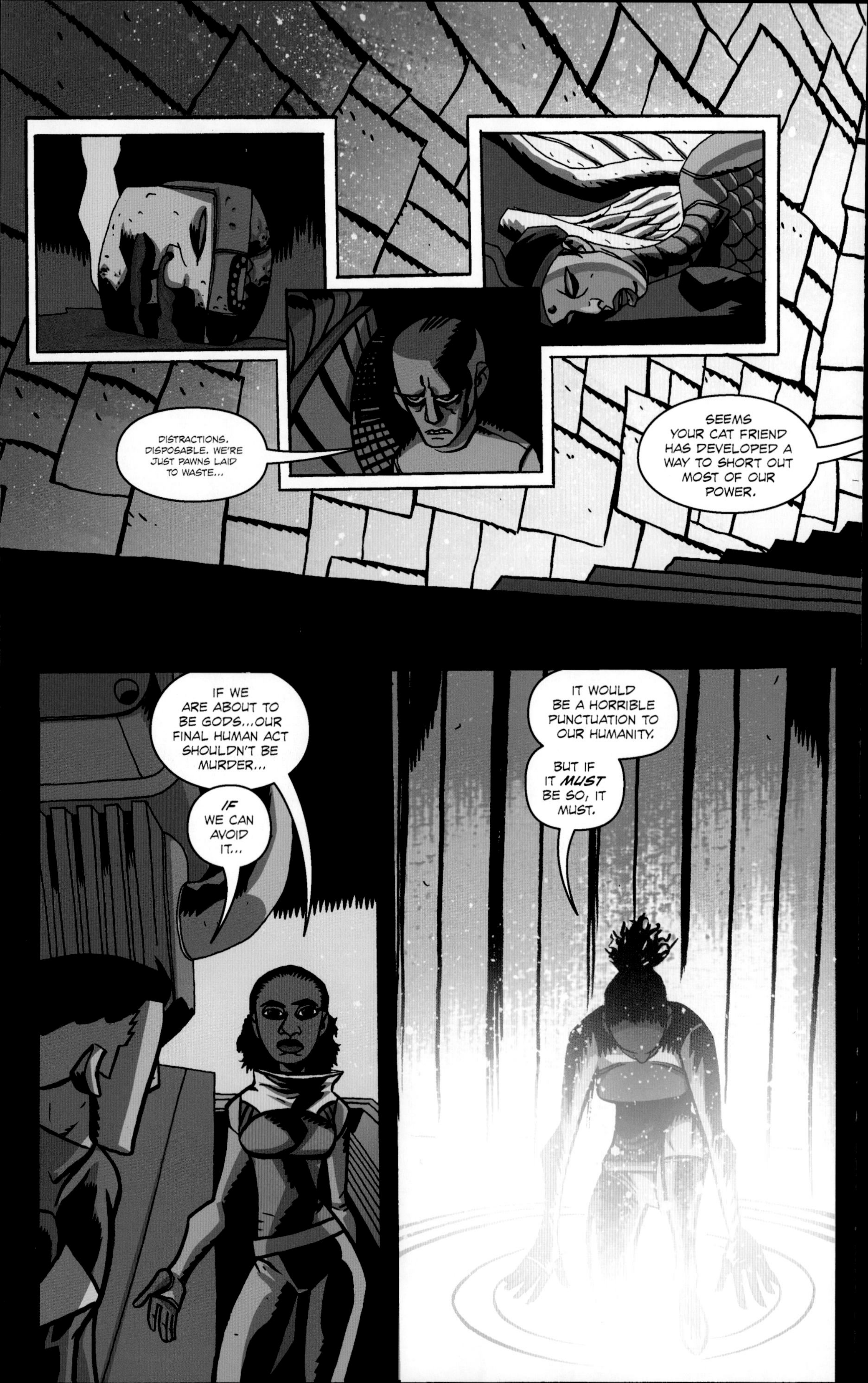
DISTRACTIONS. DISPOSABLE. WE'RE JUST PAWNS LAID TO WASTE...
SEEMS YOUR CAT FRIEND HAS DEVELOPED A WAY TO SHORT OUT MOST OF OUR POWER.
IF WE ARE ABOUT TO BE GODS...OUR FINAL HUMAN ACT SHOULDN'T BE MURDER...
IF WE CAN AVOID IT...
IT WOULD BE A HORRIBLE PUNCTUATION TO OUR HUMANITY.
BUT IF IT MUST BE SO, IT MUST.

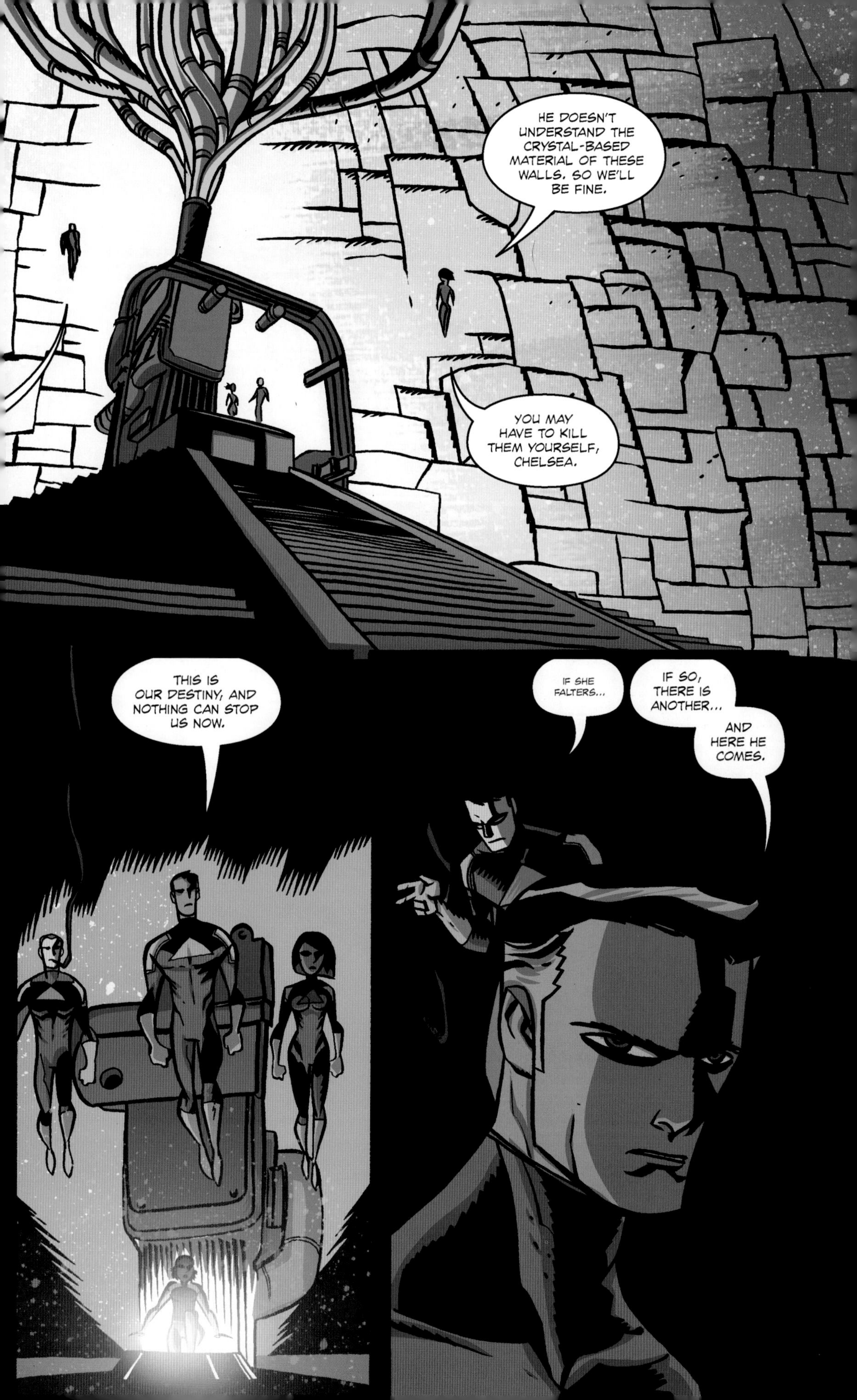
HE DOESN'T UNDERSTAND THE CRYSTAL-BASED MATERIAL OF THESE WALLS. SO WE'LL BE FINE.
YOU MAY HAVE TO KILL THEM YOURSELF, CHELSEA.
THIS IS OUR DESTINY, AND NOTHING CAN STOP US NOW.
IF SHE FALTERS...
IF SO, THERE IS ANOTHER...
AND HERE HE COMES.

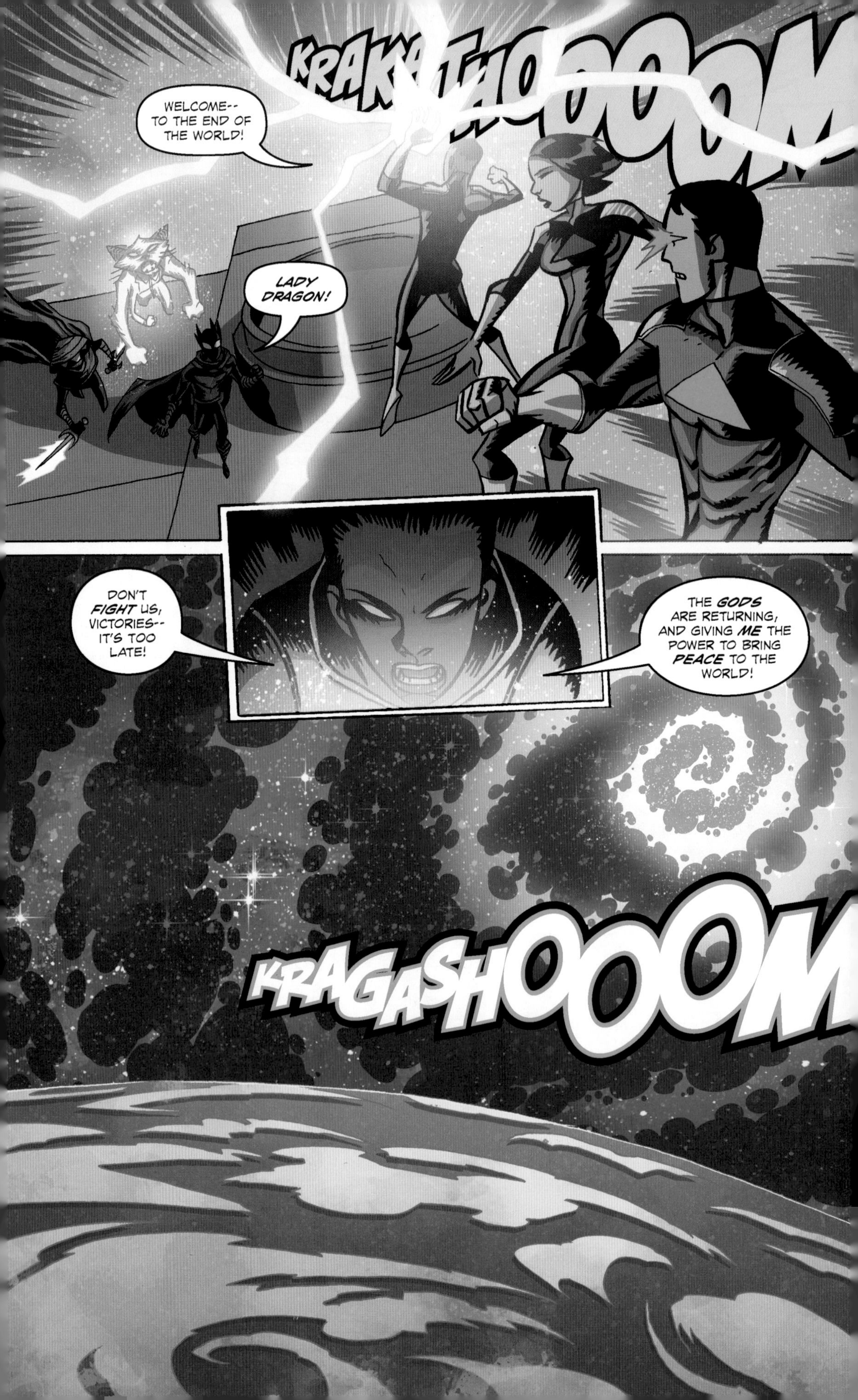
KRAKATHOOOOOM
WELCOME-- TO THE END OF THE WORLD!
LADY DRAGON!
DON'T FIGHT US, VICTORIES-- IT'S TOO LATE!
THE GODS ARE RETURNING, AND GIVING ME THE POWER TO BRING PEACE TO THE WORLD!
KRAGASHOOOOM

CHAPTER FOUR

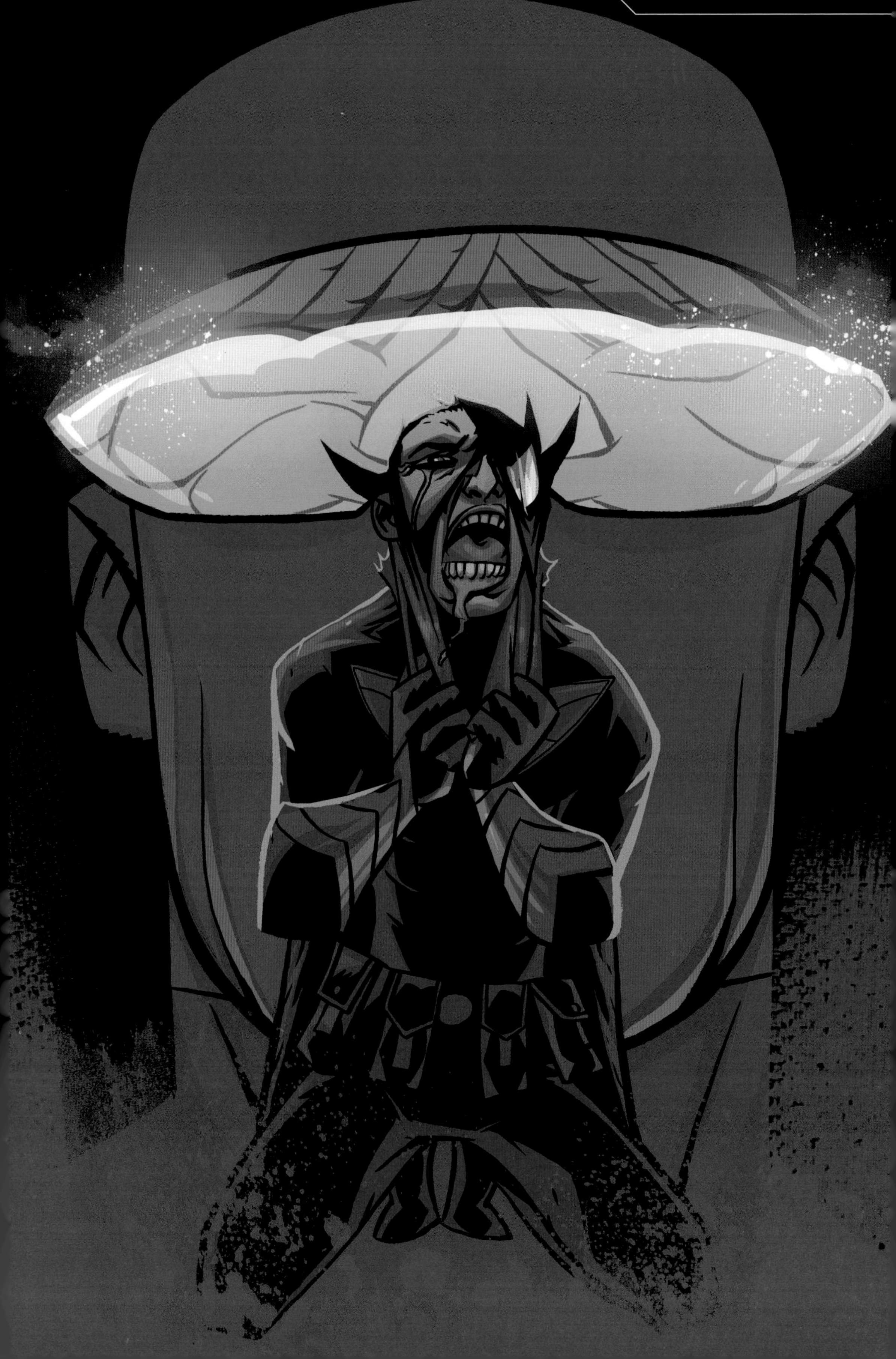

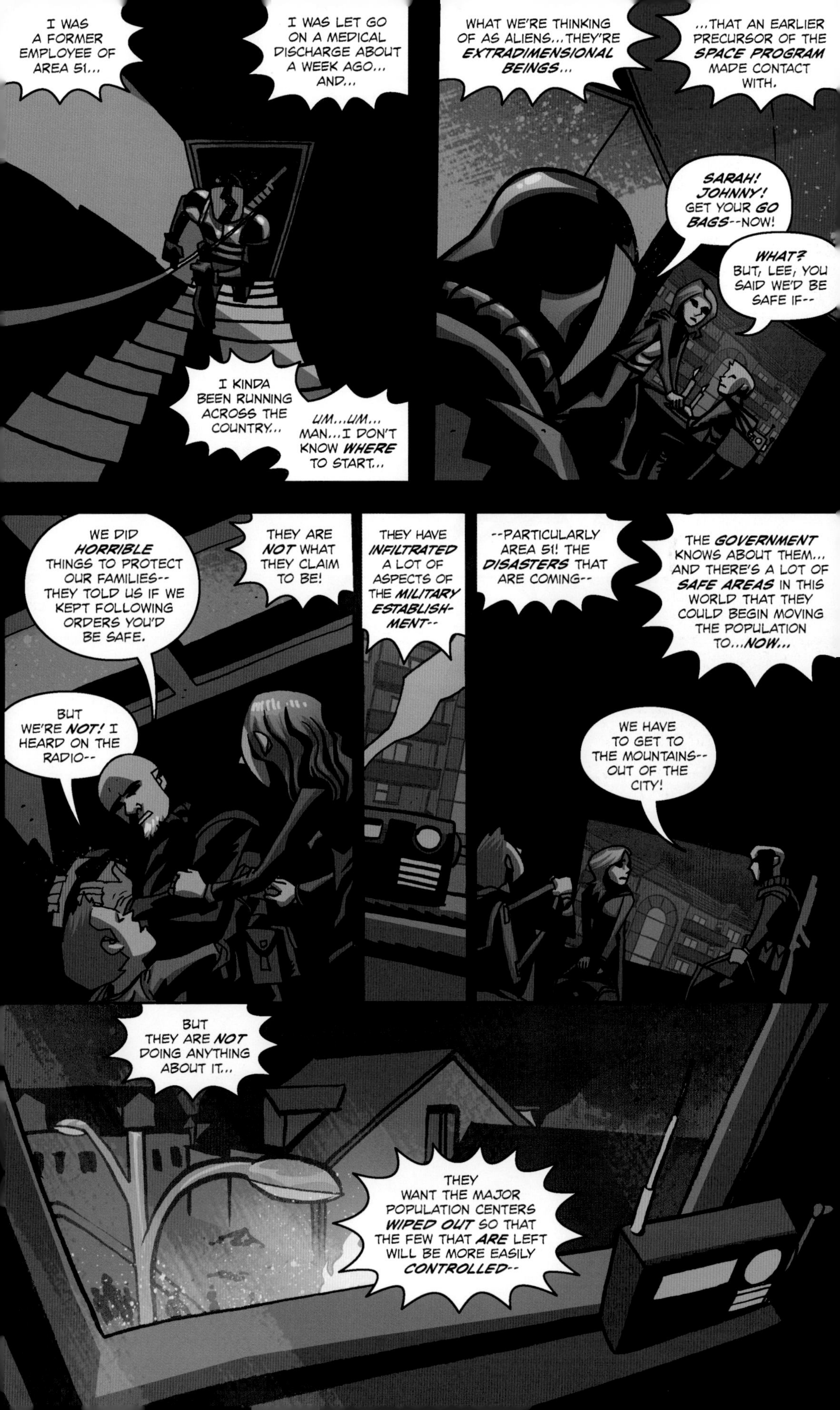
I WAS A FORMER EMPLOYEE OF AREA 51...
I WAS LET GO ON A MEDICAL DISCHARGE ABOUT A WEEK AGO... AND...
I KINDA BEEN RUNNING ACROSS THE COUNTRY...
UM...UM... MAN...I DON'T KNOW WHERE TO START...
WHAT WE'RE THINKING OF AS ALIENS...THEY'RE EXTRADIMENSIONAL BEINGS...
...THAT AN EARLIER PRECURSOR OF THE SPACE PROGRAM MADE CONTACT WITH.
SARAH! JOHNNY! GET YOUR GO BAGS--NOW!
WHAT? BUT, LEE, YOU SAID WE'D BE SAFE IF--
WE DID HORRIBLE THINGS TO PROTECT OUR FAMILIES--THEY TOLD US IF WE KEPT FOLLOWING ORDERS YOU'D BE SAFE.
THEY ARE NOT WHAT THEY CLAIM TO BE!
BUT WE'RE NOT! I HEARD ON THE RADIO--
THEY HAVE INFILTRATED A LOT OF ASPECTS OF THE MILITARY ESTABLISH-MENT--
--PARTICULARLY AREA 51! THE DISASTERS THAT ARE COMING--
THE GOVERNMENT KNOWS ABOUT THEM... AND THERE'S A LOT OF SAFE AREAS IN THIS WORLD THAT THEY COULD BEGIN MOVING THE POPULATION TO...NOW...
WE HAVE TO GET TO THE MOUNTAINS--OUT OF THE CITY!
BUT THEY ARE NOT DOING ANYTHING ABOUT IT...
THEY WANT THE MAJOR POPULATION CENTERS WIPED OUT SO THAT THE FEW THAT ARE LEFT WILL BE MORE EASILY CONTROLLED--

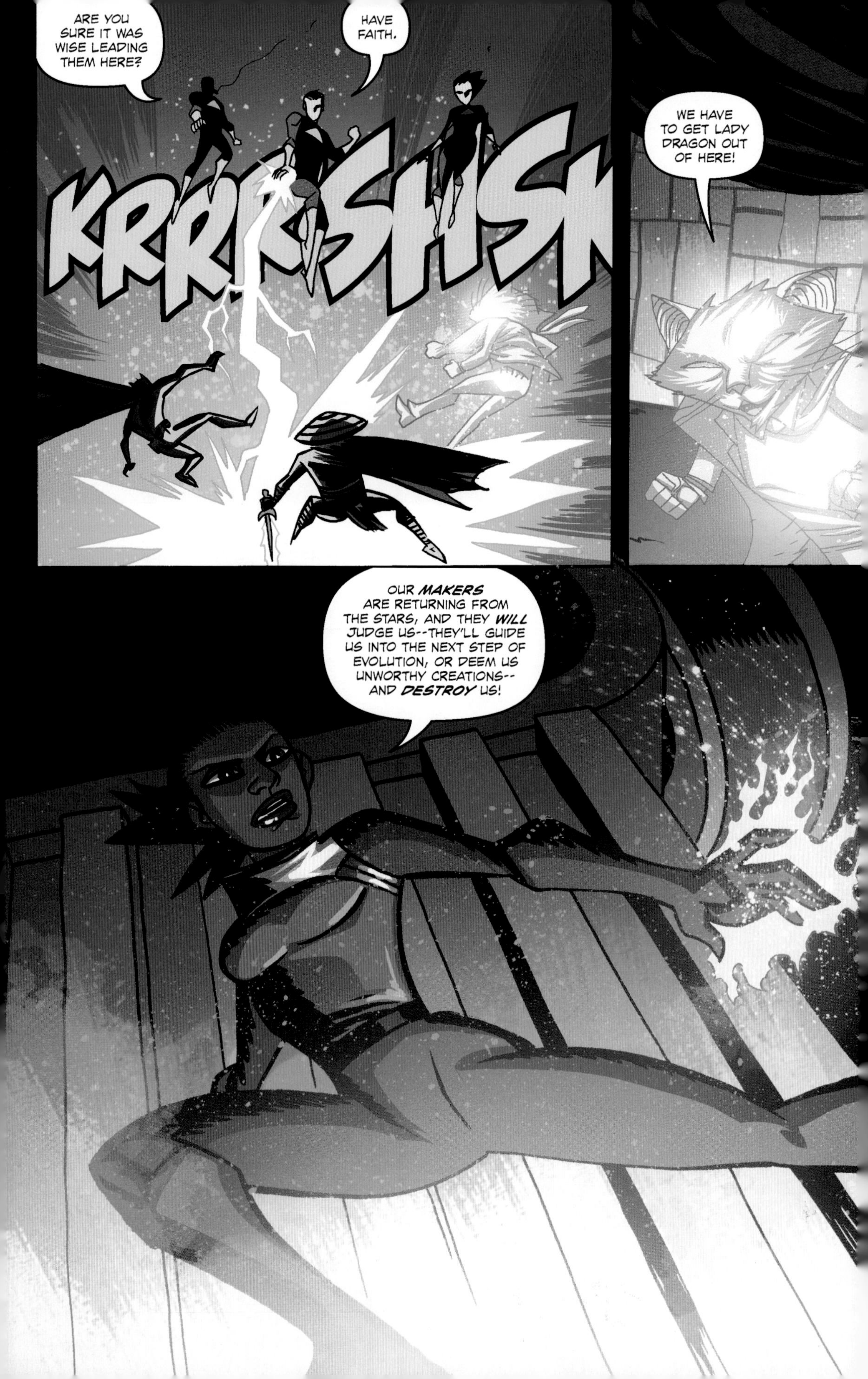
ARE YOU SURE IT WAS WISE LEADING THEM HERE?
HAVE FAITH.
KRRRSHSK
WE HAVE TO GET LADY DRAGON OUT OF HERE!
OUR MAKERS ARE RETURNING FROM THE STARS, AND THEY WILL JUDGE US--THEY'LL GUIDE US INTO THE NEXT STEP OF EVOLUTION, OR DEEM US UNWORTHY CREATIONS--AND DESTROY US!

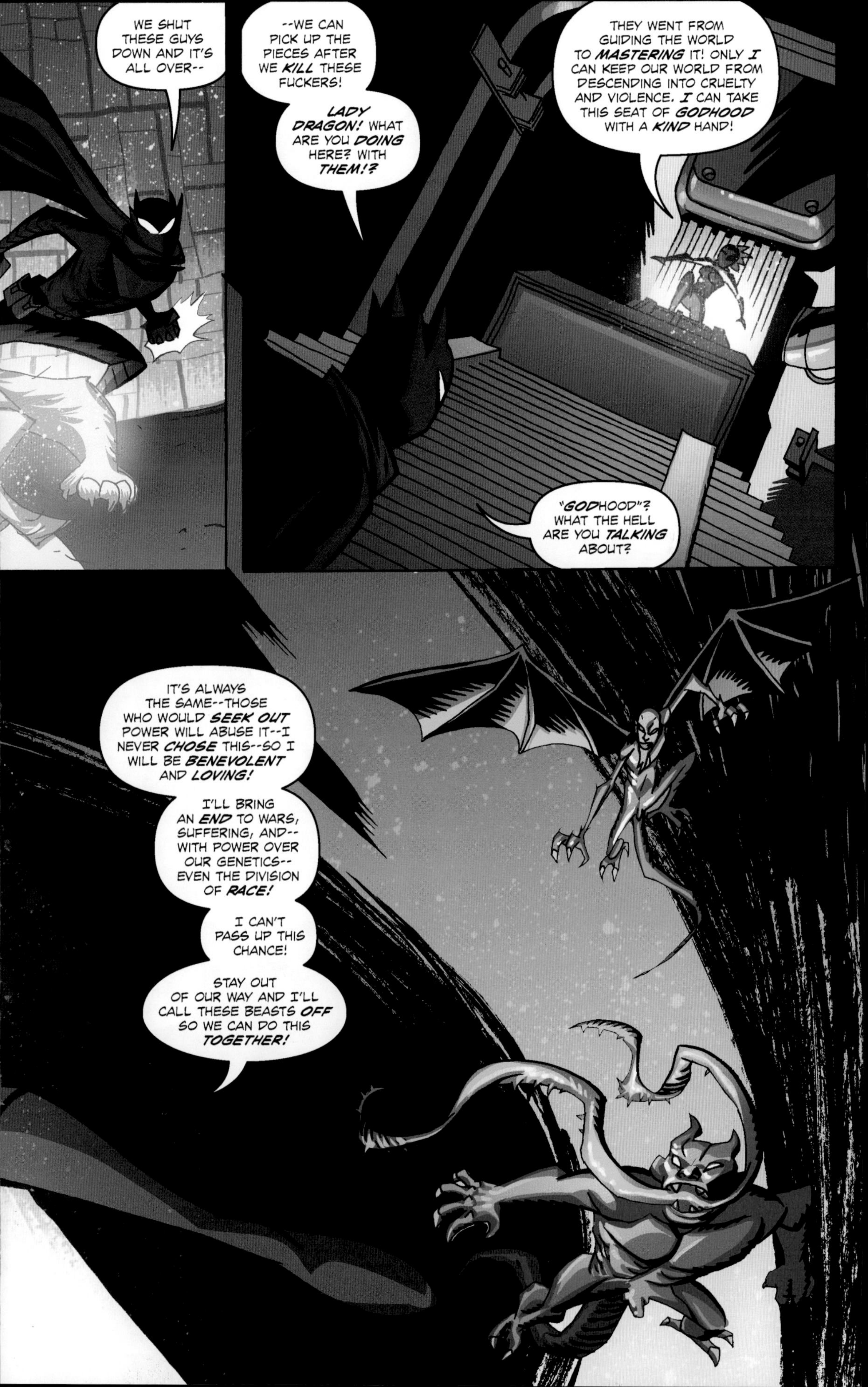
WE SHUT THESE GUYS DOWN AND IT'S ALL OVER--
--WE CAN PICK UP THE PIECES AFTER WE KILL THESE FUCKERS!
LADY DRAGON! WHAT ARE YOU DOING HERE? WITH THEM!?
THEY WENT FROM GUIDING THE WORLD TO MASTERING IT! ONLY I CAN KEEP OUR WORLD FROM DESCENDING INTO CRUELTY AND VIOLENCE. I CAN TAKE THIS SEAT OF GODHOOD WITH A KIND HAND!
"GODHOOD"? WHAT THE HELL ARE YOU TALKING ABOUT?
IT'S ALWAYS THE SAME--THOSE WHO WOULD SEEK OUT POWER WILL ABUSE IT--I NEVER CHOSE THIS--SO I WILL BE BENEVOLENT AND LOVING!
I'LL BRING AN END TO WARS, SUFFERING, AND--WITH POWER OVER OUR GENETICS--EVEN THE DIVISION OF RACE!
I CAN'T PASS UP THIS CHANCE!
STAY OUT OF OUR WAY AND I'LL CALL THESE BEASTS OFF SO WE CAN DO THIS TOGETHER!

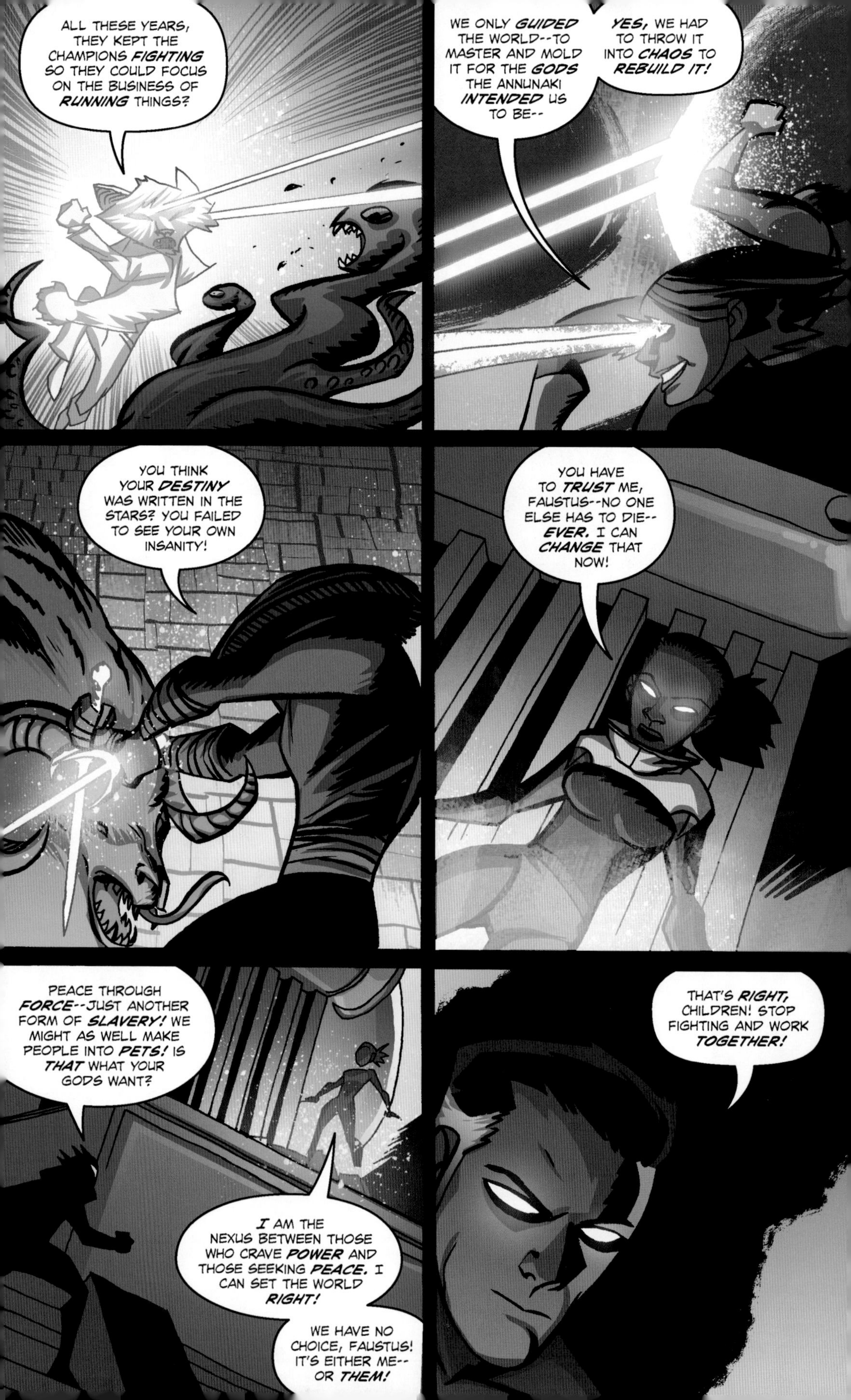
ALL THESE YEARS, THEY KEPT THE CHAMPIONS FIGHTING SO THEY COULD FOCUS ON THE BUSINESS OF RUNNING THINGS?
WE ONLY GUIDED THE WORLD--TO MASTER AND MOLD IT FOR THE GODS THE ANNUNAKI INTENDED US TO BE--
YES, WE HAD TO THROW IT INTO CHAOS TO REBUILD IT!
YOU THINK YOUR DESTINY WAS WRITTEN IN THE STARS? YOU FAILED TO SEE YOUR OWN INSANITY!
YOU HAVE TO TRUST ME, FAUSTUS--NO ONE ELSE HAS TO DIE--EVER. I CAN CHANGE THAT NOW!
PEACE THROUGH FORCE--JUST ANOTHER FORM OF SLAVERY! WE MIGHT AS WELL MAKE PEOPLE INTO PETS! IS THAT WHAT YOUR GODS WANT?
I AM THE NEXUS BETWEEN THOSE WHO CRAVE POWER AND THOSE SEEKING PEACE. I CAN SET THE WORLD RIGHT!
WE HAVE NO CHOICE, FAUSTUS! IT'S EITHER ME--OR THEM!
THAT'S RIGHT, CHILDREN! STOP FIGHTING AND WORK TOGETHER!

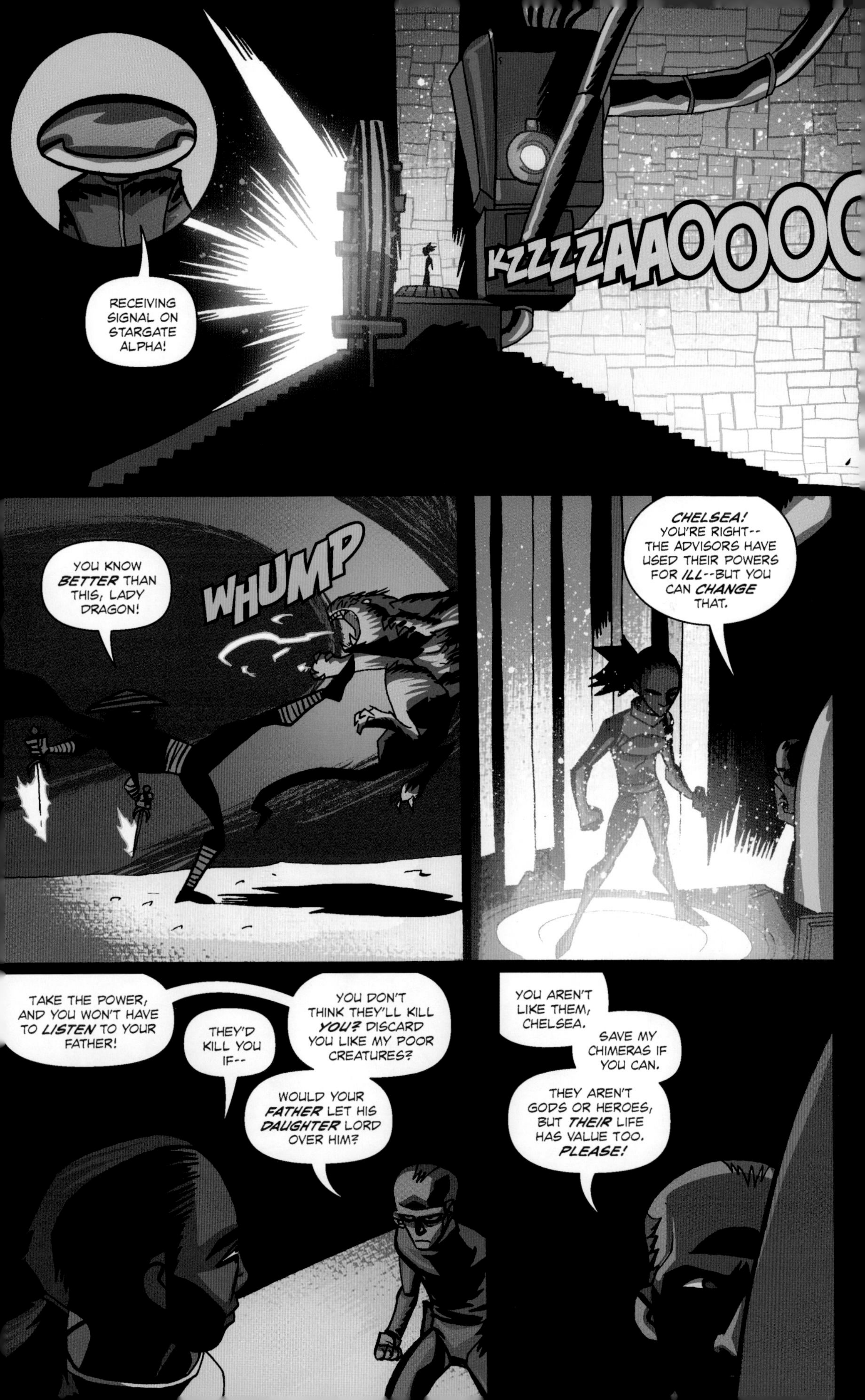
RECEIVING SIGNAL ON STARGATE ALPHA!
KZZZZAAOOOO
YOU KNOW BETTER THAN THIS, LADY DRAGON!
WHUMP
CHELSEA! YOU'RE RIGHT-- THE ADVISORS HAVE USED THEIR POWERS FOR ILL--BUT YOU CAN CHANGE THAT.
TAKE THE POWER, AND YOU WON'T HAVE TO LISTEN TO YOUR FATHER!
THEY'D KILL YOU IF--
YOU DON'T THINK THEY'LL KILL YOU? DISCARD YOU LIKE MY POOR CREATURES?
WOULD YOUR FATHER LET HIS DAUGHTER LORD OVER HIM?
YOU AREN'T LIKE THEM, CHELSEA.
SAVE MY CHIMERAS IF YOU CAN.
THEY AREN'T GODS OR HEROES, BUT THEIR LIFE HAS VALUE TOO. PLEASE!

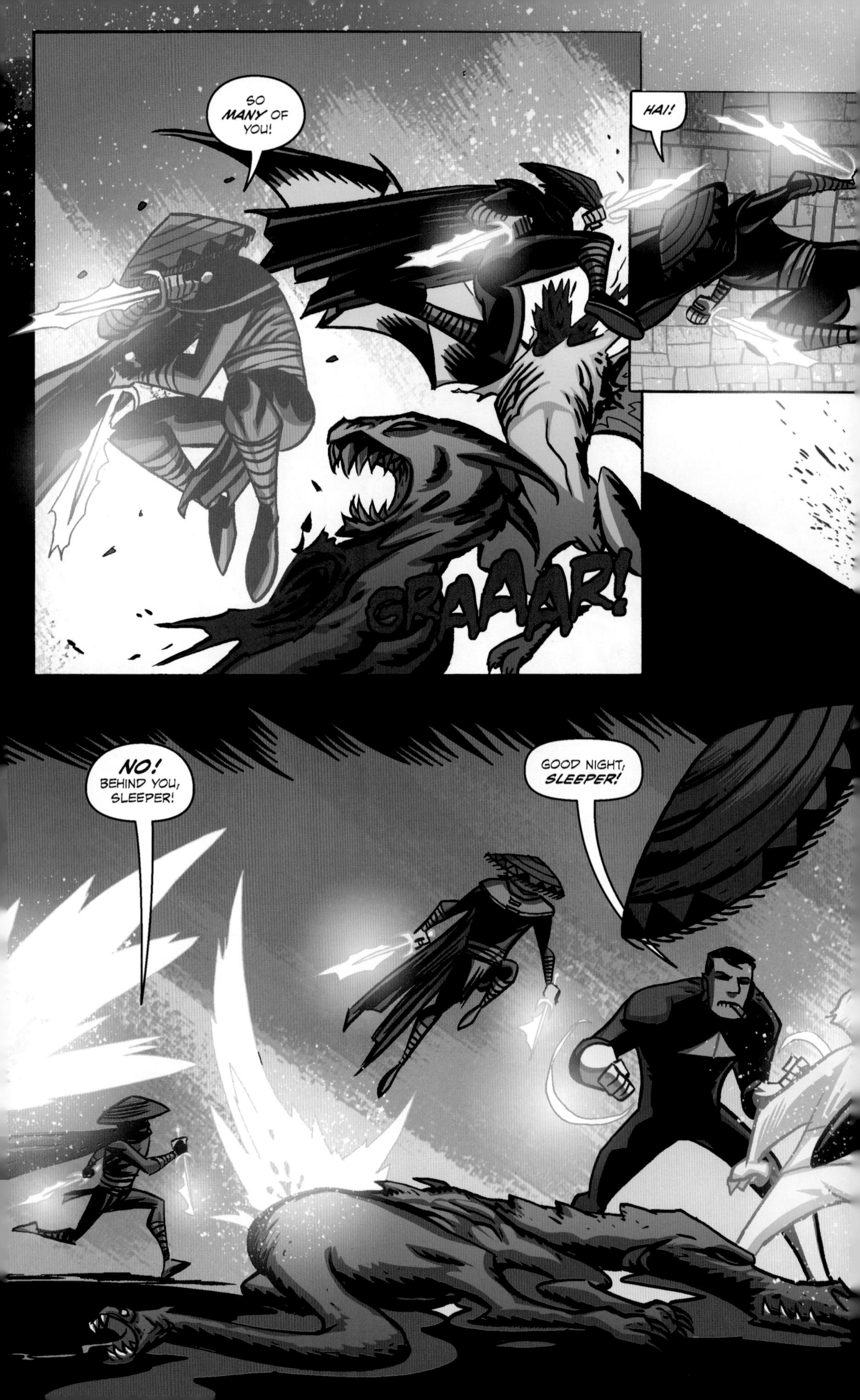
SO MANY OF YOU!
HAI!
GRAAAAR!
NO! BEHIND YOU, SLEEPER!
GOOD NIGHT, SLEEPER!

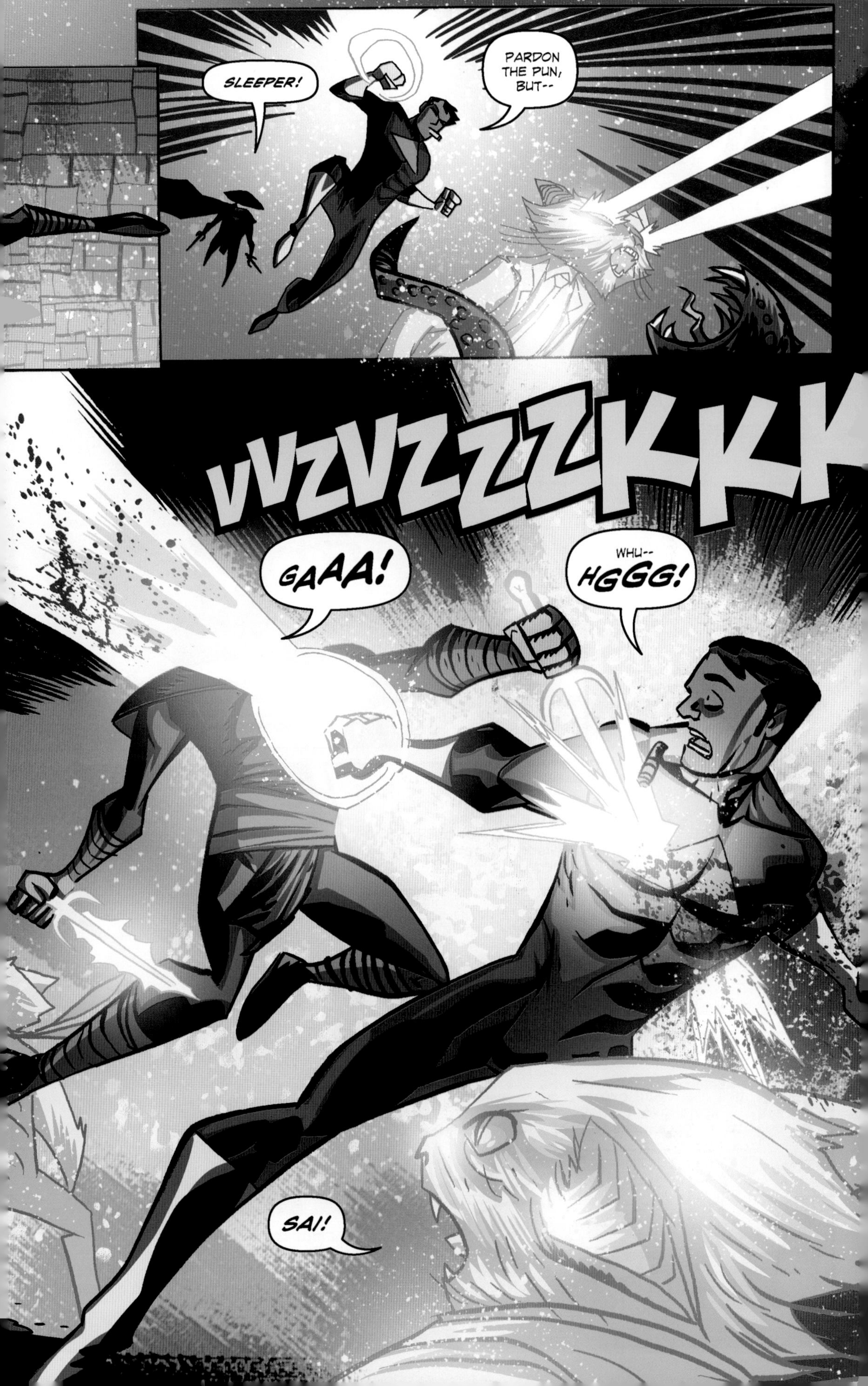
SLEEPER!
PARDON THE PUN, BUT--
VVZVZZZKKK
GAAA!
WHU-- HGGG!
SAI!

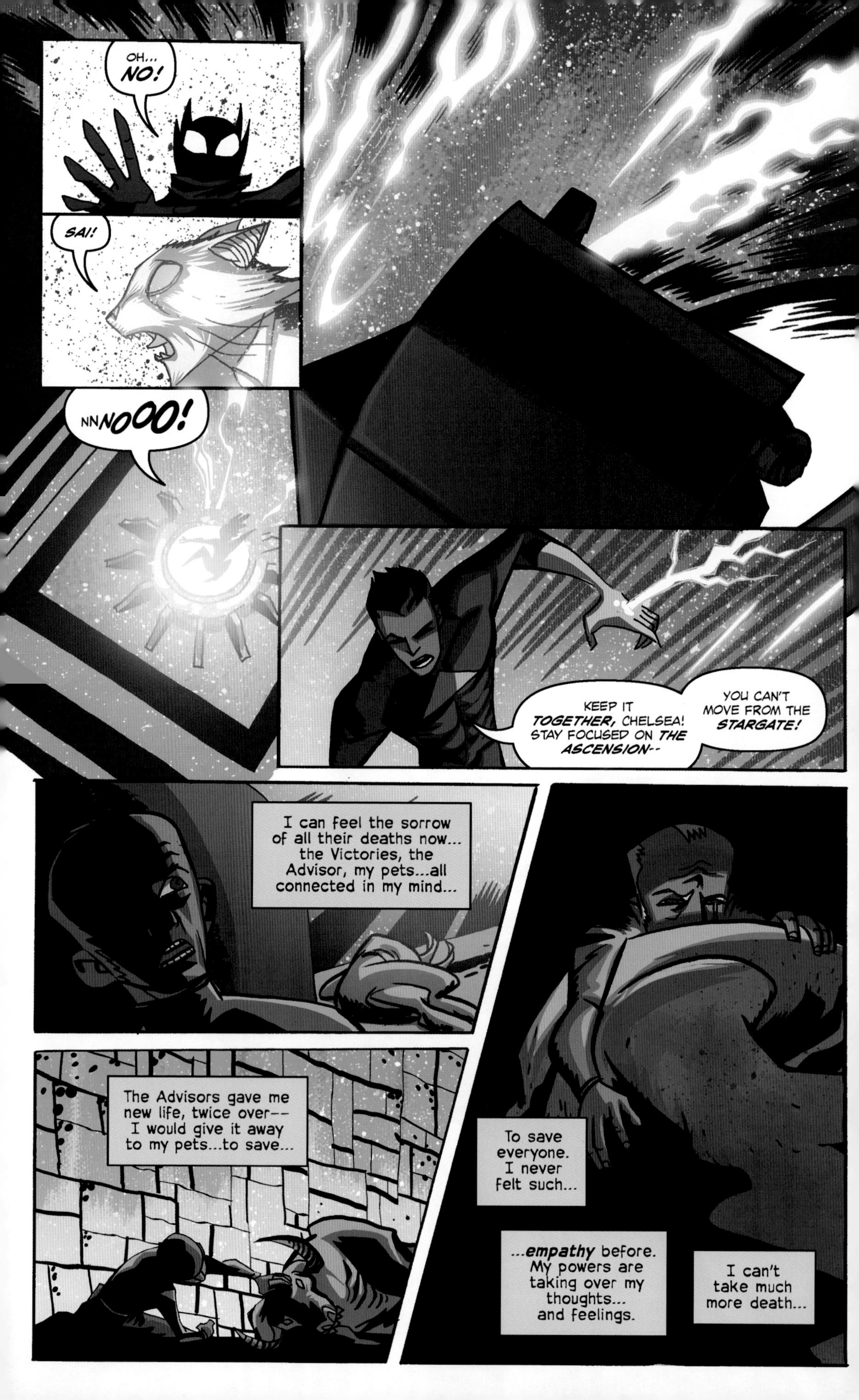
OH... NO!
SAI!
NNNOOO!
KEEP IT TOGETHER, CHELSEA! STAY FOCUSED ON THE ASCENSION--
YOU CAN'T MOVE FROM THE STARGATE!
I can feel the sorrow of all their deaths now... the Victories, the Advisor, my pets...all connected in my mind...
The Advisors gave me new life, twice over-- I would give it away to my pets...to save...
To save everyone. I never felt such...
...empathy before. My powers are taking over my thoughts... and feelings.
I can't take much more death...

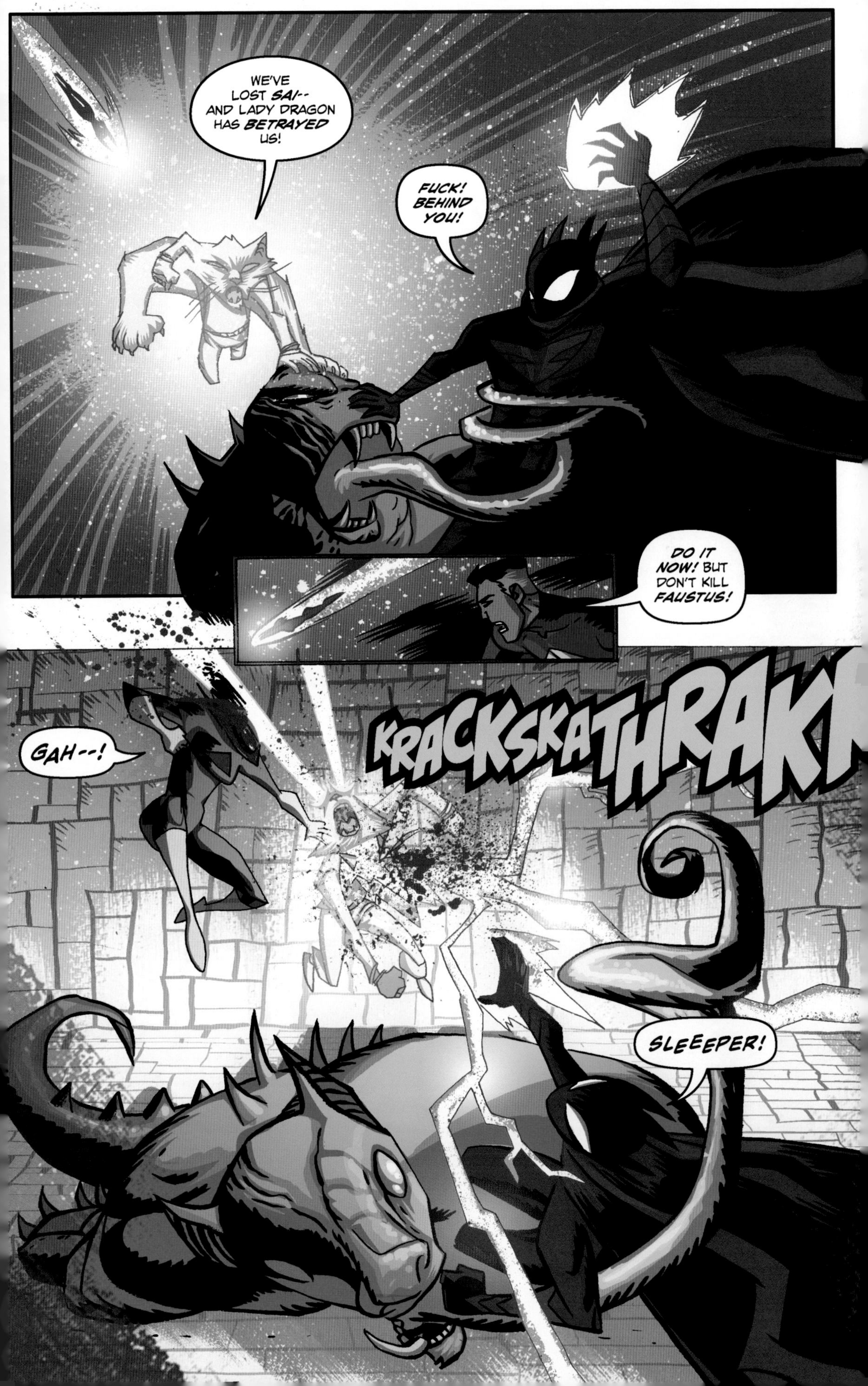
WE'VE LOST SAI-- AND LADY DRAGON HAS BETRAYED US!
FUCK! BEHIND YOU!
DO IT NOW! BUT DON'T KILL FAUSTUS!
GAH--!
KRACKSKATHRAKK
SLEEEPER!

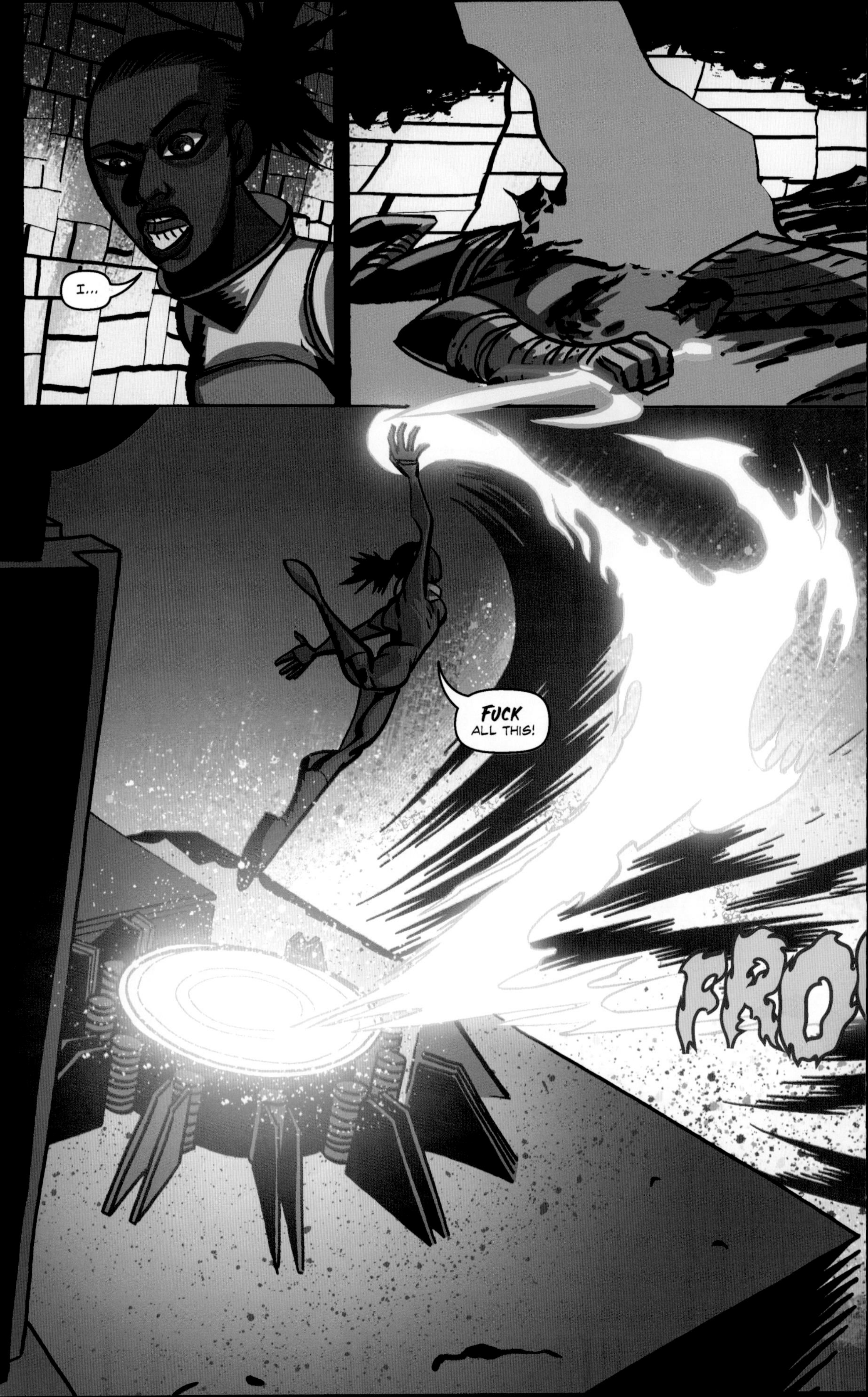
I...
FUCK ALL THIS!
FRO

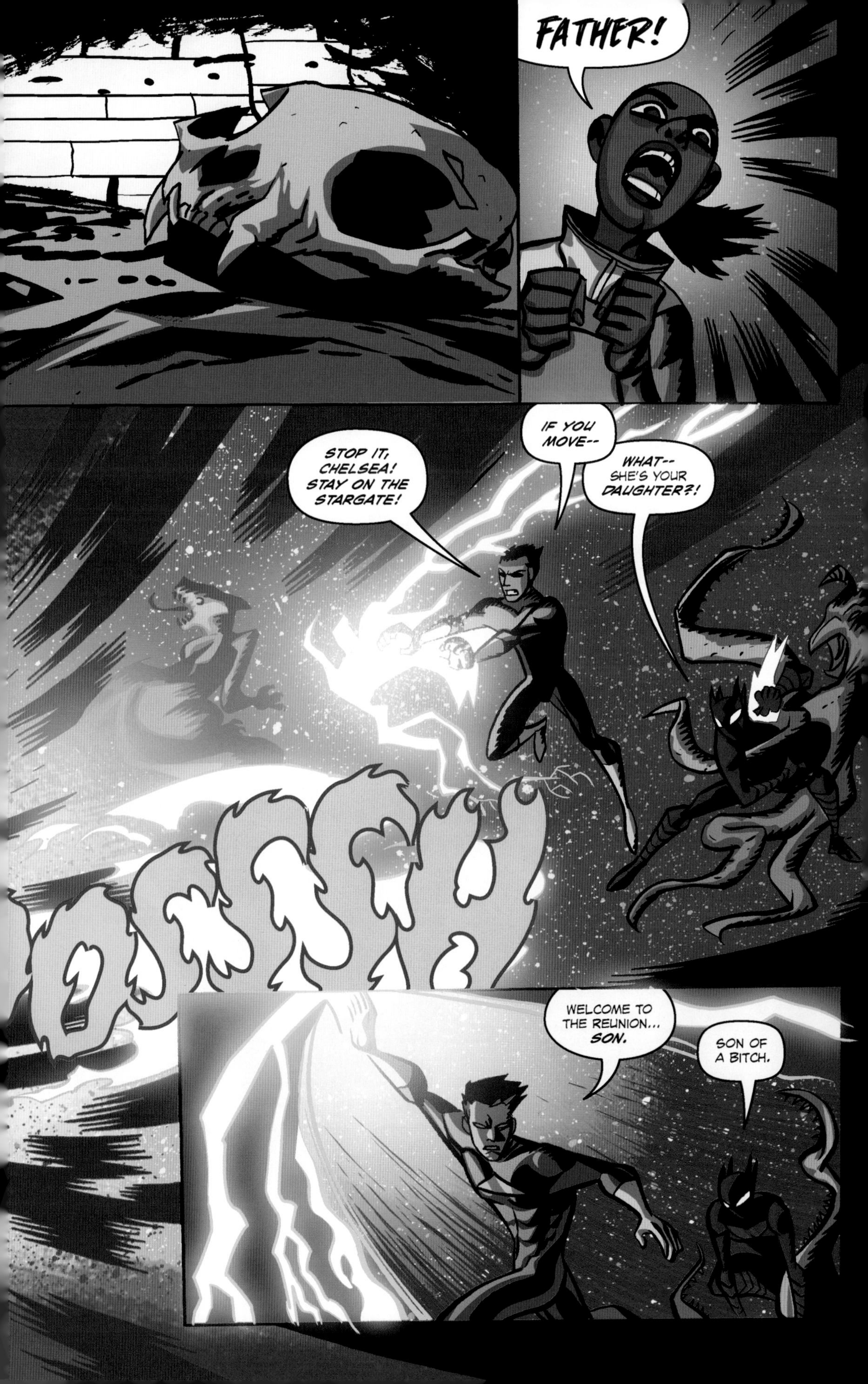
FATHER!
STOP IT, CHELSEA! STAY ON THE STARGATE!
IF YOU MOVE--
WHAT-- SHE'S YOUR DAUGHTER?!
WELCOME TO THE REUNION... SON.
SON OF A BITCH.

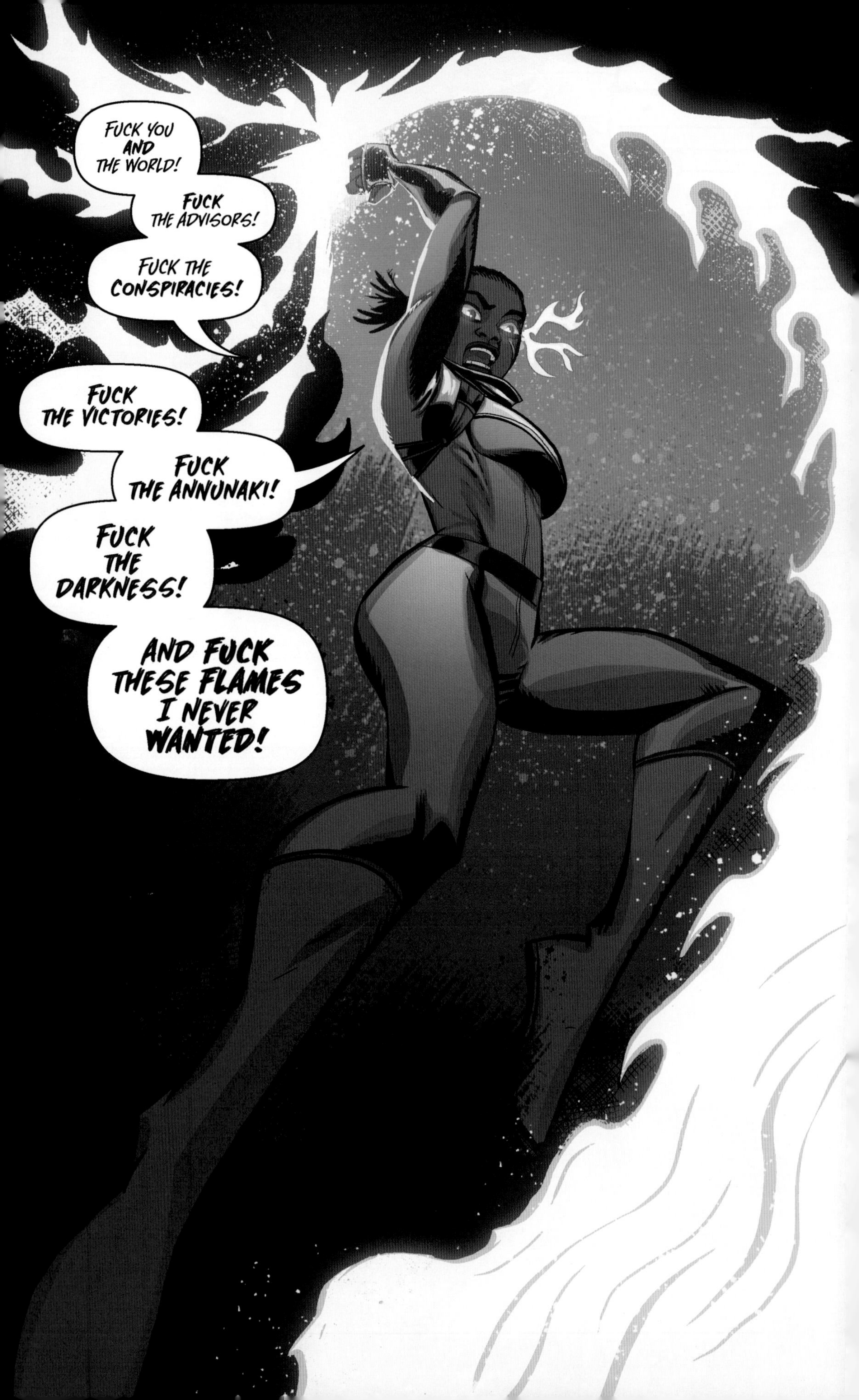
FUCK YOU AND THE WORLD!
FUCK THE ADVISORS!
FUCK THE CONSPIRACIES!
FUCK THE VICTORIES!
FUCK THE ANNUNAKI!
FUCK THE DARKNESS!
AND FUCK THESE FLAMES I NEVER WANTED!

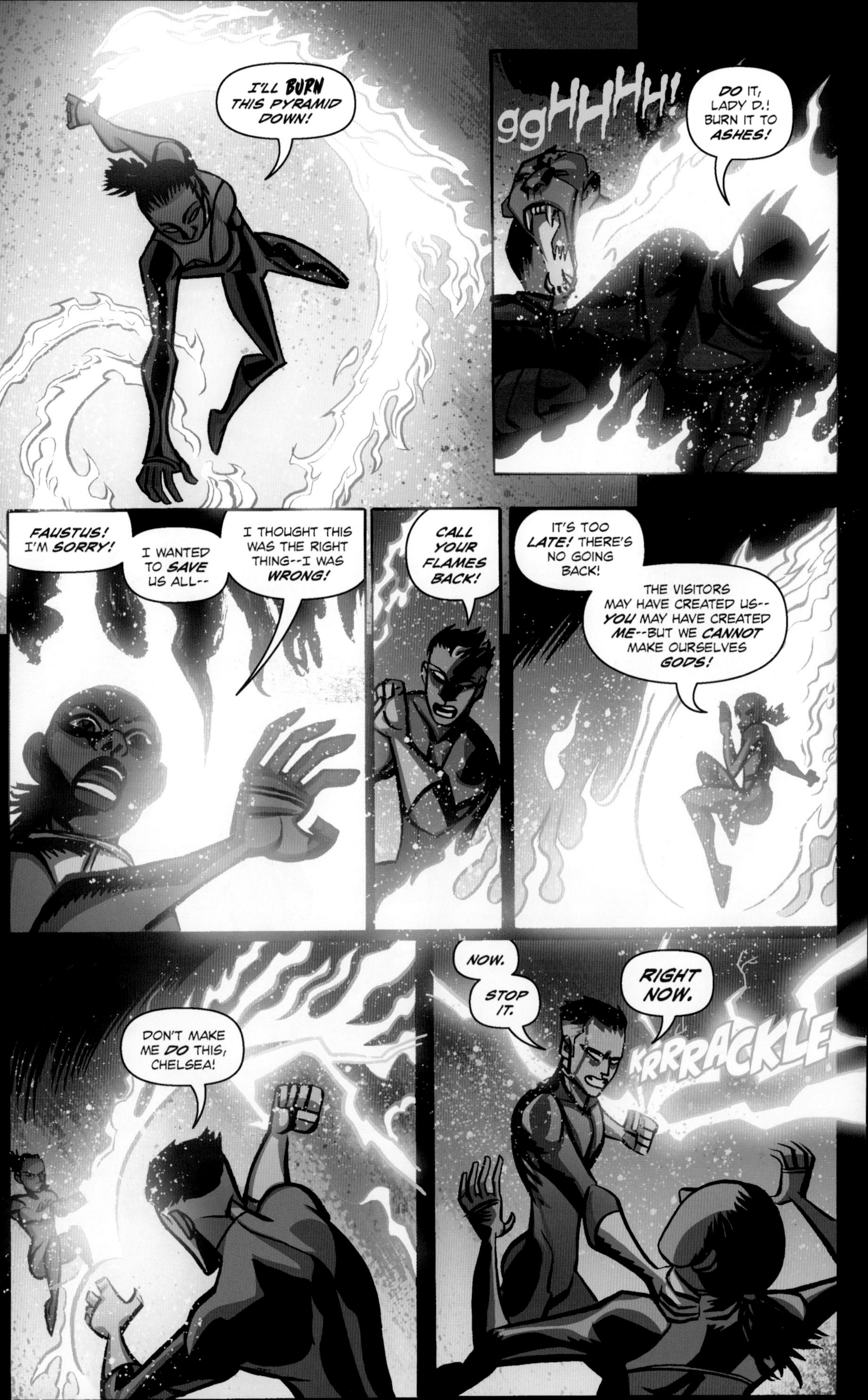

I'LL BURN THIS PYRAMID DOWN!
ggHHHH!
DO IT, LADY D.! BURN IT TO ASHES!
FAUSTUS! I'M SORRY!
I WANTED TO SAVE US ALL--
I THOUGHT THIS WAS THE RIGHT THING--I WAS WRONG!
CALL YOUR FLAMES BACK!
IT'S TOO LATE! THERE'S NO GOING BACK!
THE VISITORS MAY HAVE CREATED US-- YOU MAY HAVE CREATED ME--BUT WE CANNOT MAKE OURSELVES GODS!
DON'T MAKE ME DO THIS, CHELSEA!
NOW.
STOP IT.
RIGHT NOW.
KRRRACKLE

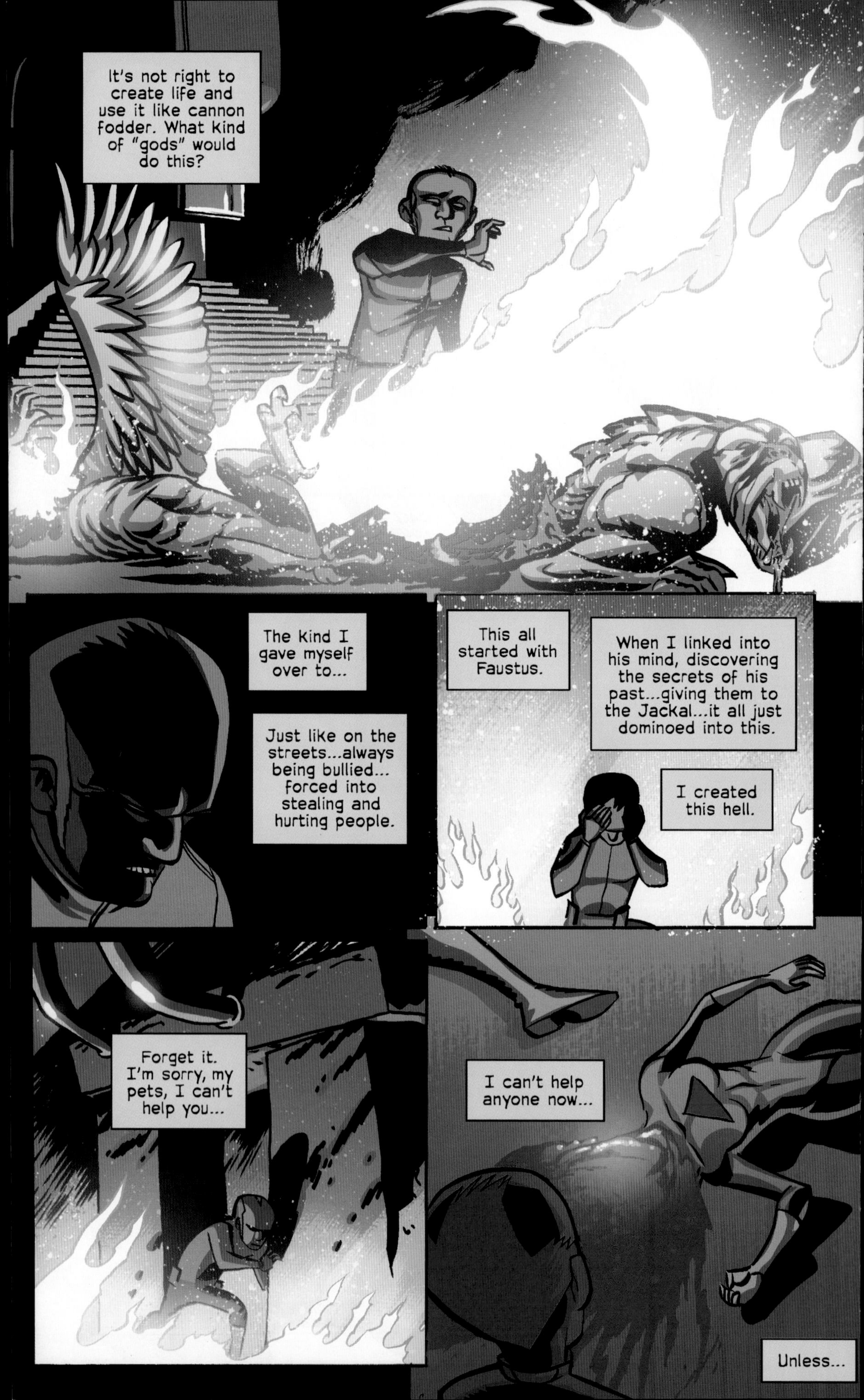
It's not right to create life and use it like cannon fodder. What kind of "gods" would do this?
The kind I gave myself over to...
Just like on the streets...always being bullied... forced into stealing and hurting people.
This all started with Faustus.
When I linked into his mind, discovering the secrets of his past...giving them to the Jackal...it all just dominoed into this.
I created this hell.
Forget it. I'm sorry, my pets, I can't help you...
I can't help anyone now...
Unless...

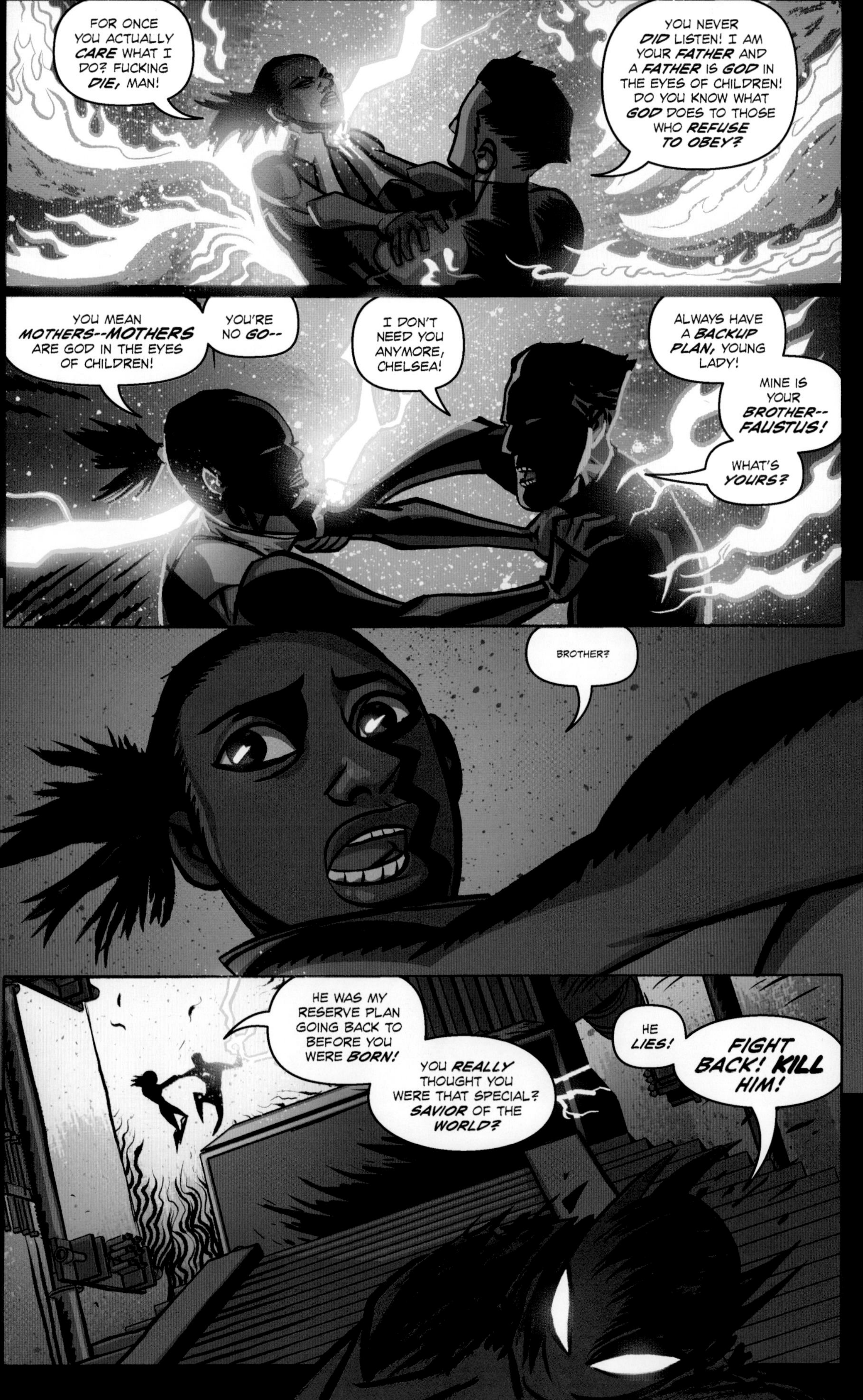
FOR ONCE YOU ACTUALLY CARE WHAT I DO? FUCKING DIE, MAN!
YOU NEVER DID LISTEN! I AM YOUR FATHER AND A FATHER IS GOD IN THE EYES OF CHILDREN! DO YOU KNOW WHAT GOD DOES TO THOSE WHO REFUSE TO OBEY?
YOU MEAN MOTHERS--MOTHERS ARE GOD IN THE EYES OF CHILDREN!
YOU'RE NO GO--
I DON'T NEED YOU ANYMORE, CHELSEA!
ALWAYS HAVE A BACKUP PLAN, YOUNG LADY!
MINE IS YOUR BROTHER-- FAUSTUS!
WHAT'S YOURS?
BROTHER?
HE WAS MY RESERVE PLAN GOING BACK TO BEFORE YOU WERE BORN!
YOU REALLY THOUGHT YOU WERE THAT SPECIAL? SAVIOR OF THE WORLD?
HE LIES!
FIGHT BACK! KILL HIM!

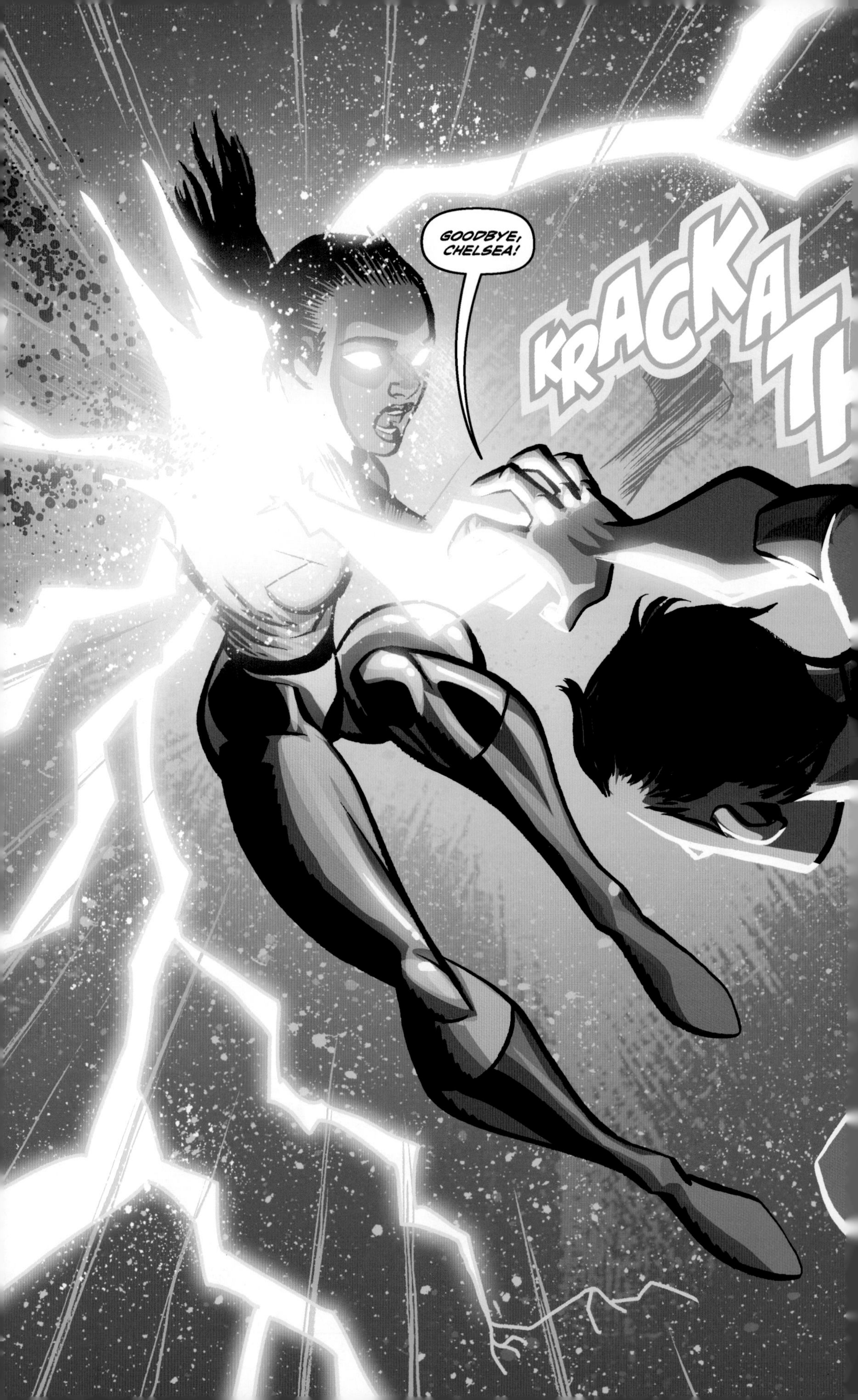
GOODBYE, CHELSEA!
KRACKATH

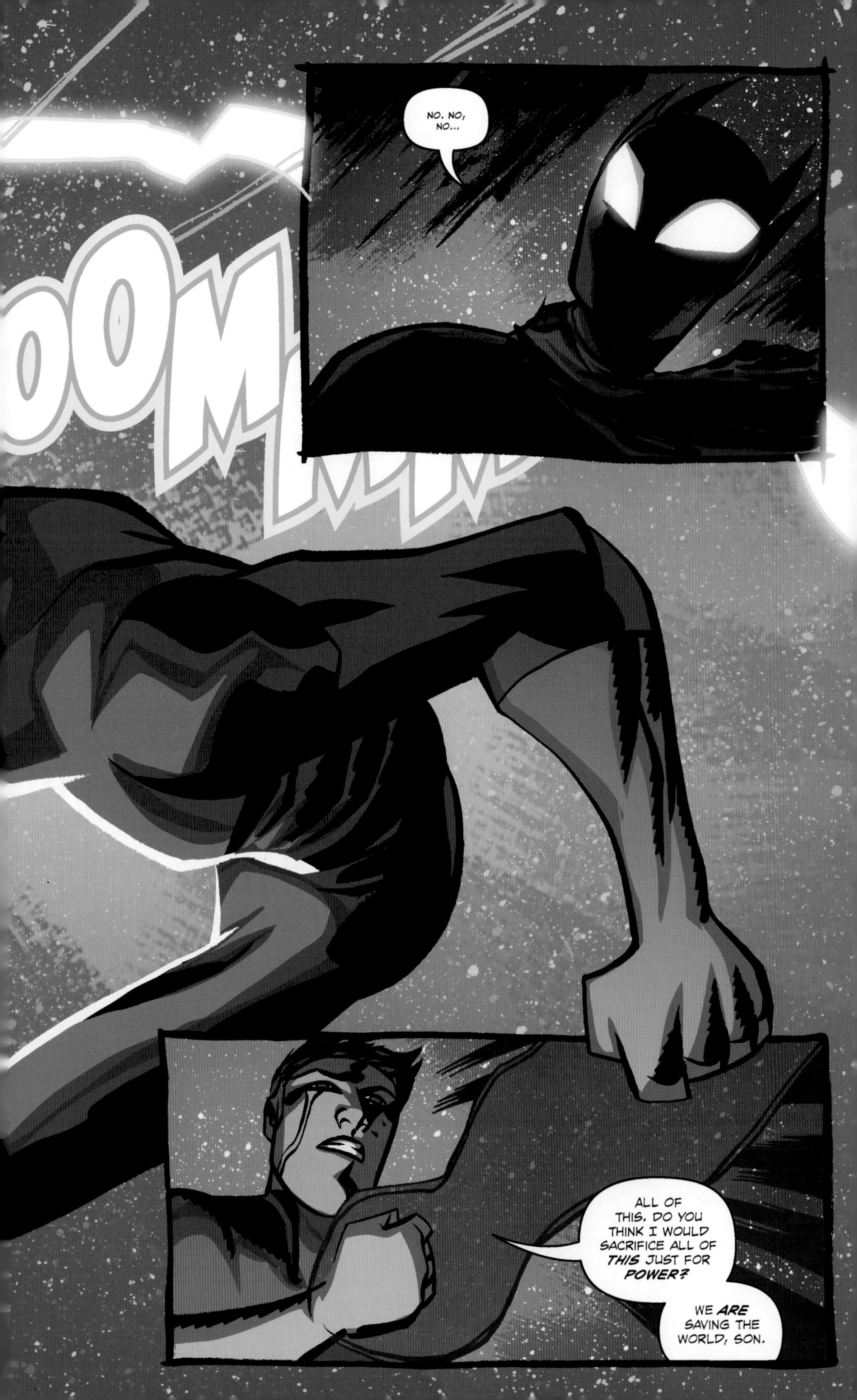
NO. NO,
NO...
ALL OF THIS. DO YOU THINK I WOULD SACRIFICE ALL OF *THIS* JUST FOR *POWER?*
WE *ARE* SAVING THE WORLD, SON.

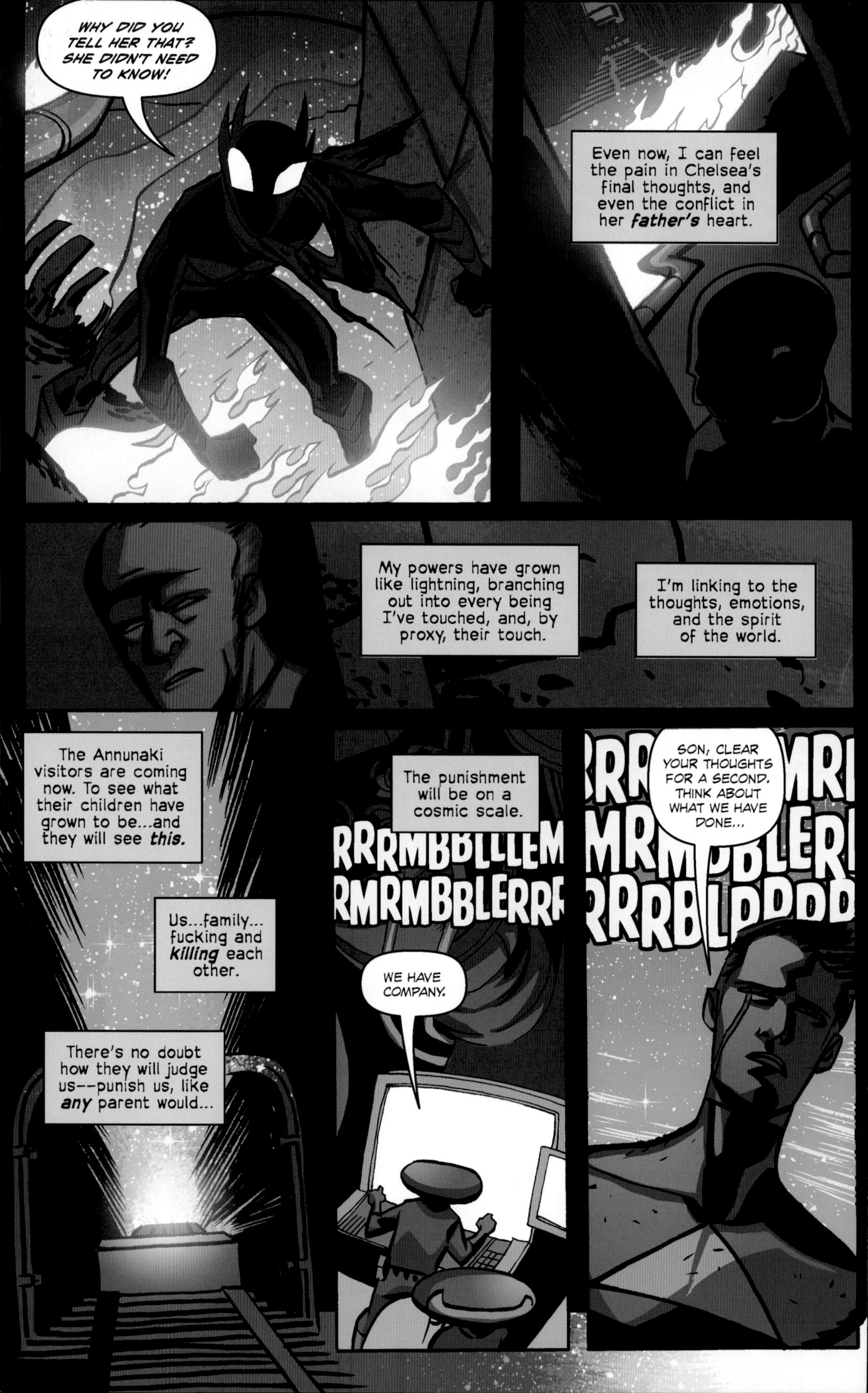

WHY DID YOU TELL HER THAT? SHE DIDN'T NEED TO KNOW!
Even now, I can feel the pain in Chelsea's final thoughts, and even the conflict in her *father's* heart.
My powers have grown like lightning, branching out into every being I've touched, and, by proxy, their touch.
I'm linking to the thoughts, emotions, and the spirit of the world.
The Annunaki visitors are coming now. To see what their children have grown to be...and they will see *this.*
Us...family... fucking and *killing* each other.
There's no doubt how they will judge us--punish us, like *any* parent would...
The punishment will be on a cosmic scale.
RRRMBBLLLEM
RMRMBBLERRR
WE HAVE COMPANY.
SON, CLEAR YOUR THOUGHTS FOR A SECOND. THINK ABOUT WHAT WE HAVE DONE...

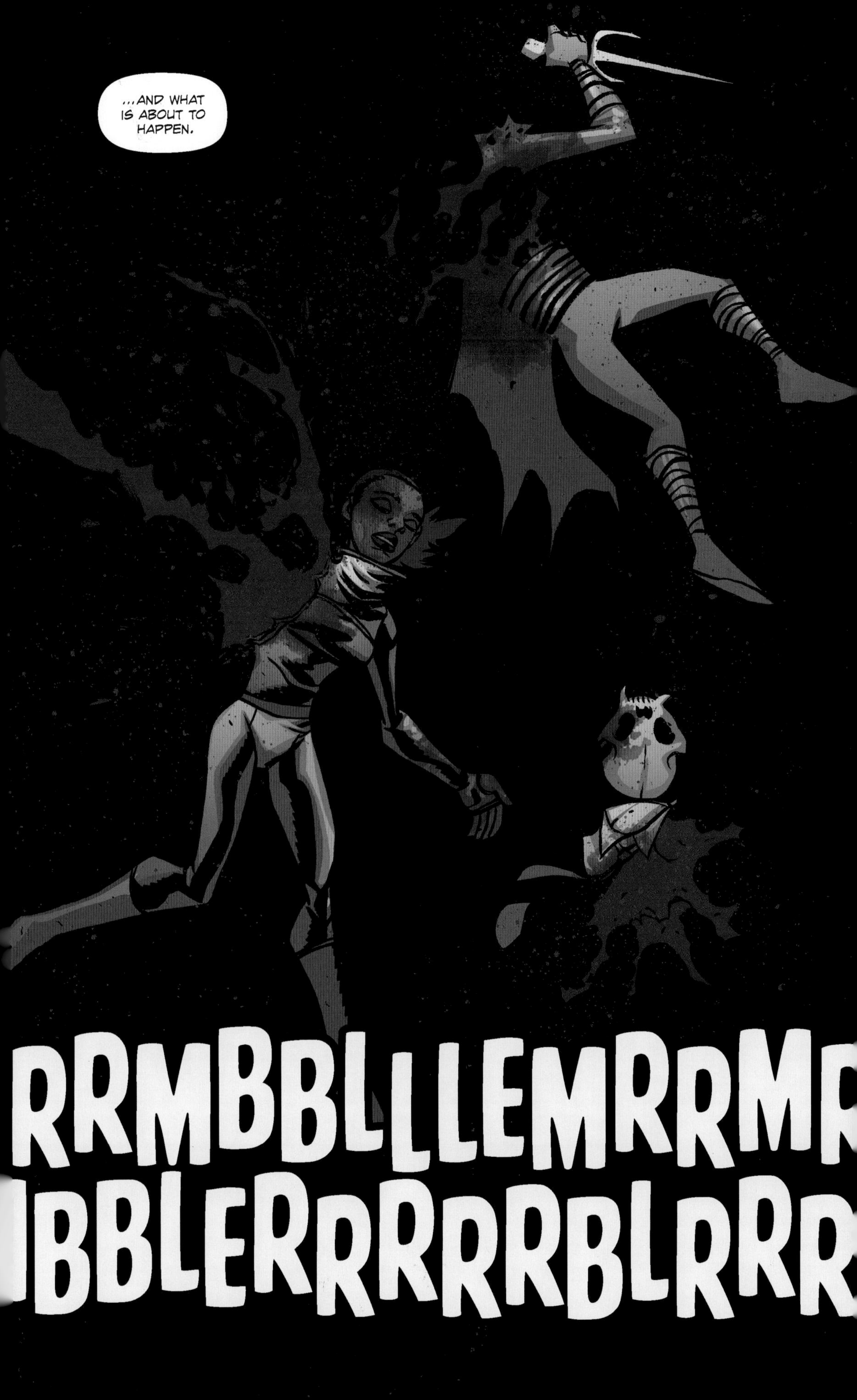
...AND WHAT IS ABOUT TO HAPPEN.
RRMBBLLLEMRRMR
IBBLERRRRRBLRRR

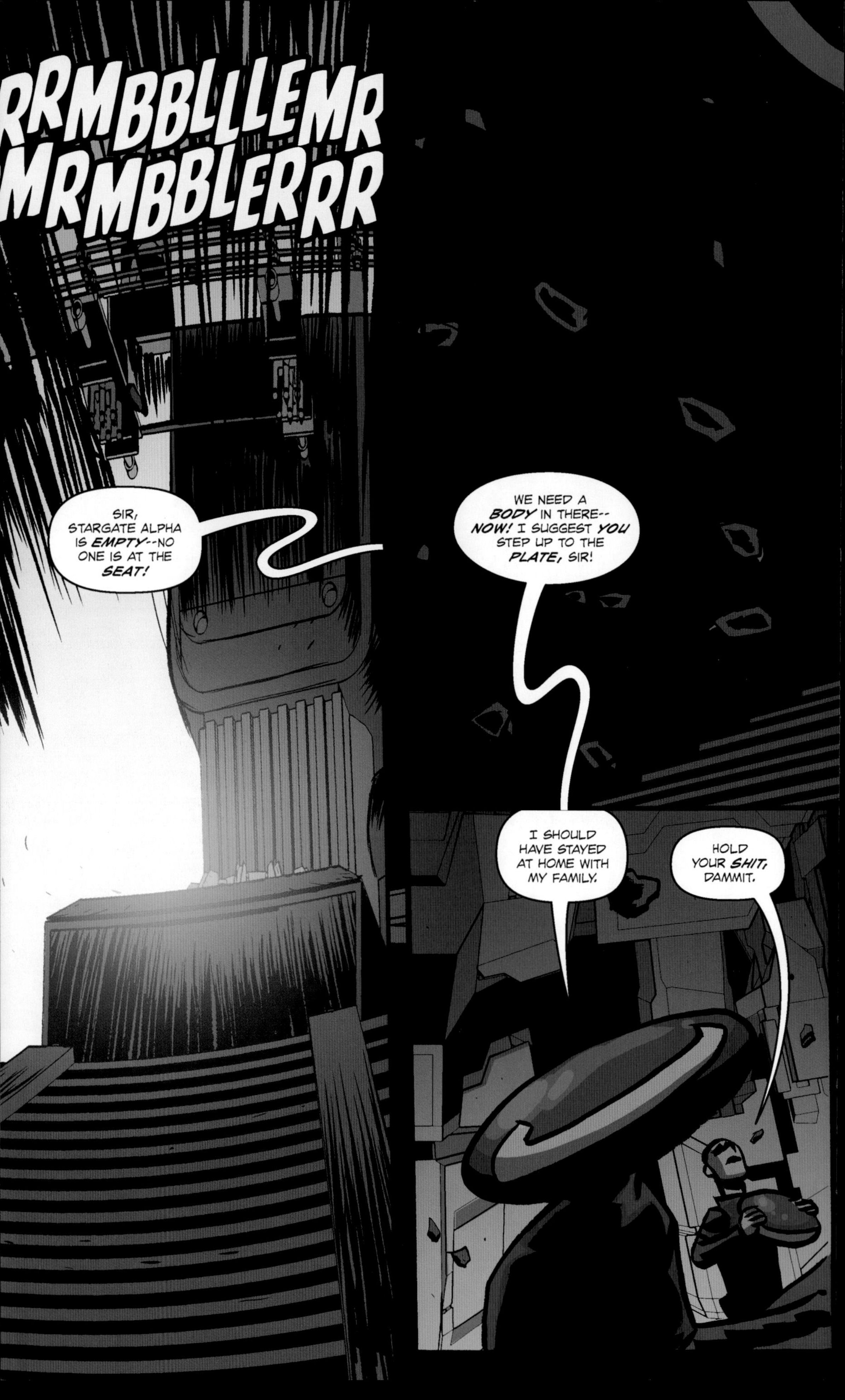
RRMBBLLLEMR MRMBBLERRR
SIR, STARGATE ALPHA IS EMPTY--NO ONE IS AT THE SEAT!
WE NEED A BODY IN THERE--NOW! I SUGGEST YOU STEP UP TO THE PLATE, SIR!
I SHOULD HAVE STAYED AT HOME WITH MY FAMILY.
HOLD YOUR SHIT, DAMMIT.

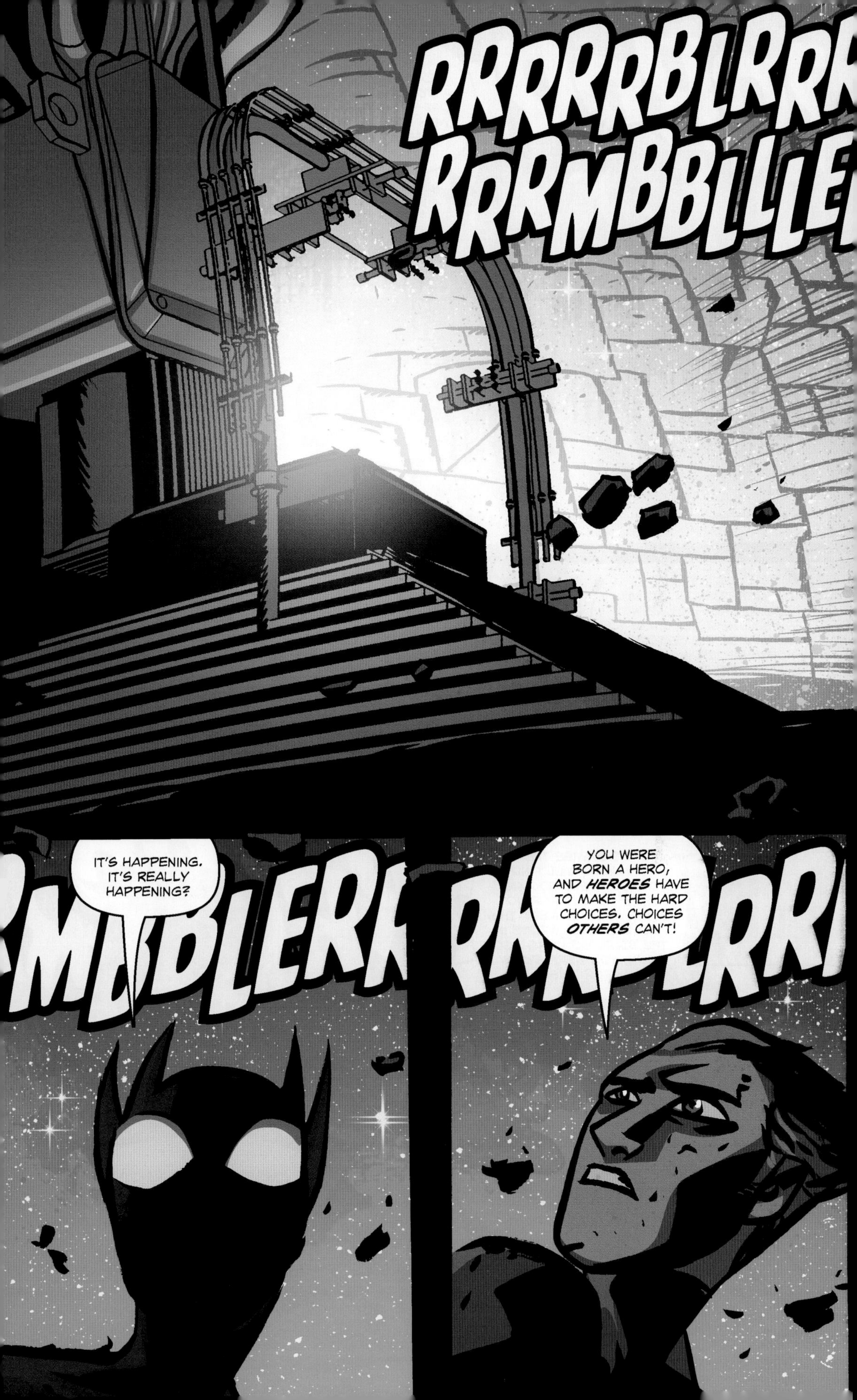
RRRRRBLRRR
RRRMBBLLE
RMBLERR
IT'S HAPPENING. IT'S REALLY HAPPENING?
RRRBLERRR
YOU WERE BORN A HERO, AND HEROES HAVE TO MAKE THE HARD CHOICES. CHOICES OTHERS CAN'T!

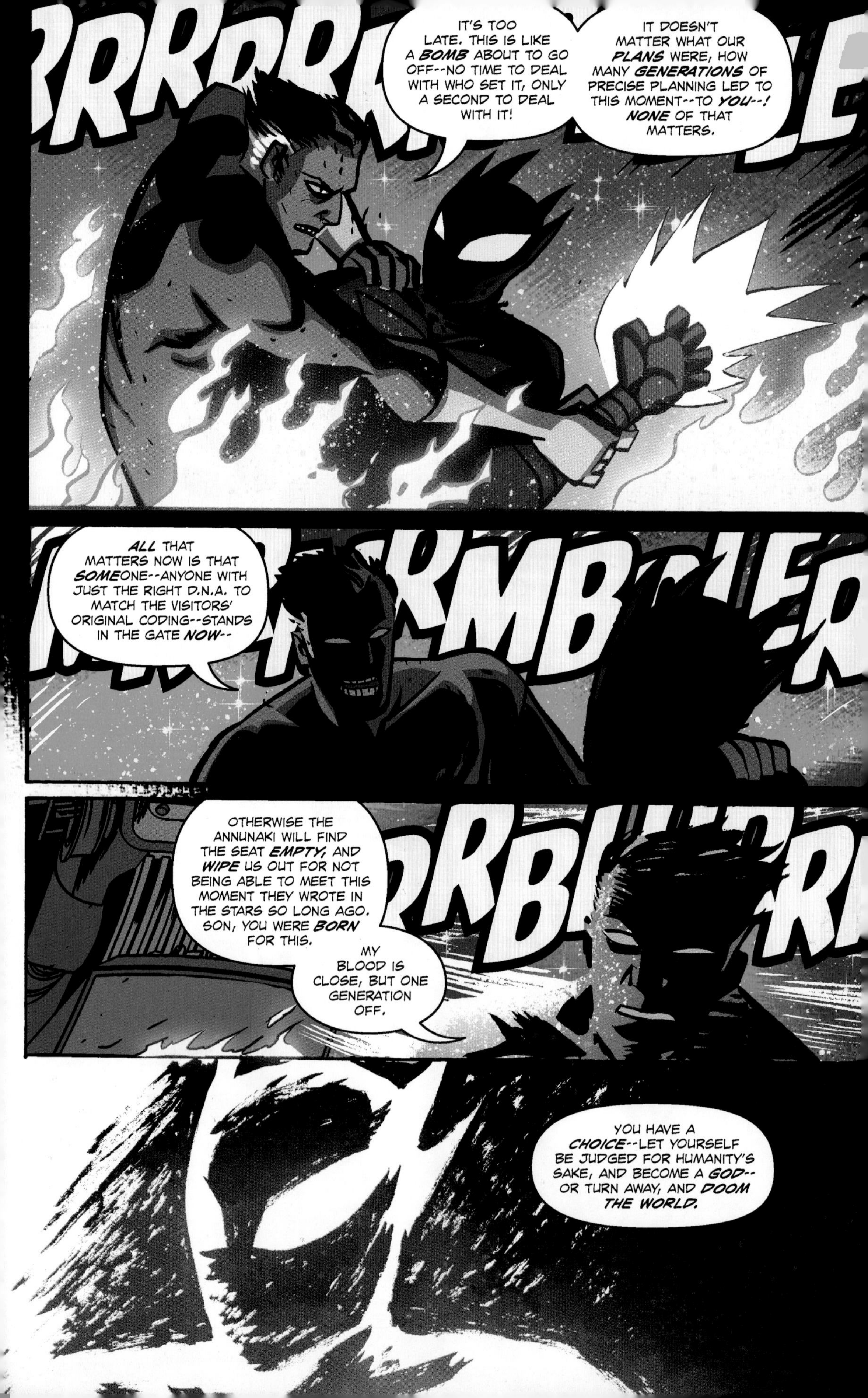
IT'S TOO LATE. THIS IS LIKE A BOMB ABOUT TO GO OFF--NO TIME TO DEAL WITH WHO SET IT, ONLY A SECOND TO DEAL WITH IT!
IT DOESN'T MATTER WHAT OUR PLANS WERE, HOW MANY GENERATIONS OF PRECISE PLANNING LED TO THIS MOMENT--TO YOU--! NONE OF THAT MATTERS.
ALL THAT MATTERS NOW IS THAT SOMEONE--ANYONE WITH JUST THE RIGHT D.N.A. TO MATCH THE VISITORS' ORIGINAL CODING--STANDS IN THE GATE NOW--
OTHERWISE THE ANNUNAKI WILL FIND THE SEAT EMPTY, AND WIPE US OUT FOR NOT BEING ABLE TO MEET THIS MOMENT THEY WROTE IN THE STARS SO LONG AGO. SON, YOU WERE BORN FOR THIS.
MY BLOOD IS CLOSE, BUT ONE GENERATION OFF.
YOU HAVE A CHOICE--LET YOURSELF BE JUDGED FOR HUMANITY'S SAKE, AND BECOME A GOD--OR TURN AWAY, AND DOOM THE WORLD.

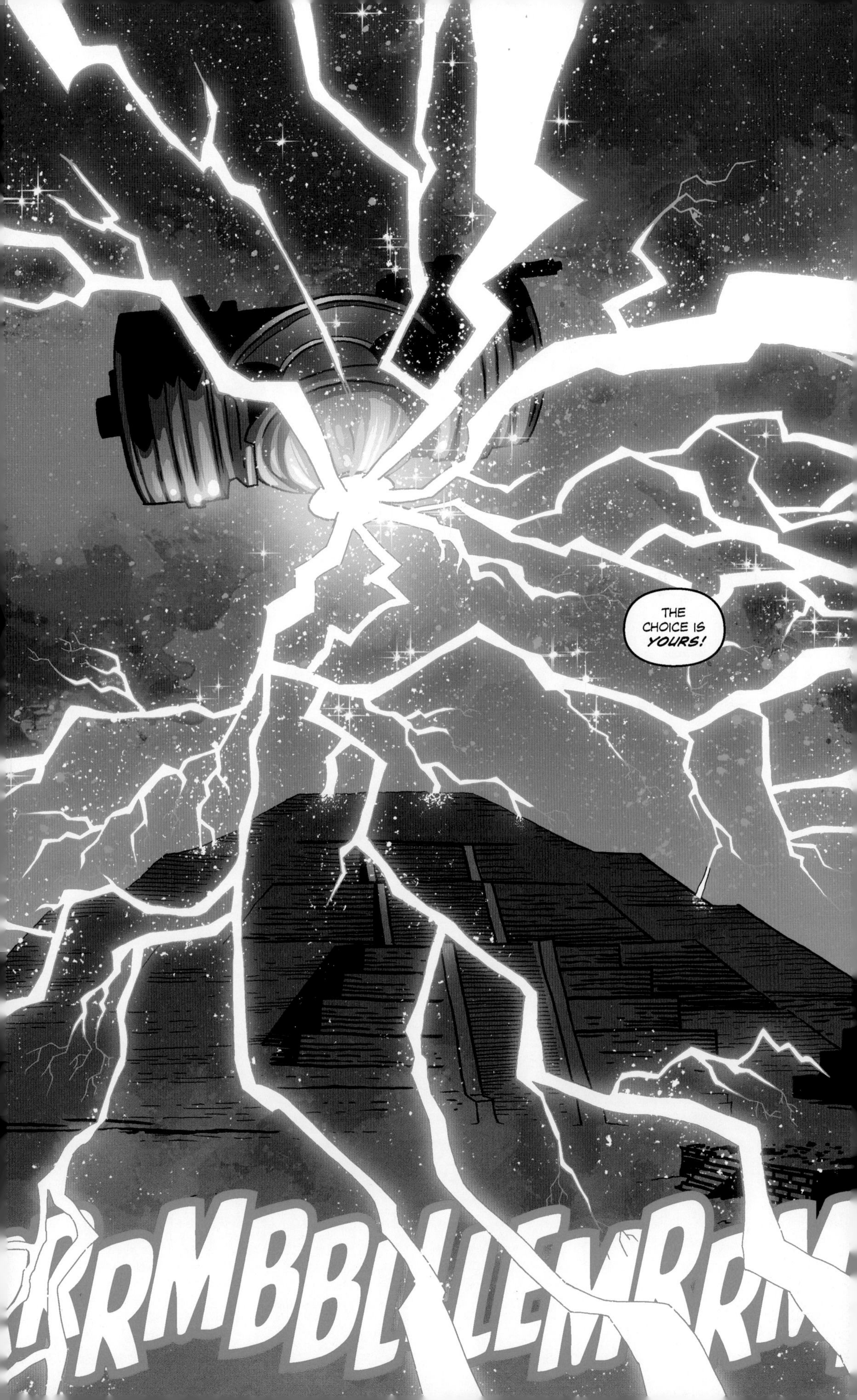
THE CHOICE IS *YOURS!*

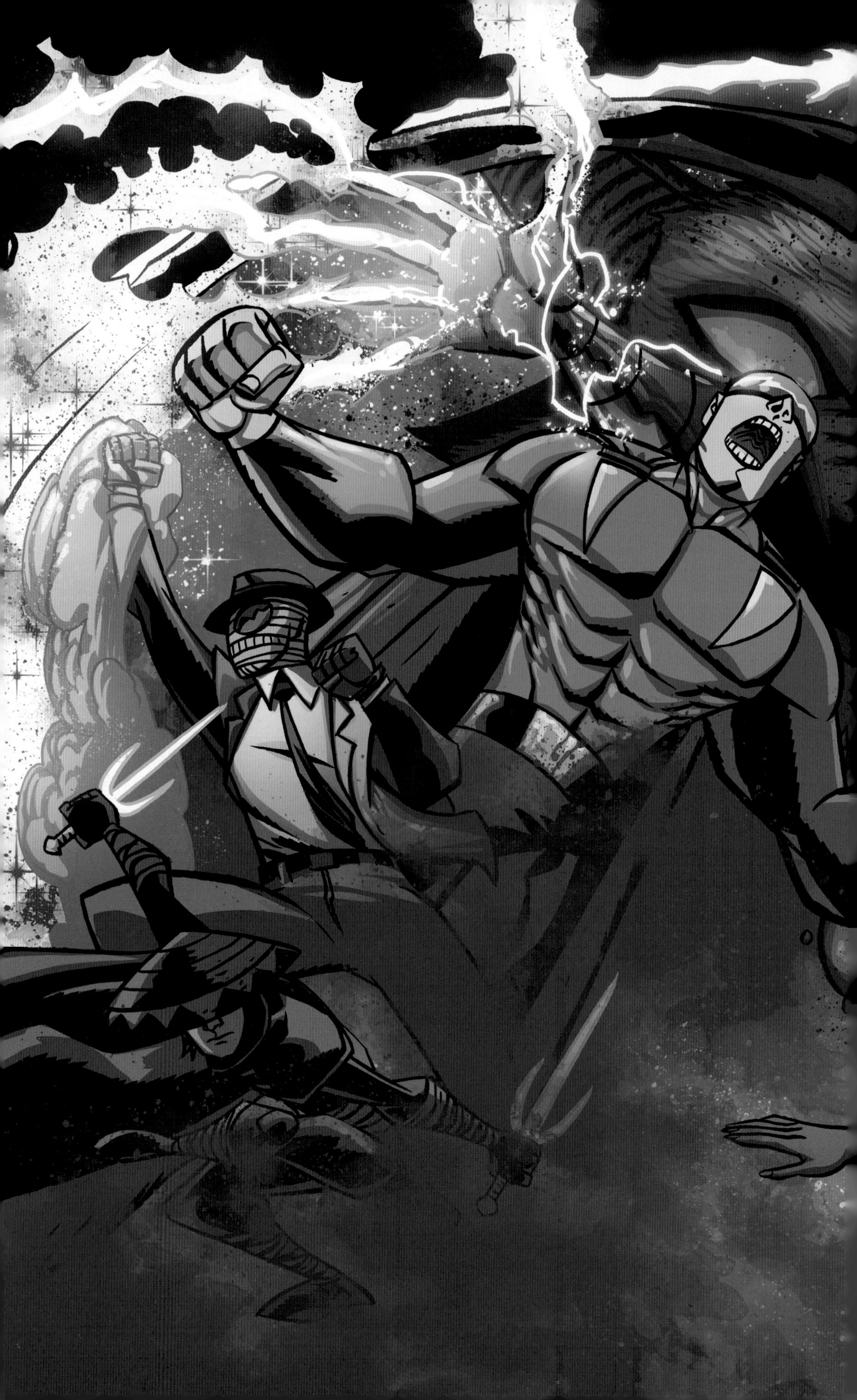

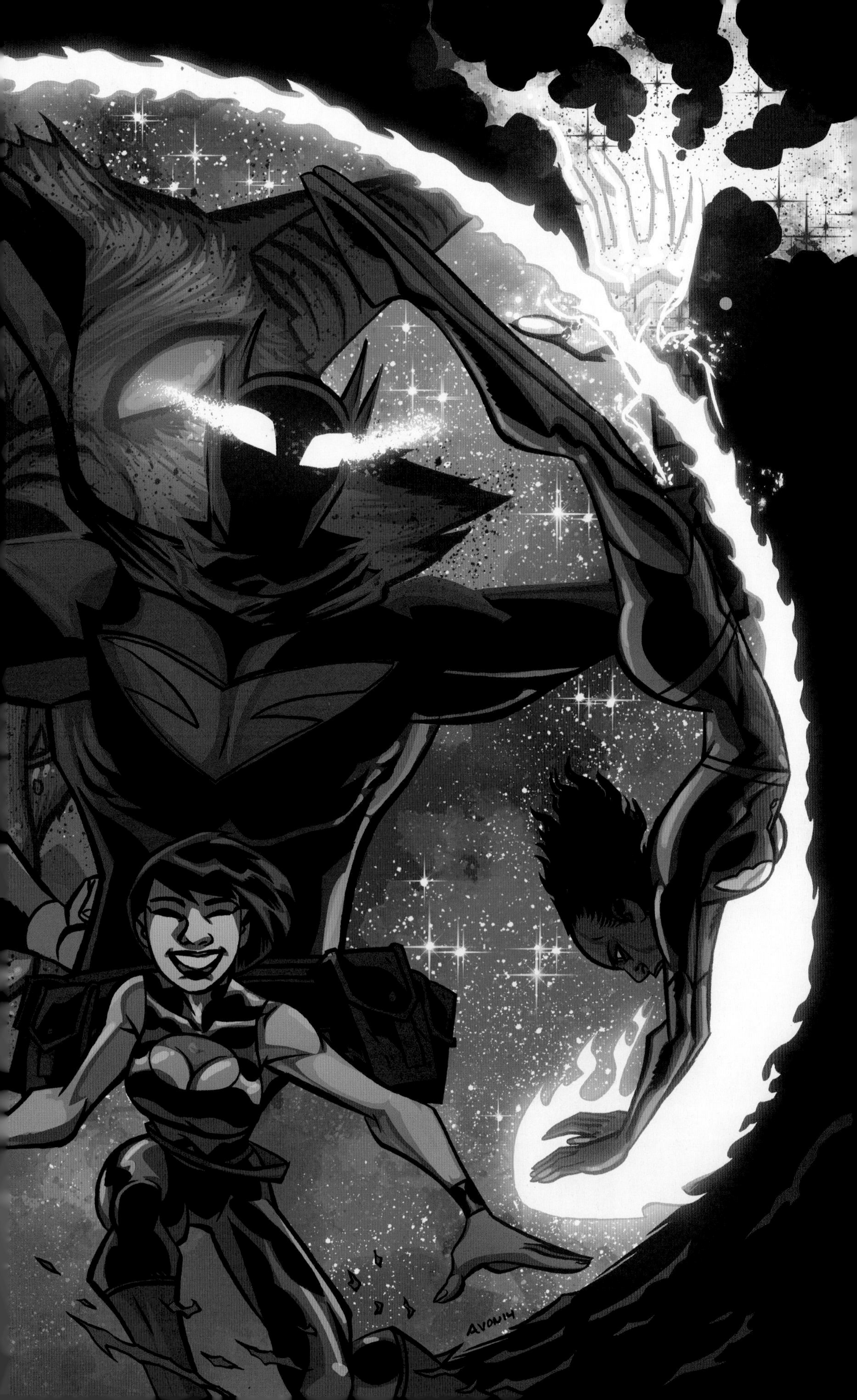
AVON14

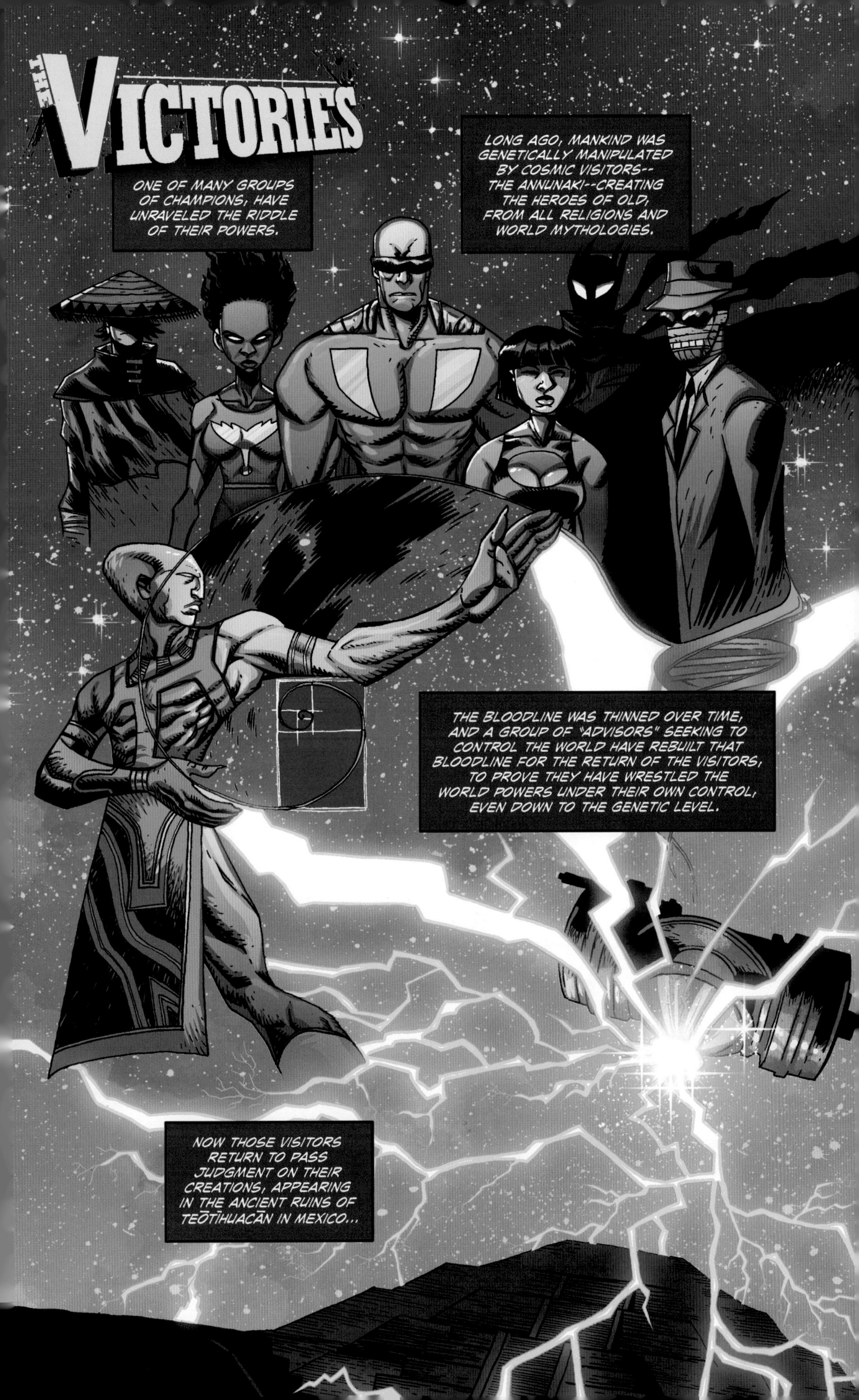
THE VICTORIES
ONE OF MANY GROUPS OF CHAMPIONS, HAVE UNRAVELED THE RIDDLE OF THEIR POWERS.
LONG AGO, MANKIND WAS GENETICALLY MANIPULATED BY COSMIC VISITORS-- THE ANNUNAKI--CREATING THE HEROES OF OLD, FROM ALL RELIGIONS AND WORLD MYTHOLOGIES.
THE BLOODLINE WAS THINNED OVER TIME, AND A GROUP OF "ADVISORS" SEEKING TO CONTROL THE WORLD HAVE REBUILT THAT BLOODLINE FOR THE RETURN OF THE VISITORS, TO PROVE THEY HAVE WRESTLED THE WORLD POWERS UNDER THEIR OWN CONTROL, EVEN DOWN TO THE GENETIC LEVEL.
NOW THOSE VISITORS RETURN TO PASS JUDGMENT ON THEIR CREATIONS, APPEARING IN THE ANCIENT RUINS OF TEŌTĪHUACĀN IN MEXICO...

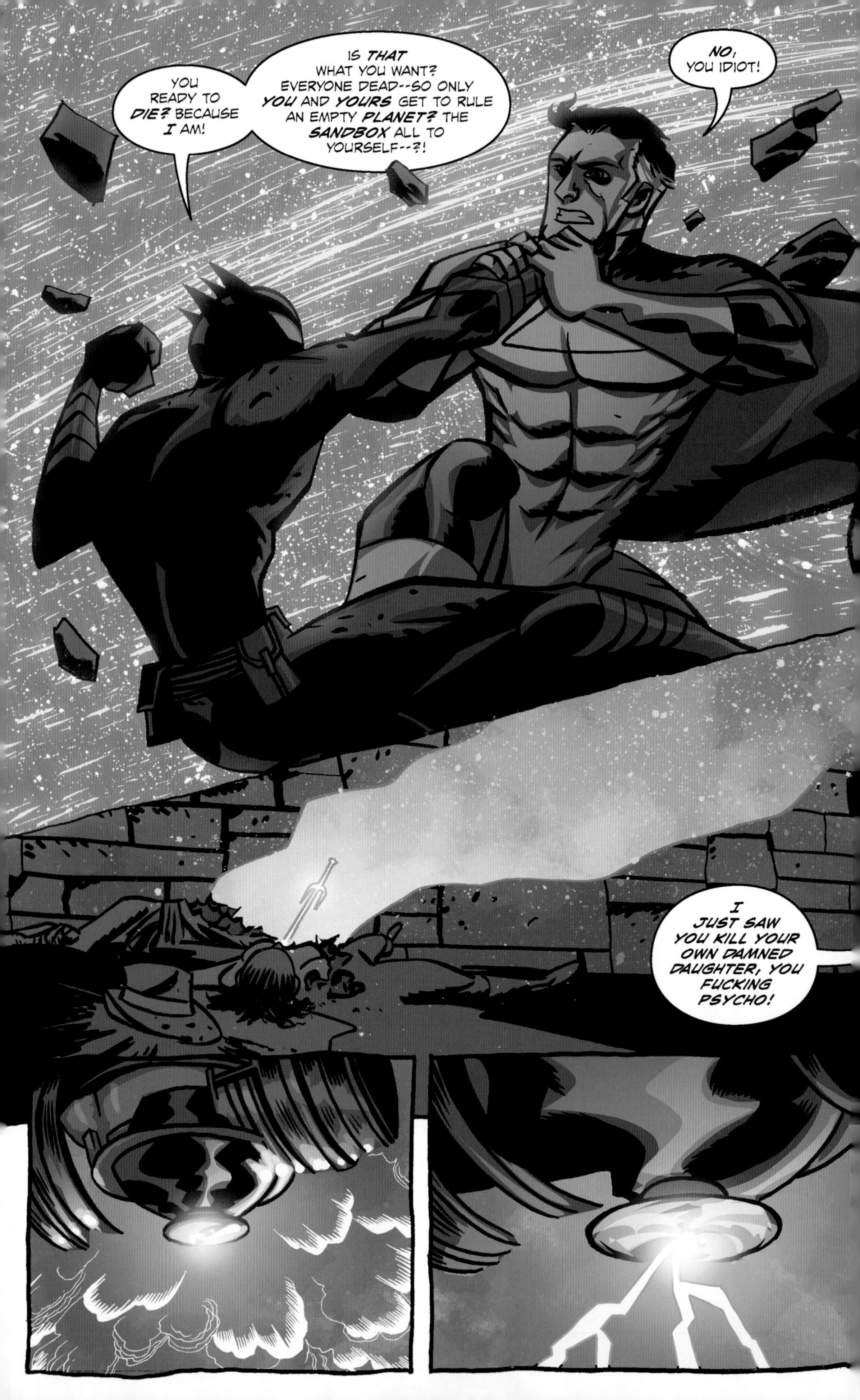

YOU READY TO DIE? BECAUSE I AM!
IS THAT WHAT YOU WANT? EVERYONE DEAD--SO ONLY YOU AND YOURS GET TO RULE AN EMPTY PLANET? THE SANDBOX ALL TO YOURSELF--?!
NO, YOU IDIOT!
I JUST SAW YOU KILL YOUR OWN DAMNED DAUGHTER, YOU FUCKING PSYCHO!

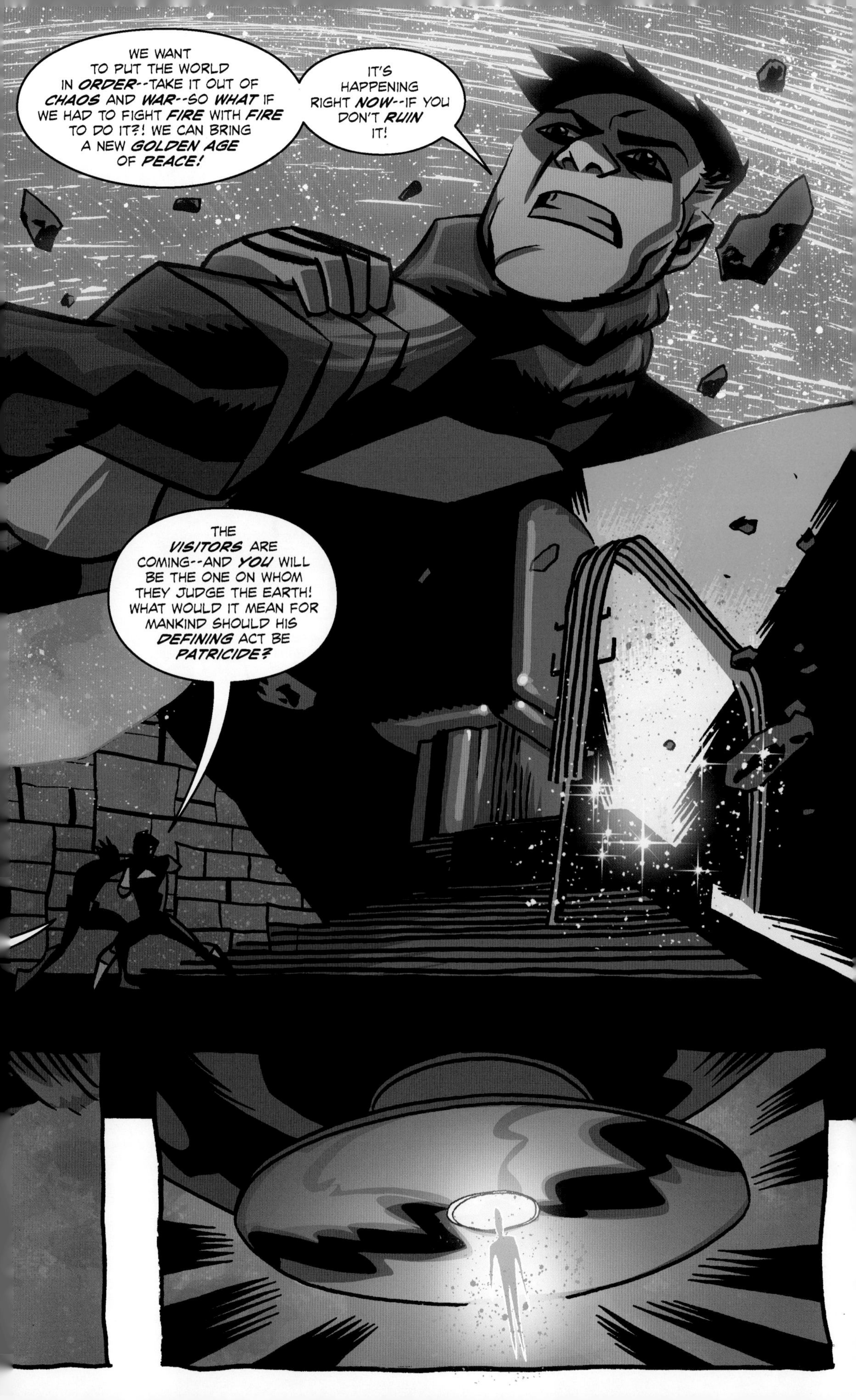
WE WANT TO PUT THE WORLD IN ORDER--TAKE IT OUT OF CHAOS AND WAR--SO WHAT IF WE HAD TO FIGHT FIRE WITH FIRE TO DO IT?! WE CAN BRING A NEW GOLDEN AGE OF PEACE!
IT'S HAPPENING RIGHT NOW--IF YOU DON'T RUIN IT!
THE VISITORS ARE COMING--AND YOU WILL BE THE ONE ON WHOM THEY JUDGE THE EARTH! WHAT WOULD IT MEAN FOR MANKIND SHOULD HIS DEFINING ACT BE PATRICIDE?

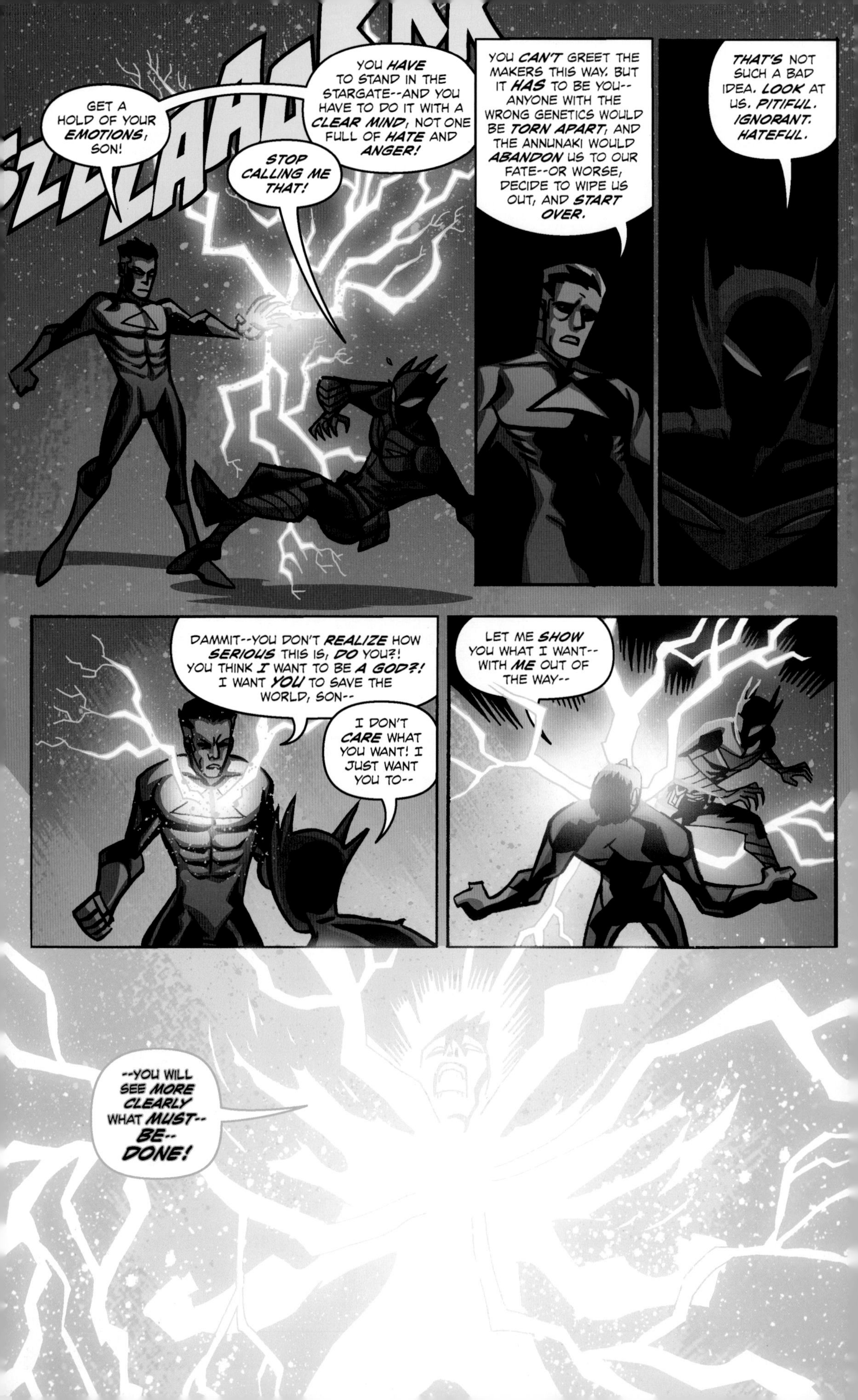

GET A HOLD OF YOUR EMOTIONS, SON!
YOU HAVE TO STAND IN THE STARGATE--AND YOU HAVE TO DO IT WITH A CLEAR MIND, NOT ONE FULL OF HATE AND ANGER!
STOP CALLING ME THAT!
YOU CAN'T GREET THE MAKERS THIS WAY. BUT IT HAS TO BE YOU--ANYONE WITH THE WRONG GENETICS WOULD BE TORN APART, AND THE ANNUNAKI WOULD ABANDON US TO OUR FATE--OR WORSE, DECIDE TO WIPE US OUT, AND START OVER.
THAT'S NOT SUCH A BAD IDEA. LOOK AT US. PITIFUL. IGNORANT. HATEFUL.
DAMMIT--YOU DON'T REALIZE HOW SERIOUS THIS IS, DO YOU?! YOU THINK I WANT TO BE A GOD?! I WANT YOU TO SAVE THE WORLD, SON--
I DON'T CARE WHAT YOU WANT! I JUST WANT YOU TO--
LET ME SHOW YOU WHAT I WANT--WITH ME OUT OF THE WAY--
--YOU WILL SEE MORE CLEARLY WHAT MUST--BE--DONE!

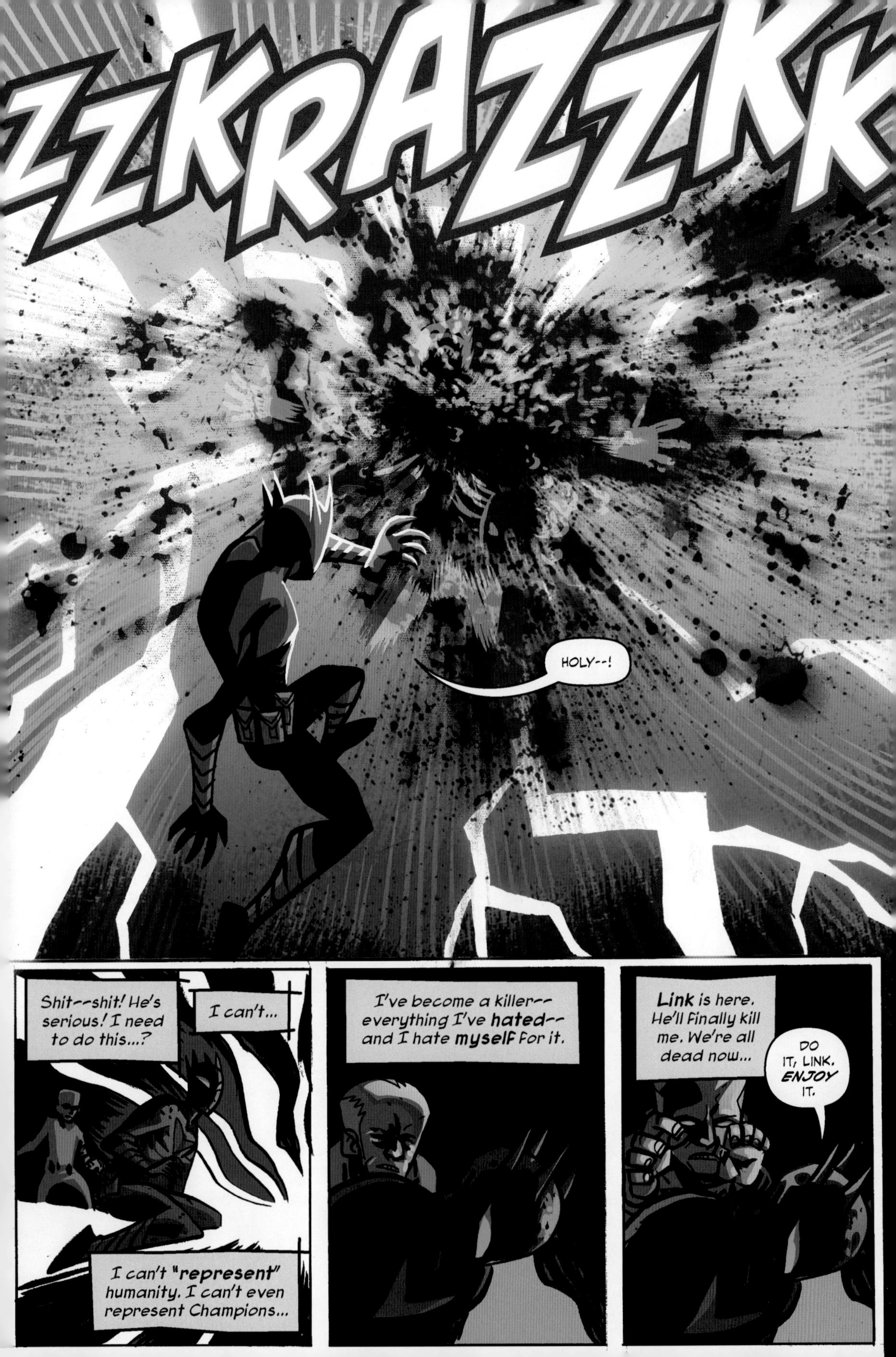
ZZKRAZZKK
HOLY--!
Shit--shit! He's serious! I need to do this...?
I can't...
I can't "represent" humanity. I can't even represent Champions...
I've become a killer--everything I've hated--and I hate myself for it.
Link is here. He'll finally kill me. We're all dead now...
DO IT, LINK. ENJOY IT.

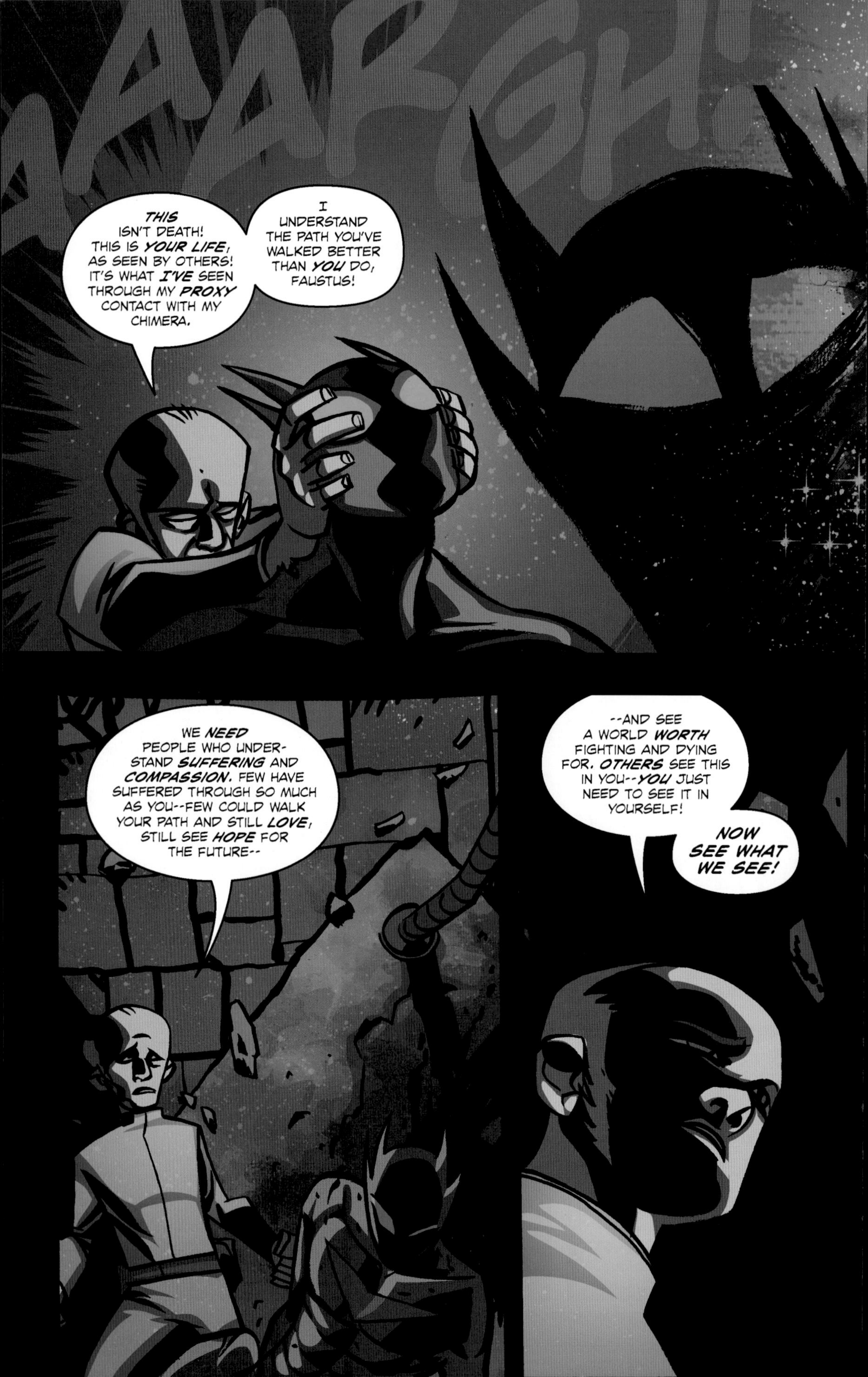
THIS ISN'T DEATH! THIS IS YOUR LIFE, AS SEEN BY OTHERS! IT'S WHAT I'VE SEEN THROUGH MY PROXY CONTACT WITH MY CHIMERA.
I UNDERSTAND THE PATH YOU'VE WALKED BETTER THAN YOU DO, FAUSTUS!
WE NEED PEOPLE WHO UNDER-STAND SUFFERING AND COMPASSION. FEW HAVE SUFFERED THROUGH SO MUCH AS YOU--FEW COULD WALK YOUR PATH AND STILL LOVE, STILL SEE HOPE FOR THE FUTURE--
--AND SEE A WORLD WORTH FIGHTING AND DYING FOR. OTHERS SEE THIS IN YOU--YOU JUST NEED TO SEE IT IN YOURSELF!
NOW SEE WHAT WE SEE!

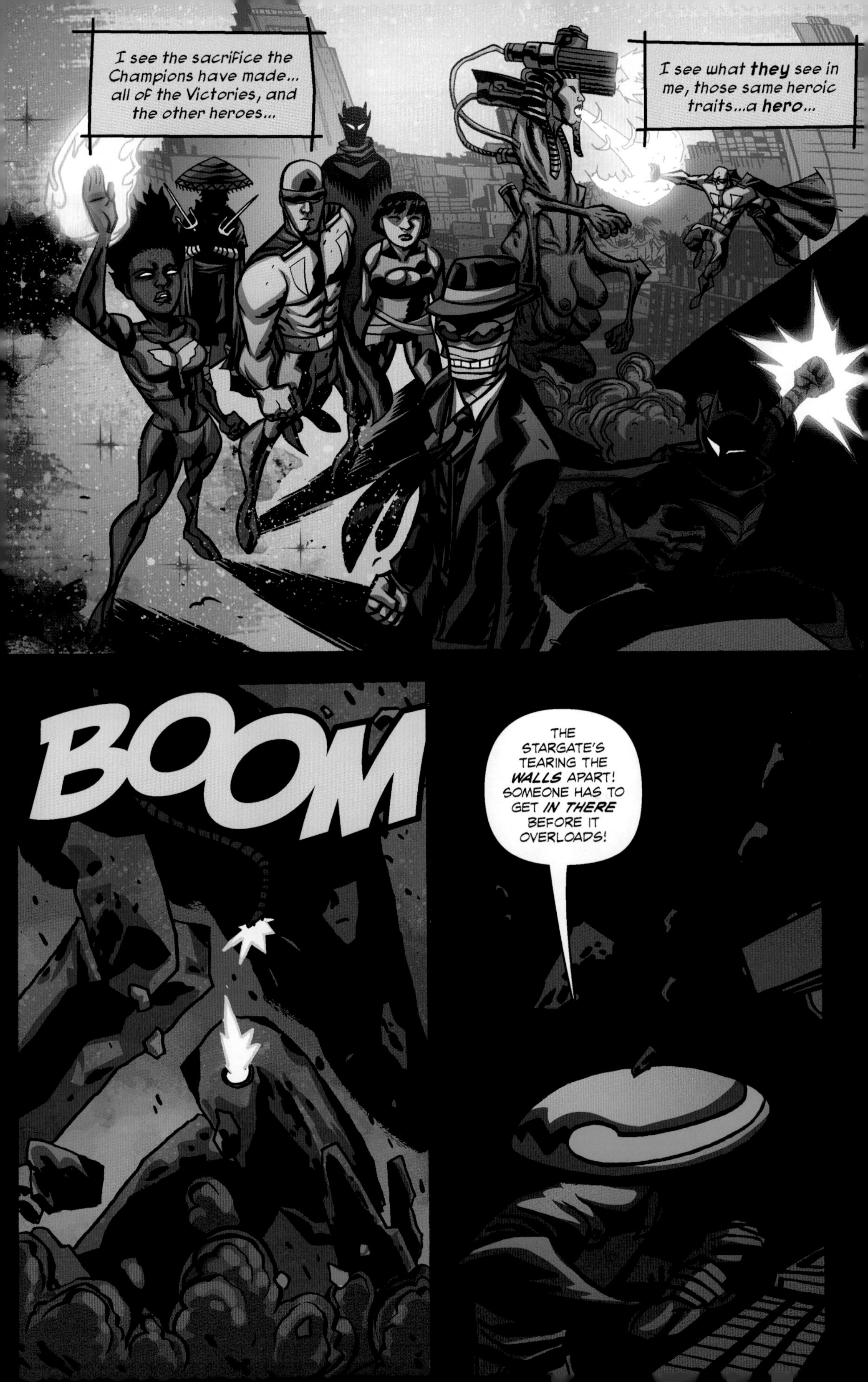
I see the sacrifice the Champions have made... all of the Victories, and the other heroes...
I see what **they** see in me, those same heroic traits...a **hero**...
BOOM
THE STARGATE'S TEARING THE ***WALLS*** APART! SOMEONE HAS TO GET ***IN THERE*** BEFORE IT OVERLOADS!

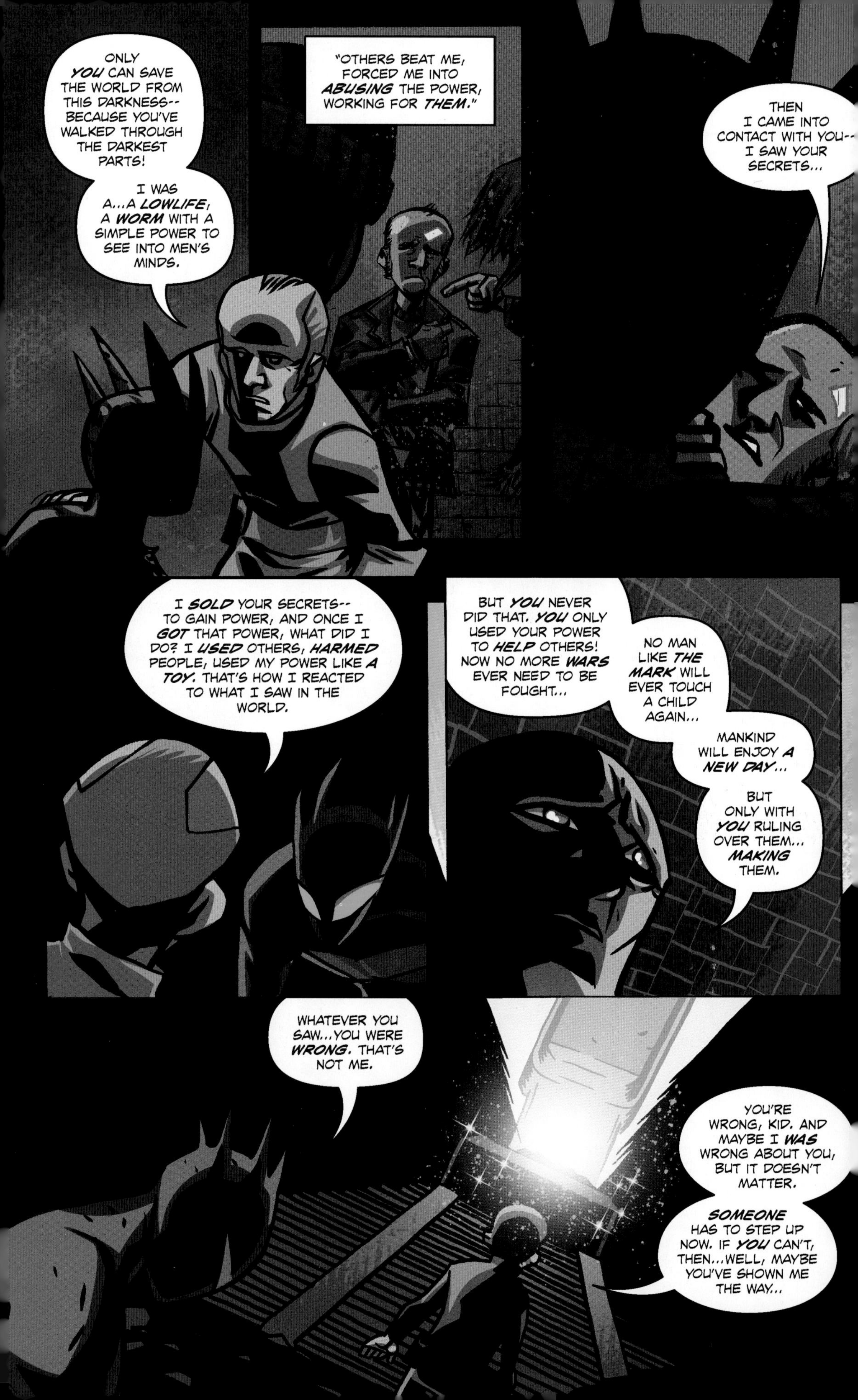
ONLY *YOU* CAN SAVE THE WORLD FROM THIS DARKNESS-- BECAUSE YOU'VE WALKED THROUGH THE DARKEST PARTS!
I WAS A...A *LOWLIFE*, A *WORM* WITH A SIMPLE POWER TO SEE INTO MEN'S MINDS.
"OTHERS BEAT ME, FORCED ME INTO *ABUSING* THE POWER, WORKING FOR *THEM*."
THEN I CAME INTO CONTACT WITH YOU-- I SAW YOUR SECRETS...
I *SOLD* YOUR SECRETS-- TO GAIN POWER, AND ONCE I *GOT* THAT POWER, WHAT DID I DO? I *USED* OTHERS, *HARMED* PEOPLE, USED MY POWER LIKE *A TOY*. THAT'S HOW I REACTED TO WHAT I SAW IN THE WORLD.
BUT *YOU* NEVER DID THAT. *YOU* ONLY USED YOUR POWER TO *HELP* OTHERS! NOW NO MORE *WARS* EVER NEED TO BE FOUGHT...
NO MAN LIKE *THE MARK* WILL EVER TOUCH A CHILD AGAIN...
MANKIND WILL ENJOY *A NEW DAY*...
BUT ONLY WITH *YOU* RULING OVER THEM... *MAKING* THEM.
WHATEVER YOU SAW...YOU WERE *WRONG*. THAT'S NOT ME.
YOU'RE WRONG, KID. AND MAYBE I *WAS* WRONG ABOUT YOU, BUT IT DOESN'T MATTER.
SOMEONE HAS TO STEP UP NOW. IF *YOU* CAN'T, THEN...WELL, MAYBE YOU'VE SHOWN ME THE WAY...

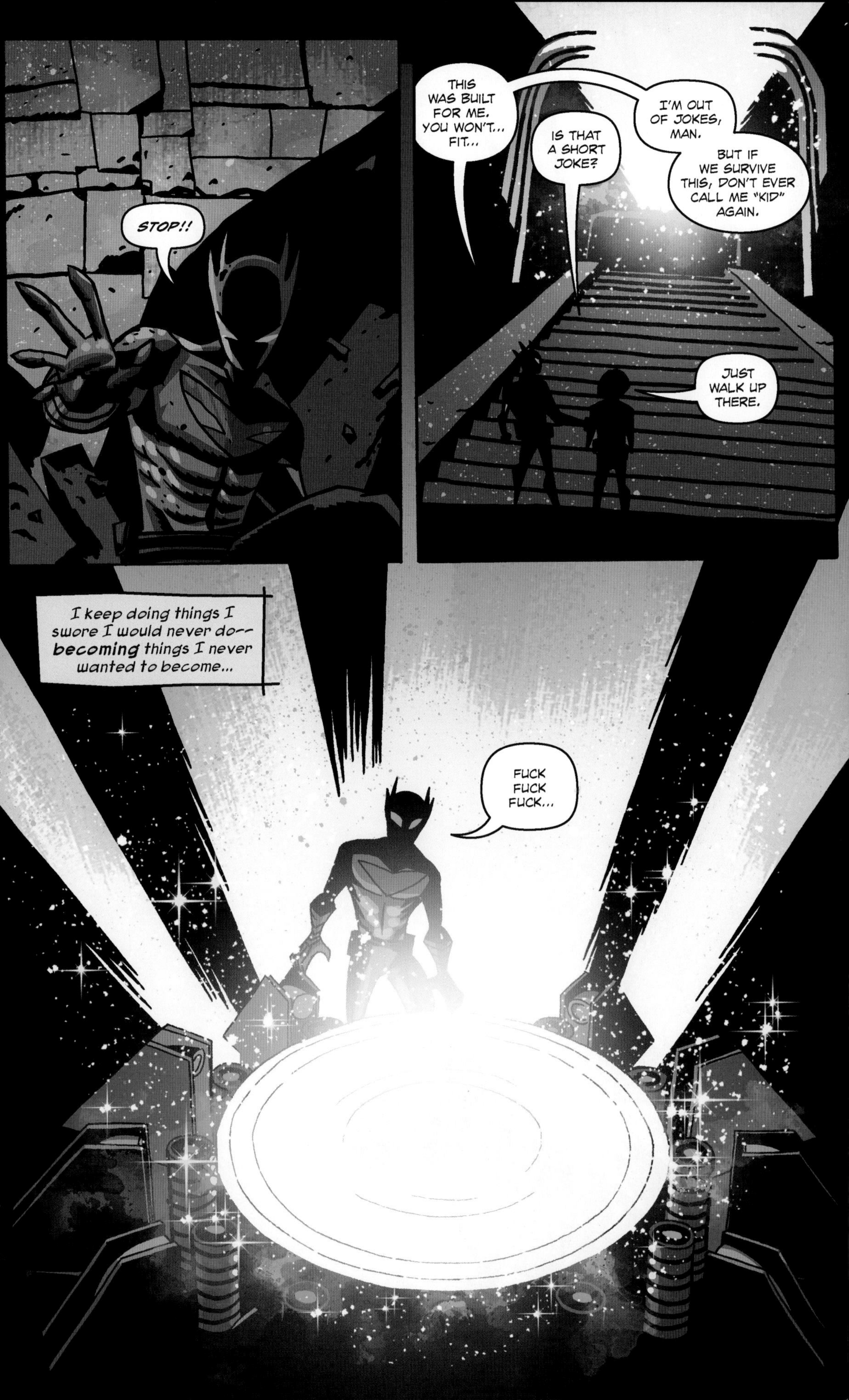
STOP!!
THIS WAS BUILT FOR ME. YOU WON'T... FIT...
IS THAT A SHORT JOKE?
I'M OUT OF JOKES, MAN.
BUT IF WE SURVIVE THIS, DON'T EVER CALL ME "KID" AGAIN.
JUST WALK UP THERE.
I keep doing things I swore I would never do-- **becoming** things I never wanted to become...
FUCK FUCK FUCK...

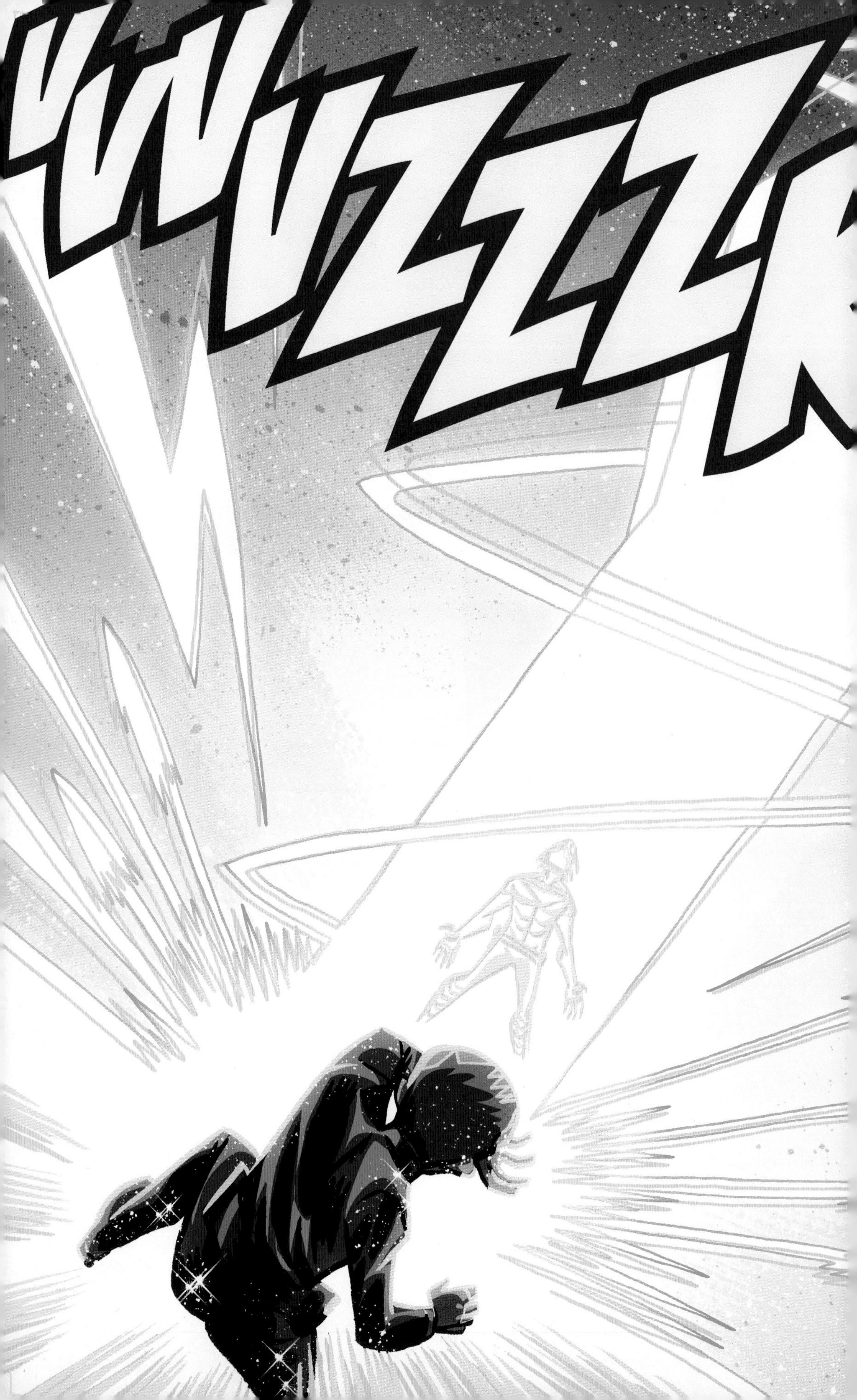

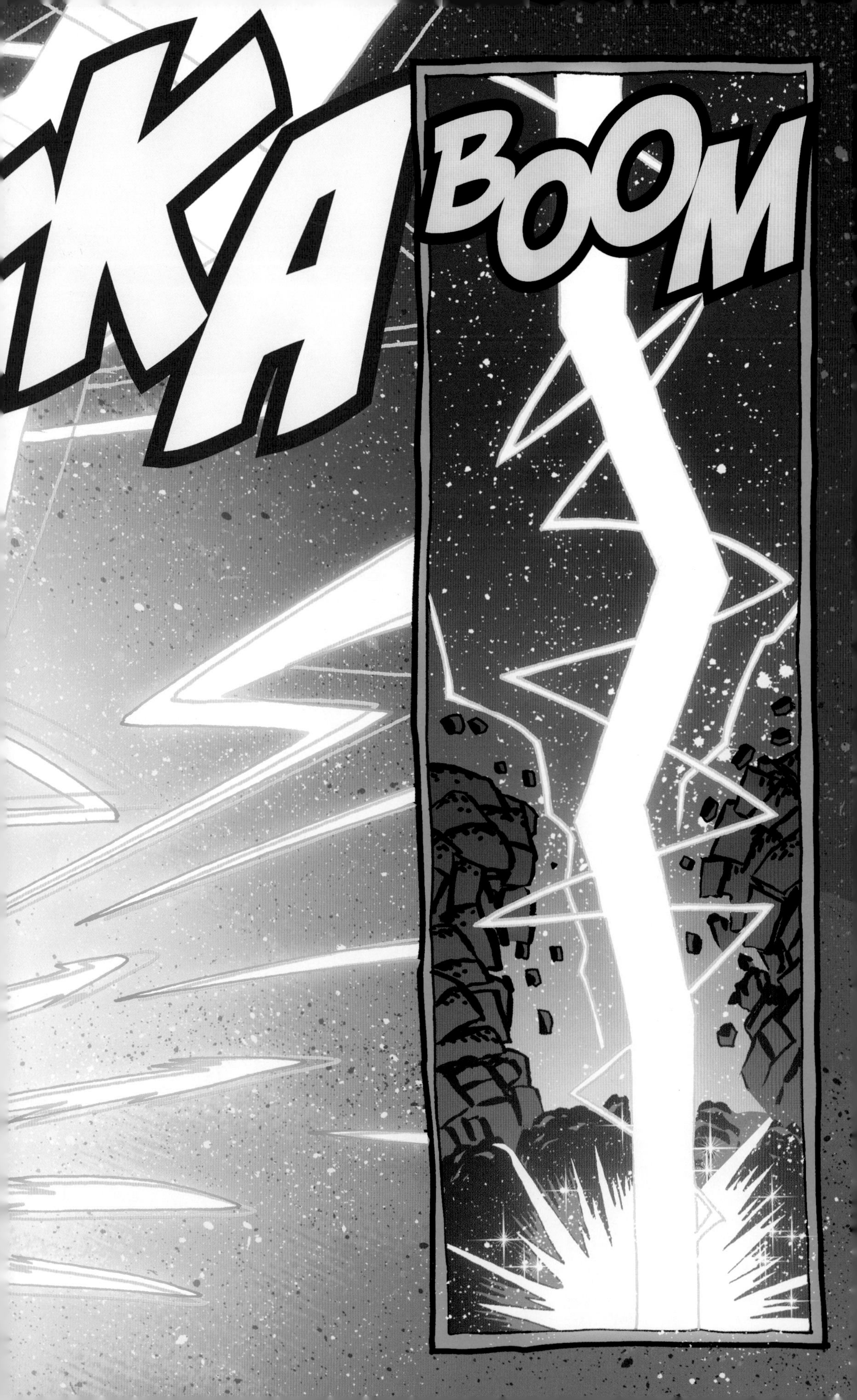
KABOOM

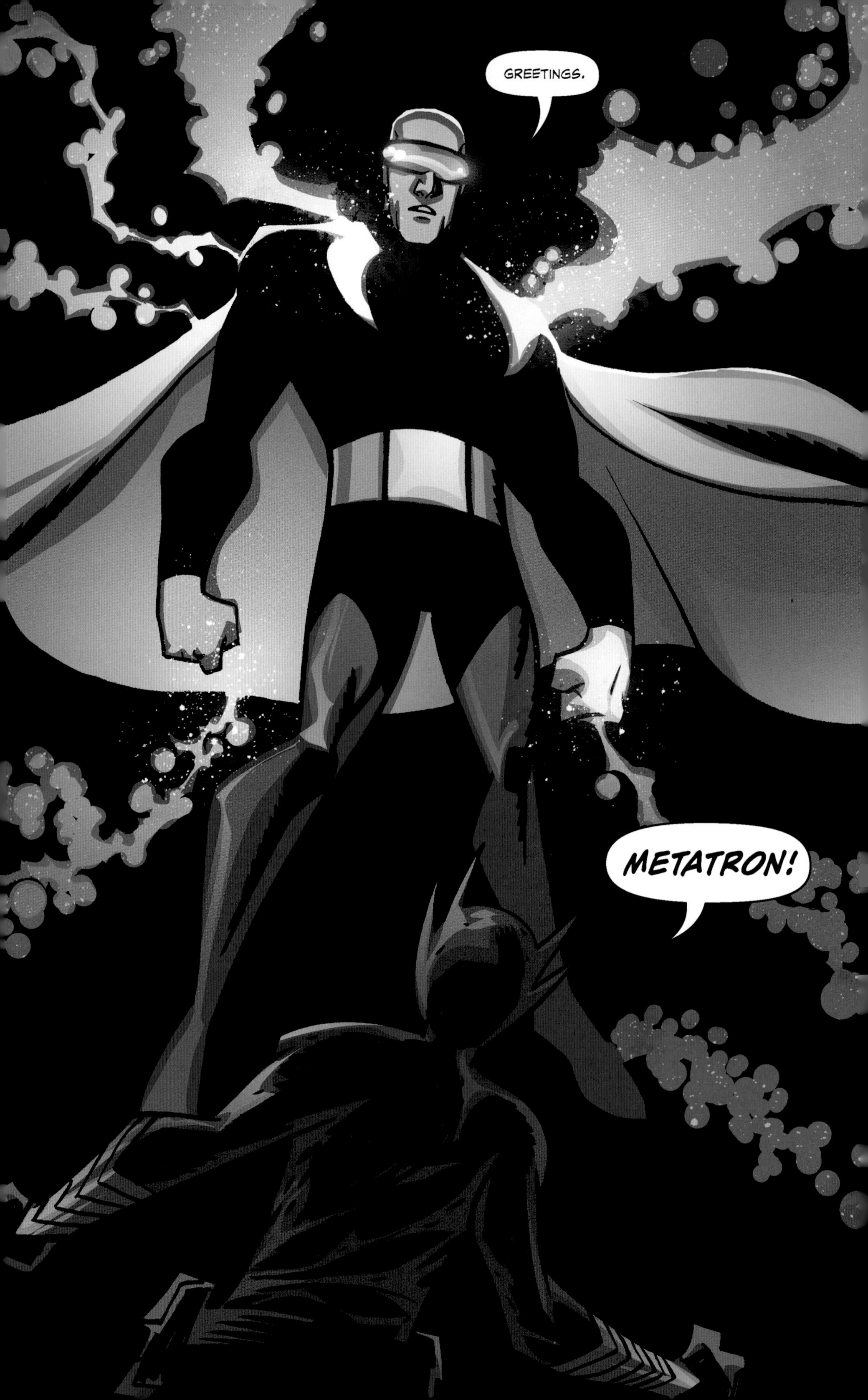
GREETINGS.
METATRON!

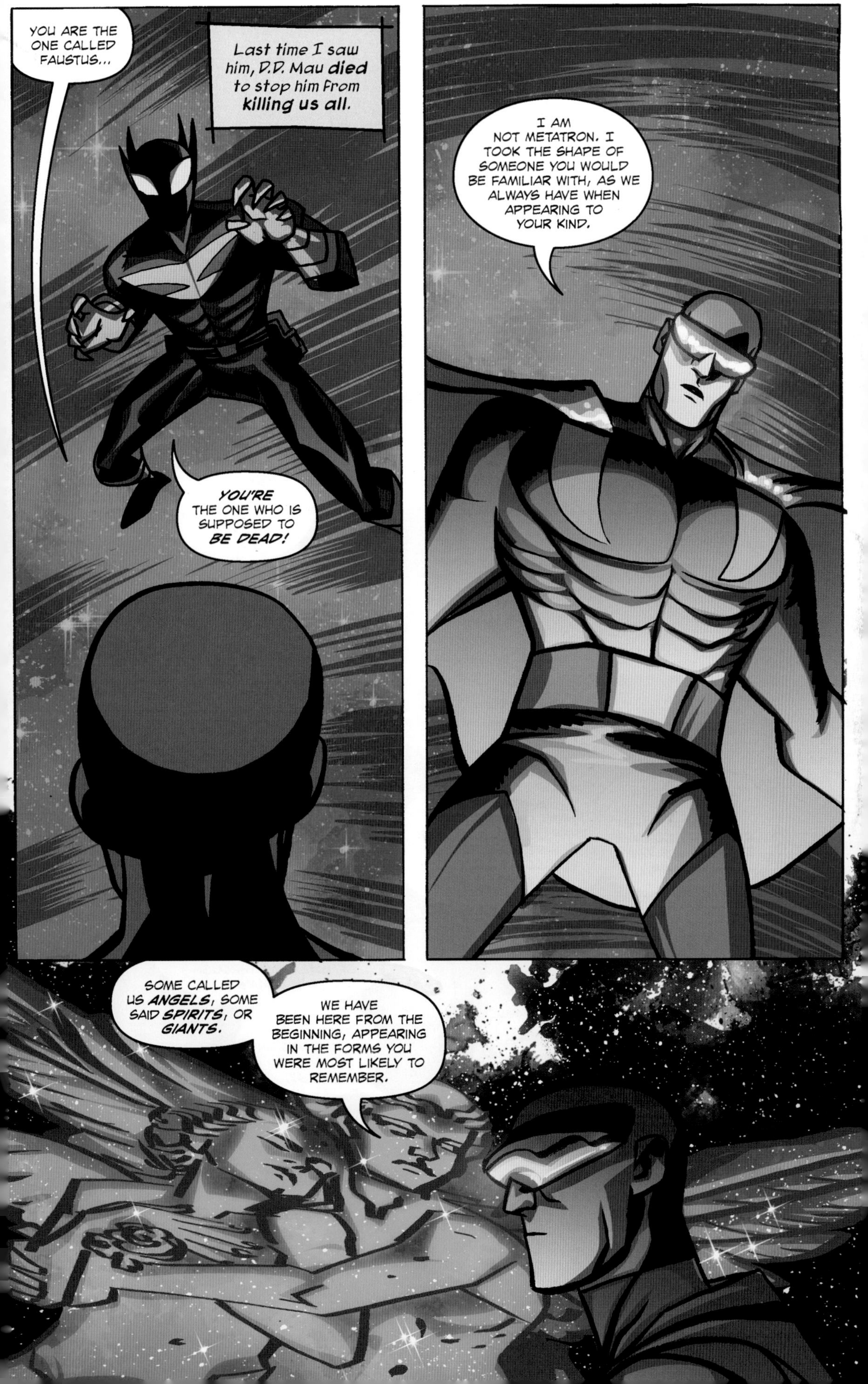
YOU ARE THE ONE CALLED FAUSTUS...
Last time I saw him, D.D. Mau died to stop him from killing us all.
YOU'RE THE ONE WHO IS SUPPOSED TO BE DEAD!
I AM NOT METATRON. I TOOK THE SHAPE OF SOMEONE YOU WOULD BE FAMILIAR WITH, AS WE ALWAYS HAVE WHEN APPEARING TO YOUR KIND.
SOME CALLED US ANGELS, SOME SAID SPIRITS, OR GIANTS.
WE HAVE BEEN HERE FROM THE BEGINNING, APPEARING IN THE FORMS YOU WERE MOST LIKELY TO REMEMBER.

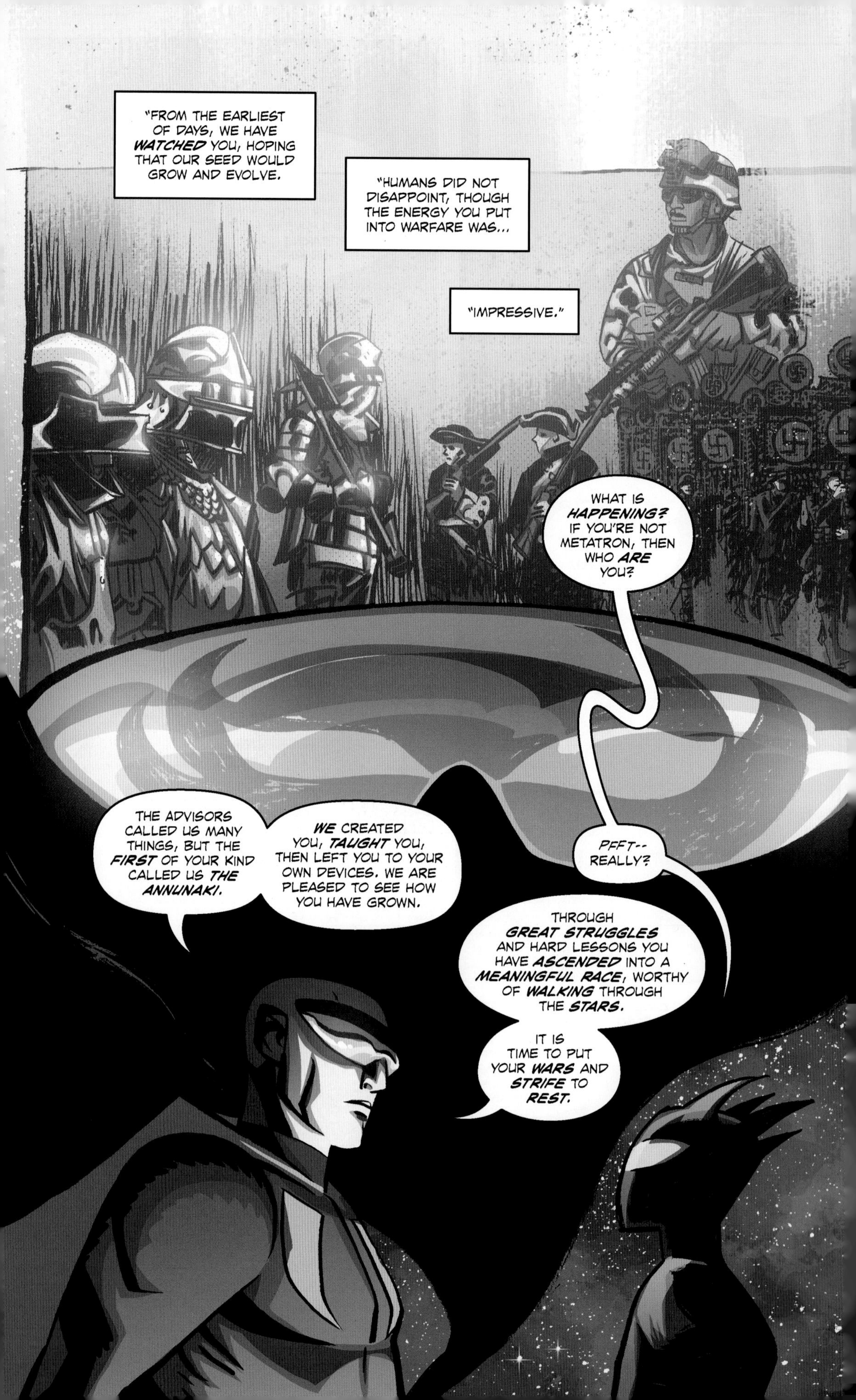
"FROM THE EARLIEST OF DAYS, WE HAVE WATCHED YOU, HOPING THAT OUR SEED WOULD GROW AND EVOLVE.
"HUMANS DID NOT DISAPPOINT, THOUGH THE ENERGY YOU PUT INTO WARFARE WAS...
"IMPRESSIVE."
WHAT IS HAPPENING? IF YOU'RE NOT METATRON, THEN WHO ARE YOU?
THE ADVISORS CALLED US MANY THINGS, BUT THE FIRST OF YOUR KIND CALLED US THE ANNUNAKI.
WE CREATED YOU, TAUGHT YOU, THEN LEFT YOU TO YOUR OWN DEVICES. WE ARE PLEASED TO SEE HOW YOU HAVE GROWN.
PFFT-- REALLY?
THROUGH GREAT STRUGGLES AND HARD LESSONS YOU HAVE ASCENDED INTO A MEANINGFUL RACE, WORTHY OF WALKING THROUGH THE STARS.
IT IS TIME TO PUT YOUR WARS AND STRIFE TO REST.

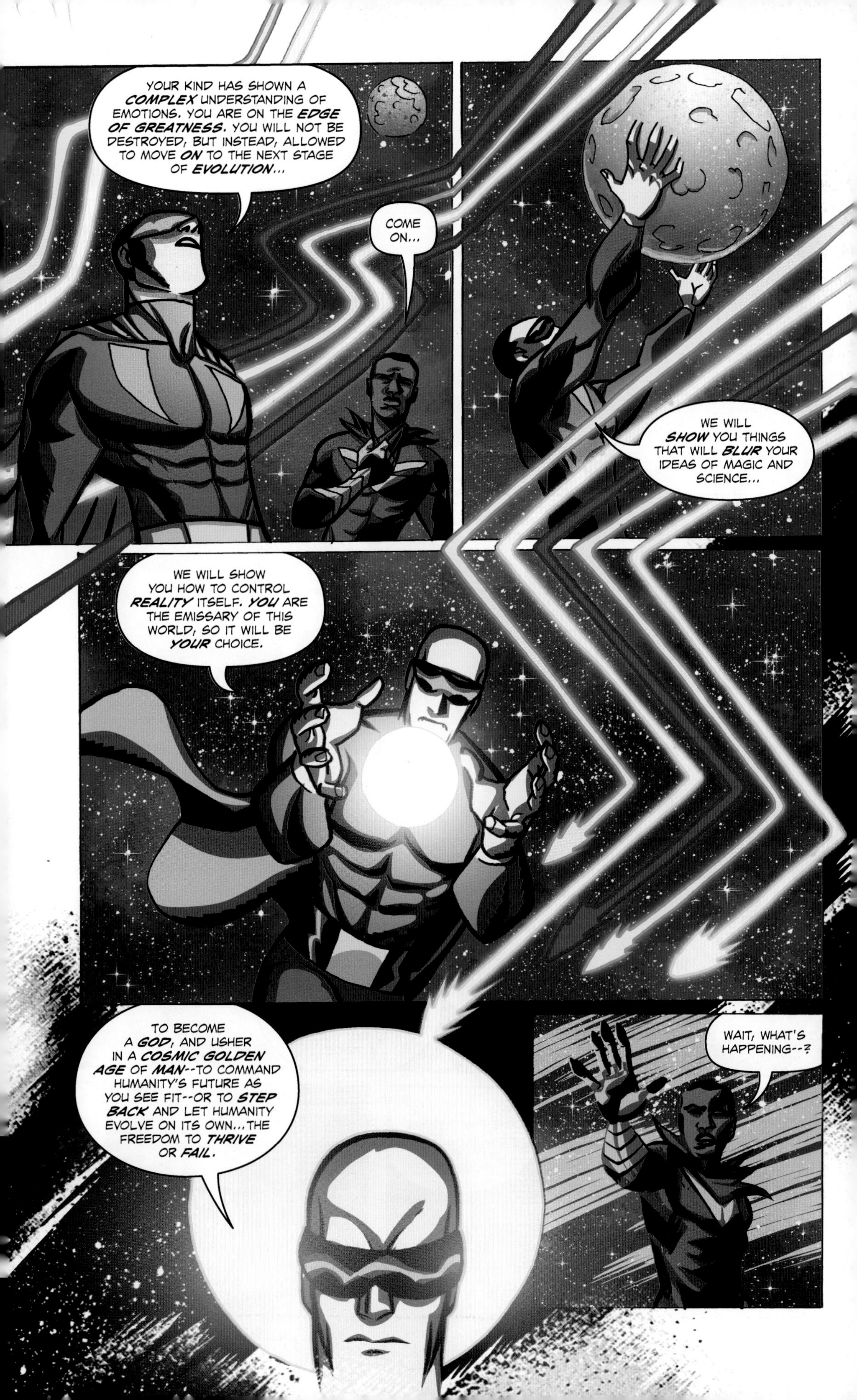
YOUR KIND HAS SHOWN A COMPLEX UNDERSTANDING OF EMOTIONS. YOU ARE ON THE EDGE OF GREATNESS. YOU WILL NOT BE DESTROYED, BUT INSTEAD, ALLOWED TO MOVE ON TO THE NEXT STAGE OF EVOLUTION...
COME ON...
WE WILL SHOW YOU THINGS THAT WILL BLUR YOUR IDEAS OF MAGIC AND SCIENCE...
WE WILL SHOW YOU HOW TO CONTROL REALITY ITSELF. YOU ARE THE EMISSARY OF THIS WORLD, SO IT WILL BE YOUR CHOICE.
TO BECOME A GOD, AND USHER IN A COSMIC GOLDEN AGE OF MAN--TO COMMAND HUMANITY'S FUTURE AS YOU SEE FIT--OR TO STEP BACK AND LET HUMANITY EVOLVE ON ITS OWN... THE FREEDOM TO THRIVE OR FAIL.
WAIT, WHAT'S HAPPENING--?

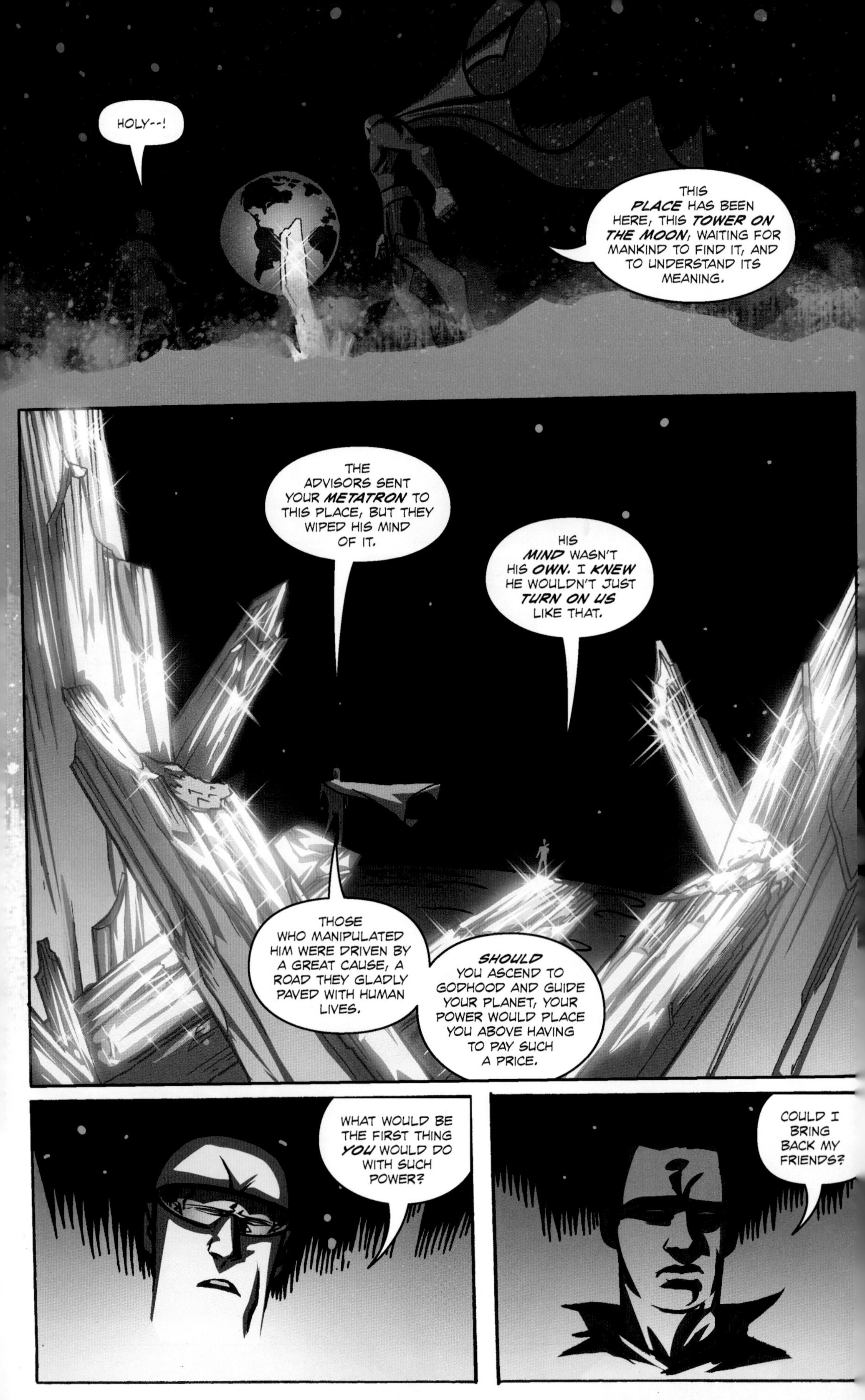
HOLY--!
THIS PLACE HAS BEEN HERE, THIS TOWER ON THE MOON, WAITING FOR MANKIND TO FIND IT, AND TO UNDERSTAND ITS MEANING.
THE ADVISORS SENT YOUR METATRON TO THIS PLACE, BUT THEY WIPED HIS MIND OF IT.
HIS MIND WASN'T HIS OWN. I KNEW HE WOULDN'T JUST TURN ON US LIKE THAT.
THOSE WHO MANIPULATED HIM WERE DRIVEN BY A GREAT CAUSE, A ROAD THEY GLADLY PAVED WITH HUMAN LIVES.
SHOULD YOU ASCEND TO GODHOOD AND GUIDE YOUR PLANET, YOUR POWER WOULD PLACE YOU ABOVE HAVING TO PAY SUCH A PRICE.
WHAT WOULD BE THE FIRST THING YOU WOULD DO WITH SUCH POWER?
COULD I BRING BACK MY FRIENDS?

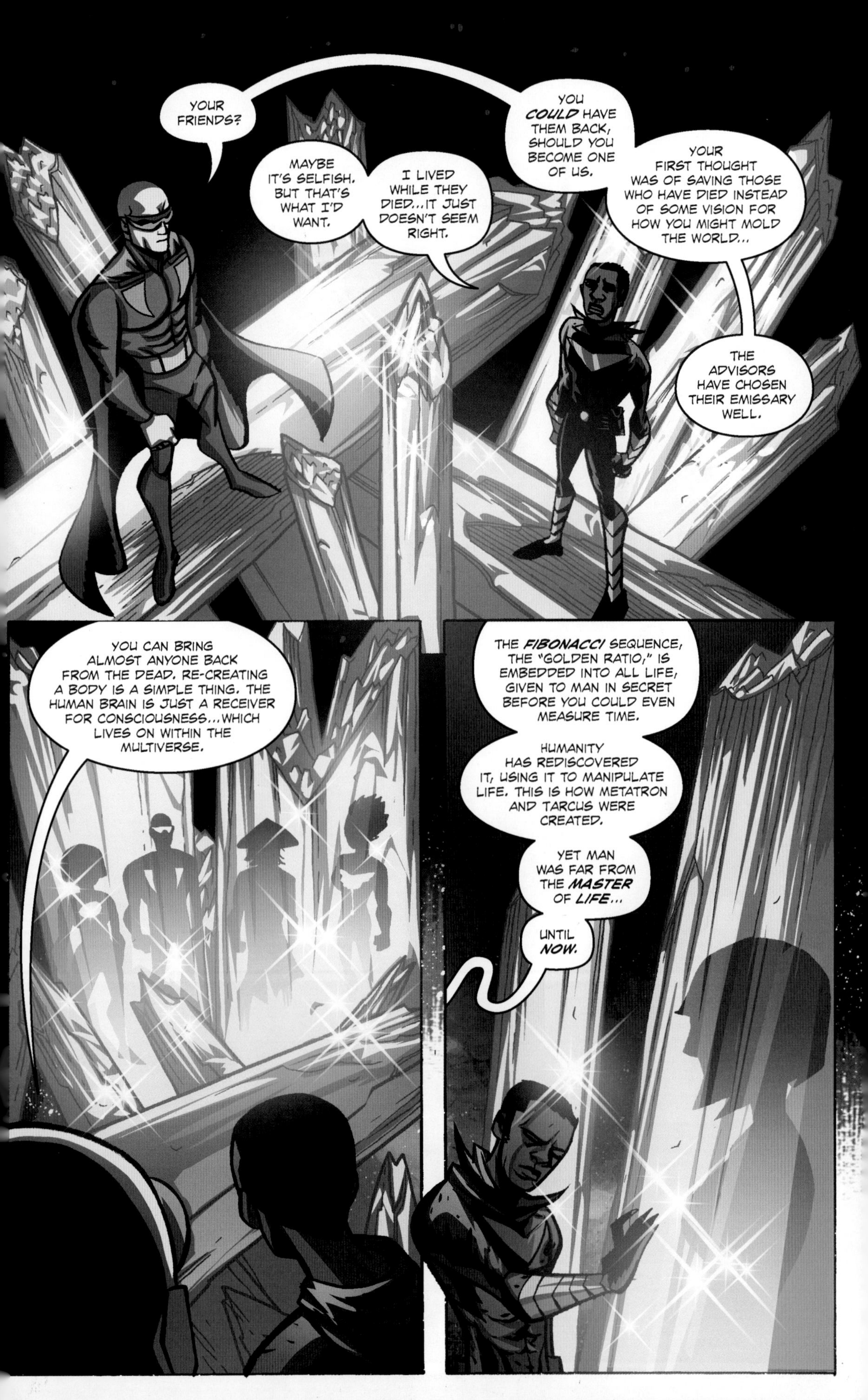
YOUR FRIENDS?
MAYBE IT'S SELFISH. BUT THAT'S WHAT I'D WANT.
I LIVED WHILE THEY DIED... IT JUST DOESN'T SEEM RIGHT.
YOU COULD HAVE THEM BACK, SHOULD YOU BECOME ONE OF US.
YOUR FIRST THOUGHT WAS OF SAVING THOSE WHO HAVE DIED INSTEAD OF SOME VISION FOR HOW YOU MIGHT MOLD THE WORLD...
THE ADVISORS HAVE CHOSEN THEIR EMISSARY WELL.
YOU CAN BRING ALMOST ANYONE BACK FROM THE DEAD. RE-CREATING A BODY IS A SIMPLE THING. THE HUMAN BRAIN IS JUST A RECEIVER FOR CONSCIOUSNESS... WHICH LIVES ON WITHIN THE MULTIVERSE.
THE FIBONACCI SEQUENCE, THE "GOLDEN RATIO," IS EMBEDDED INTO ALL LIFE, GIVEN TO MAN IN SECRET BEFORE YOU COULD EVEN MEASURE TIME.
HUMANITY HAS REDISCOVERED IT, USING IT TO MANIPULATE LIFE. THIS IS HOW METATRON AND TARCUS WERE CREATED.
YET MAN WAS FAR FROM THE MASTER OF LIFE...
UNTIL NOW.

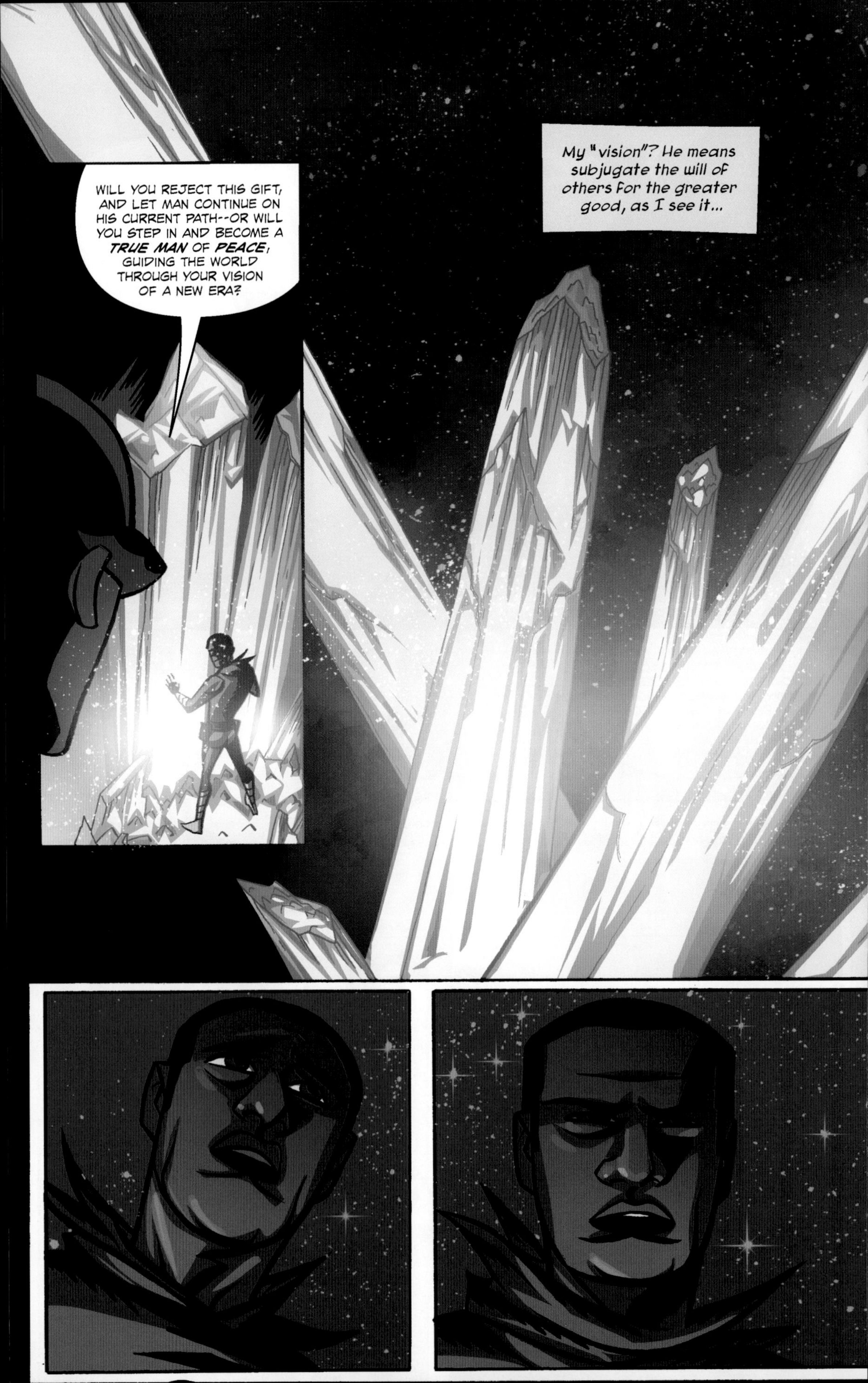
WILL YOU REJECT THIS GIFT, AND LET MAN CONTINUE ON HIS CURRENT PATH--OR WILL YOU STEP IN AND BECOME A TRUE MAN OF PEACE, GUIDING THE WORLD THROUGH YOUR VISION OF A NEW ERA?
My "vision"? He means subjugate the will of others for the greater good, as I see it...

To step into my father's shoes, to finish out his plan...and throw away everything I believe about freedom, deny everyone else the chance to walk their **own** path, all for...

For the sake of the world...

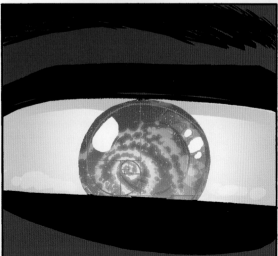

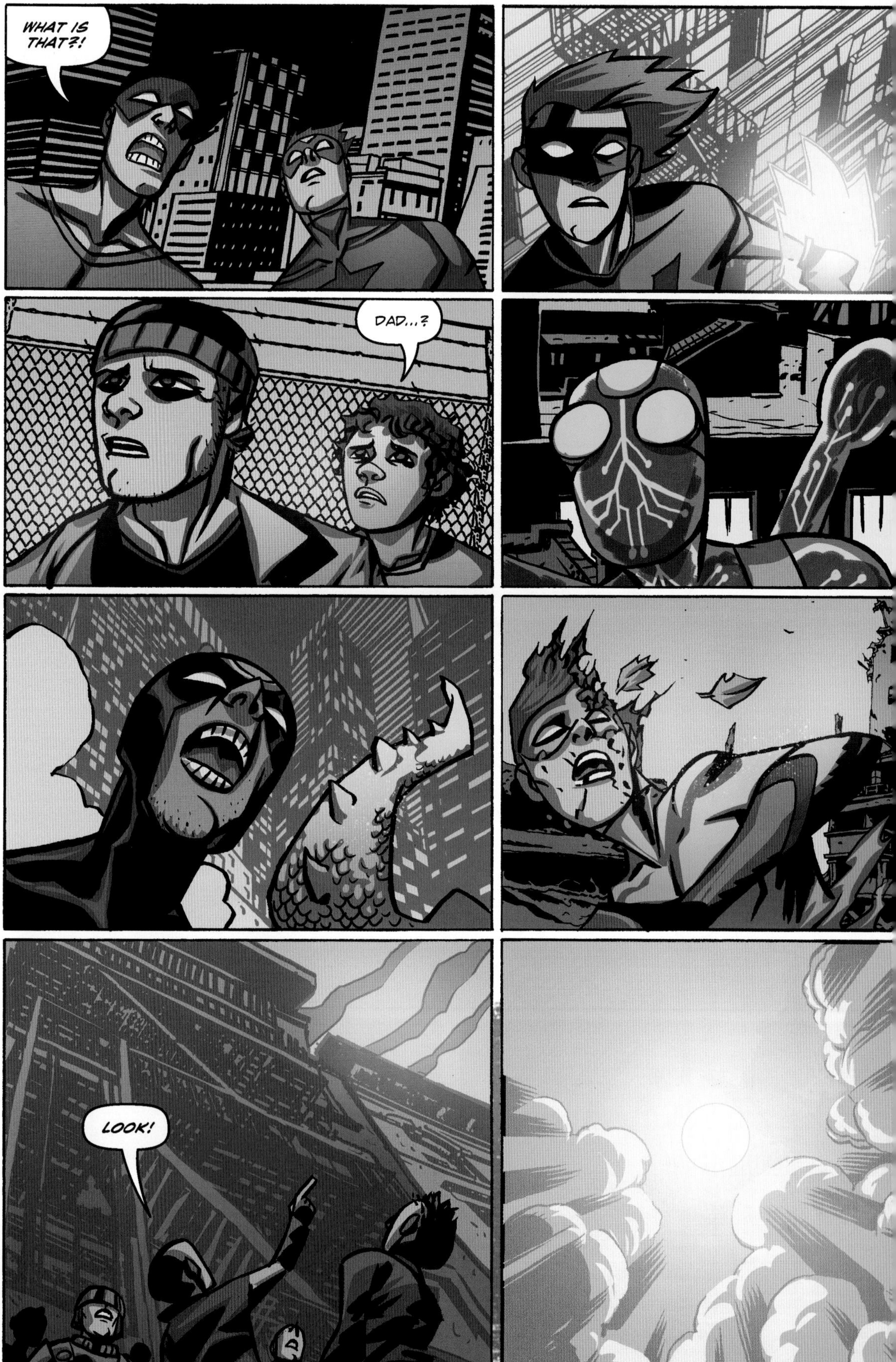
WHAT IS THAT?!
DAD...?
LOOK!

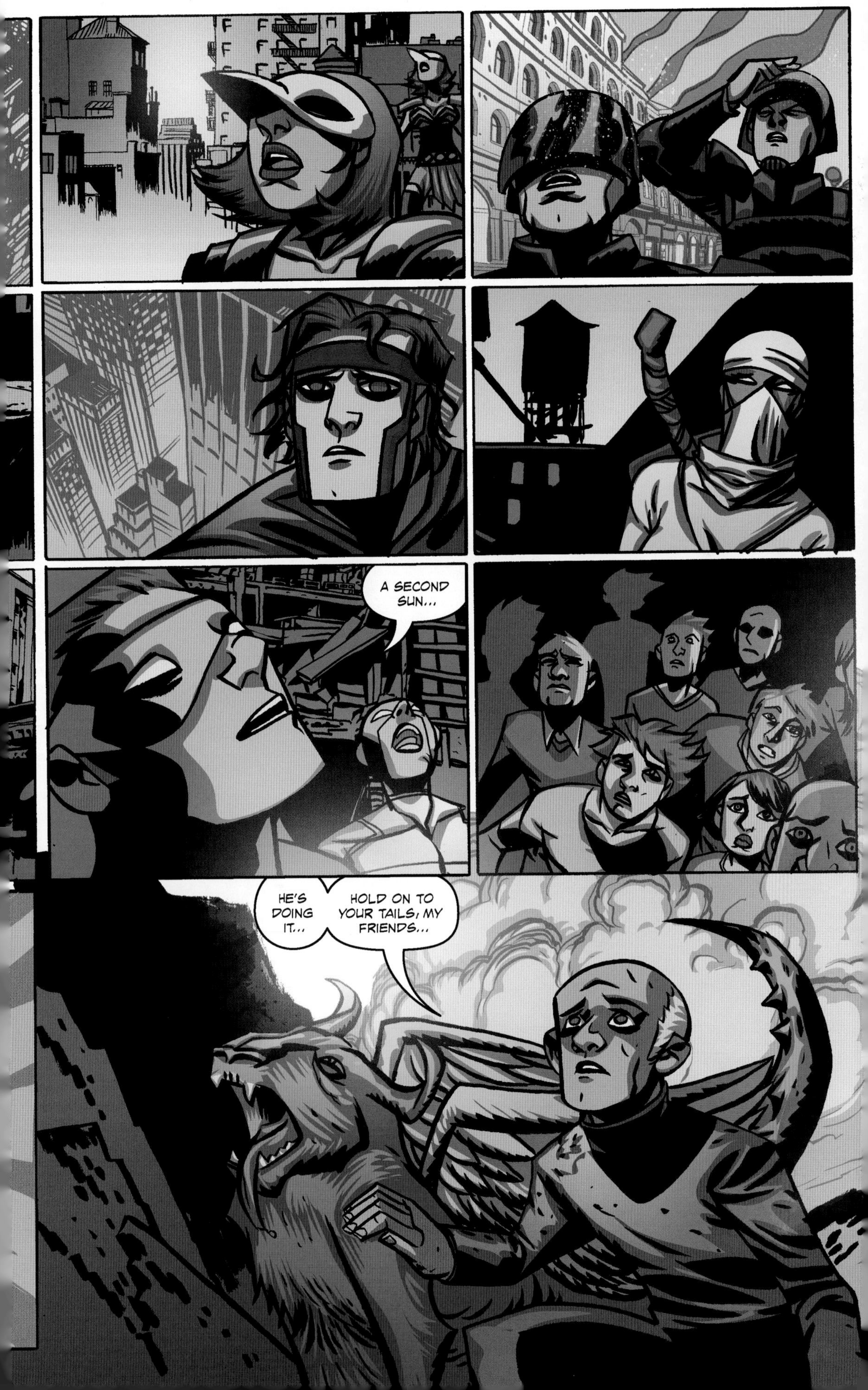
A SECOND SUN...
HE'S DOING IT...
HOLD ON TO YOUR TAILS, MY FRIENDS...

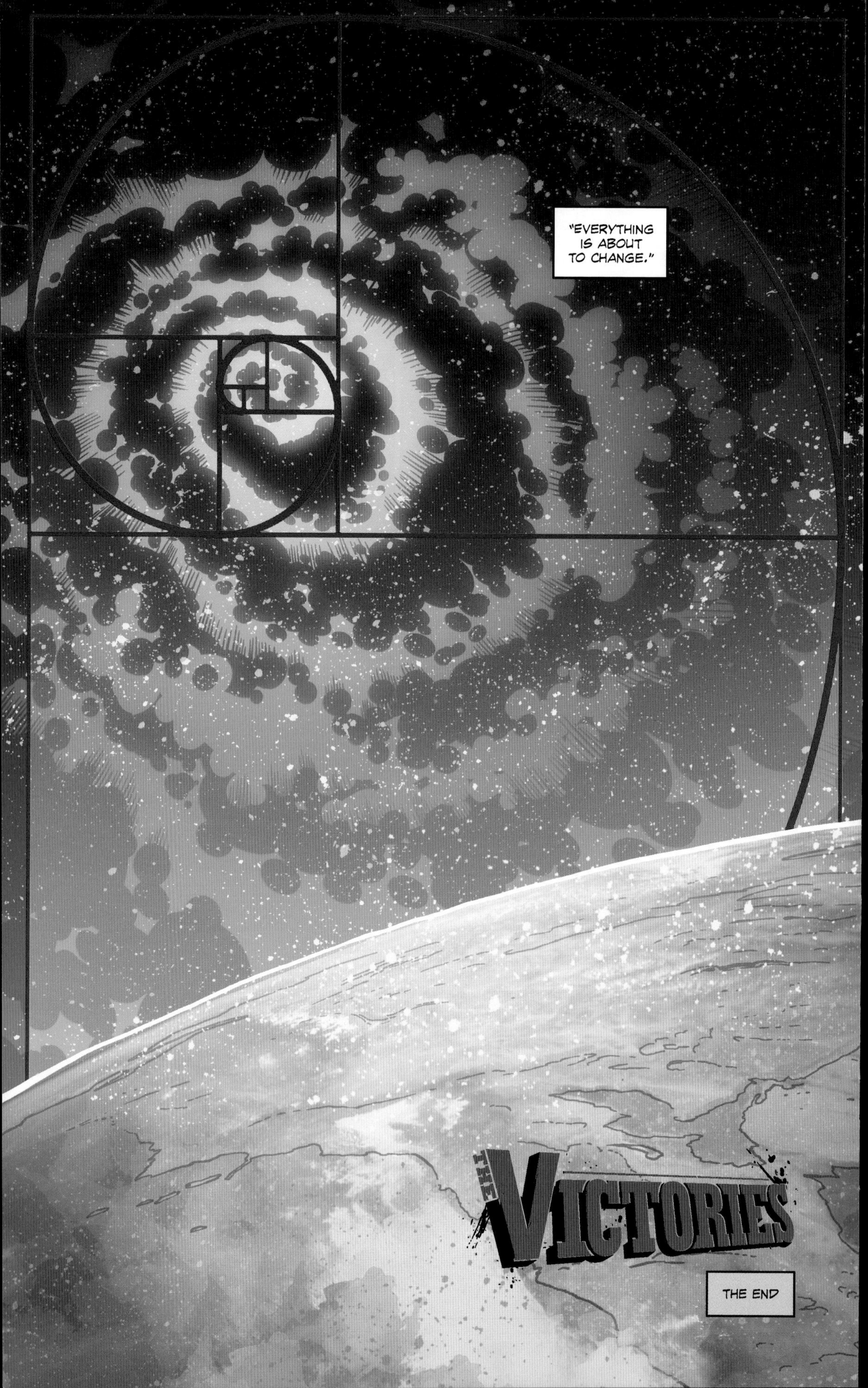
"EVERYTHING IS ABOUT TO CHANGE."
THE VICTORIES
THE END

SHORT STORIES

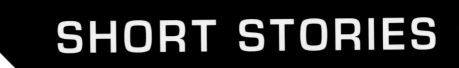

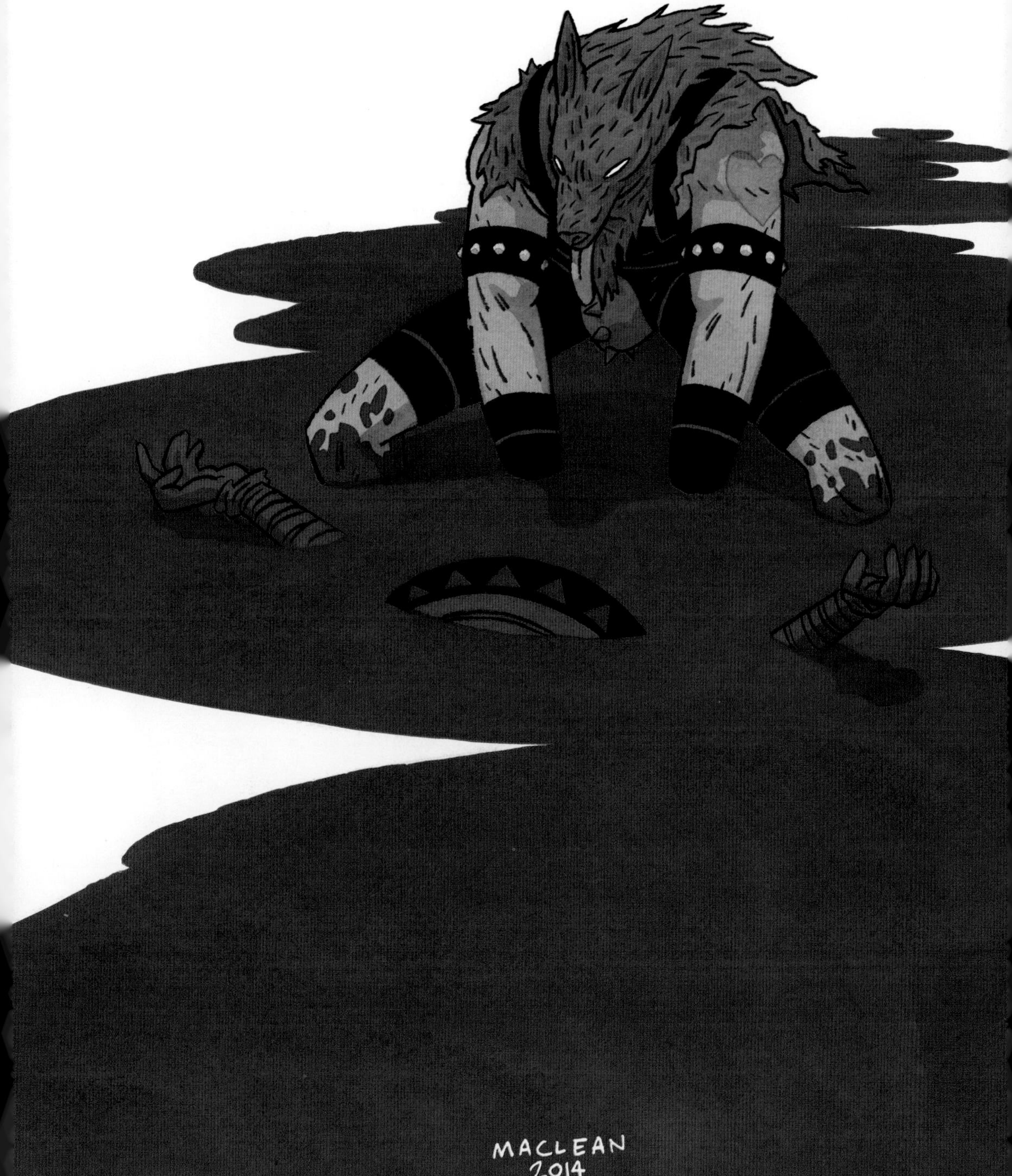
MACLEAN
2014

Illustration by Andrew MacLean

FLOAT

STORY Michael Avon Oeming
ART Agnes Garbowska
COLORS Nick Filardi
LETTERS Aaron Walker

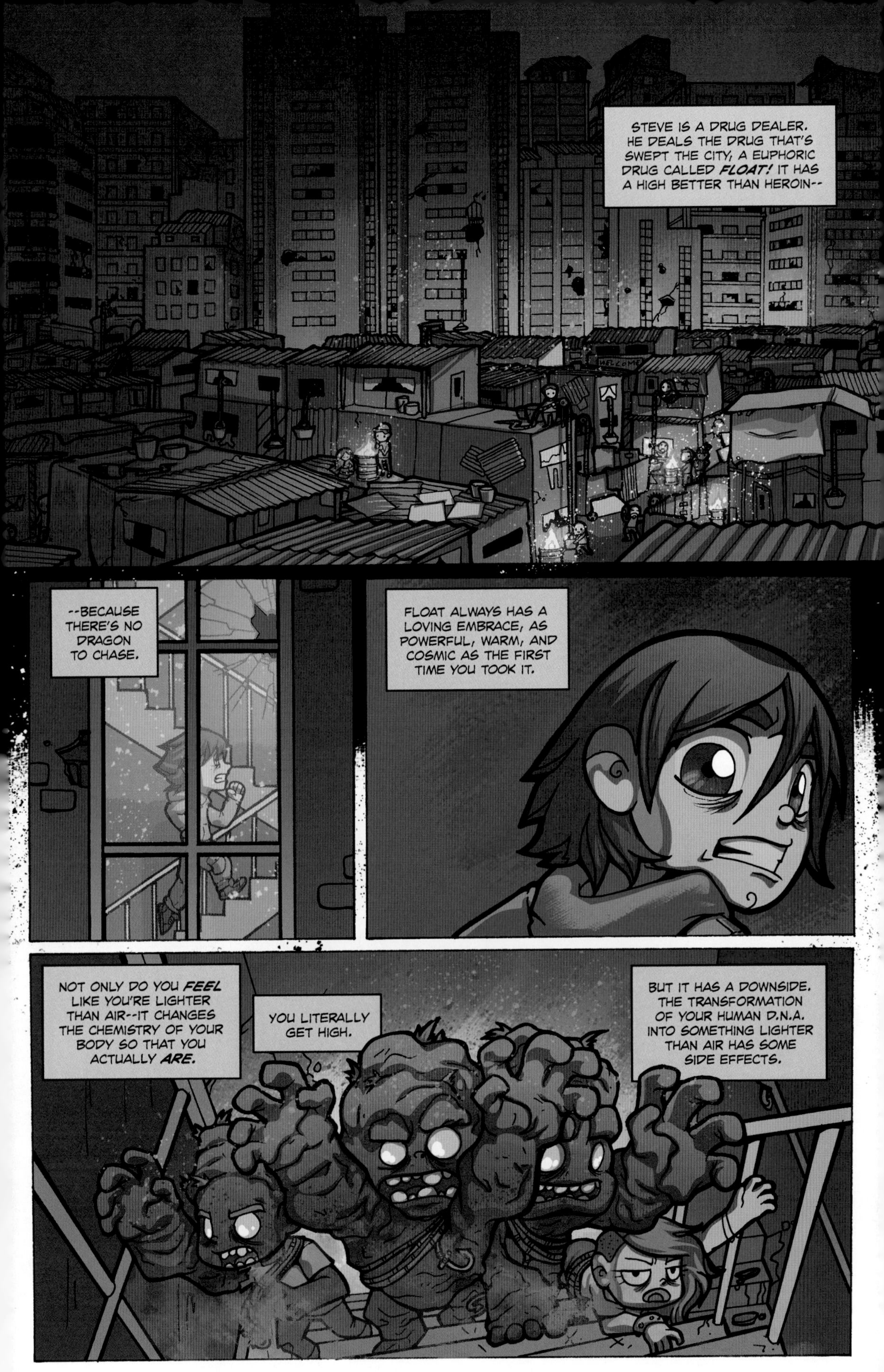
STEVE IS A DRUG DEALER. HE DEALS THE DRUG THAT'S SWEPT THE CITY; A EUPHORIC DRUG CALLED *FLOAT!* IT HAS A HIGH BETTER THAN HEROIN--
--BECAUSE THERE'S NO DRAGON TO CHASE.
FLOAT ALWAYS HAS A LOVING EMBRACE, AS POWERFUL, WARM, AND COSMIC AS THE FIRST TIME YOU TOOK IT.
NOT ONLY DO YOU *FEEL* LIKE YOU'RE LIGHTER THAN AIR--IT CHANGES THE CHEMISTRY OF YOUR BODY SO THAT YOU ACTUALLY *ARE.*
YOU LITERALLY GET HIGH.
BUT IT HAS A DOWNSIDE. THE TRANSFORMATION OF YOUR HUMAN D.N.A. INTO SOMETHING LIGHTER THAN AIR HAS SOME SIDE EFFECTS.

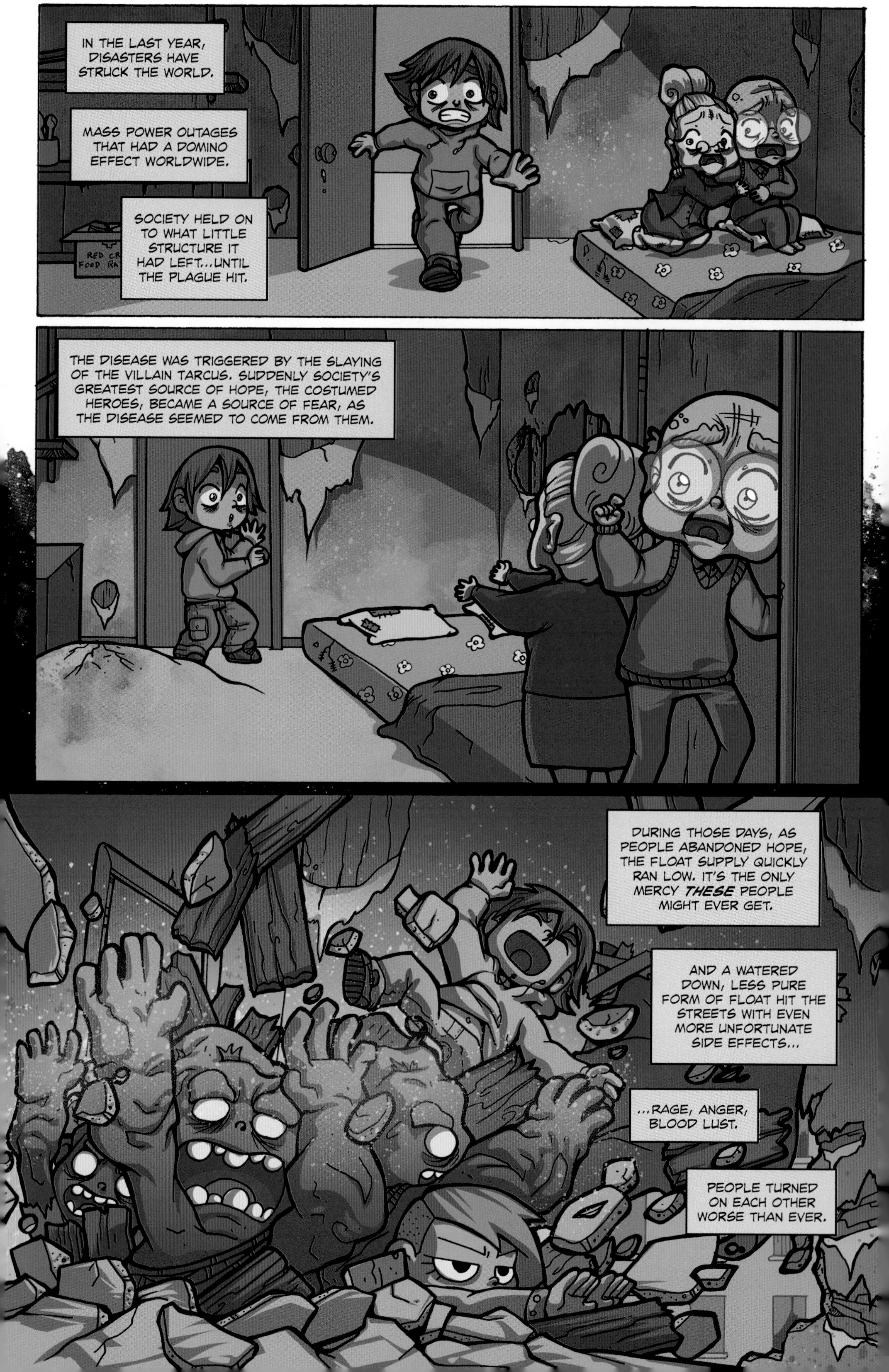
IN THE LAST YEAR, DISASTERS HAVE STRUCK THE WORLD.
MASS POWER OUTAGES THAT HAD A DOMINO EFFECT WORLDWIDE.
SOCIETY HELD ON TO WHAT LITTLE STRUCTURE IT HAD LEFT...UNTIL THE PLAGUE HIT.
THE DISEASE WAS TRIGGERED BY THE SLAYING OF THE VILLAIN TARCUS. SUDDENLY SOCIETY'S GREATEST SOURCE OF HOPE, THE COSTUMED HEROES, BECAME A SOURCE OF FEAR, AS THE DISEASE SEEMED TO COME FROM THEM.
DURING THOSE DAYS, AS PEOPLE ABANDONED HOPE, THE FLOAT SUPPLY QUICKLY RAN LOW. IT'S THE ONLY MERCY *THESE* PEOPLE MIGHT EVER GET.
AND A WATERED DOWN, LESS PURE FORM OF FLOAT HIT THE STREETS WITH EVEN MORE UNFORTUNATE SIDE EFFECTS...
...RAGE, ANGER, BLOOD LUST.
PEOPLE TURNED ON EACH OTHER WORSE THAN EVER.

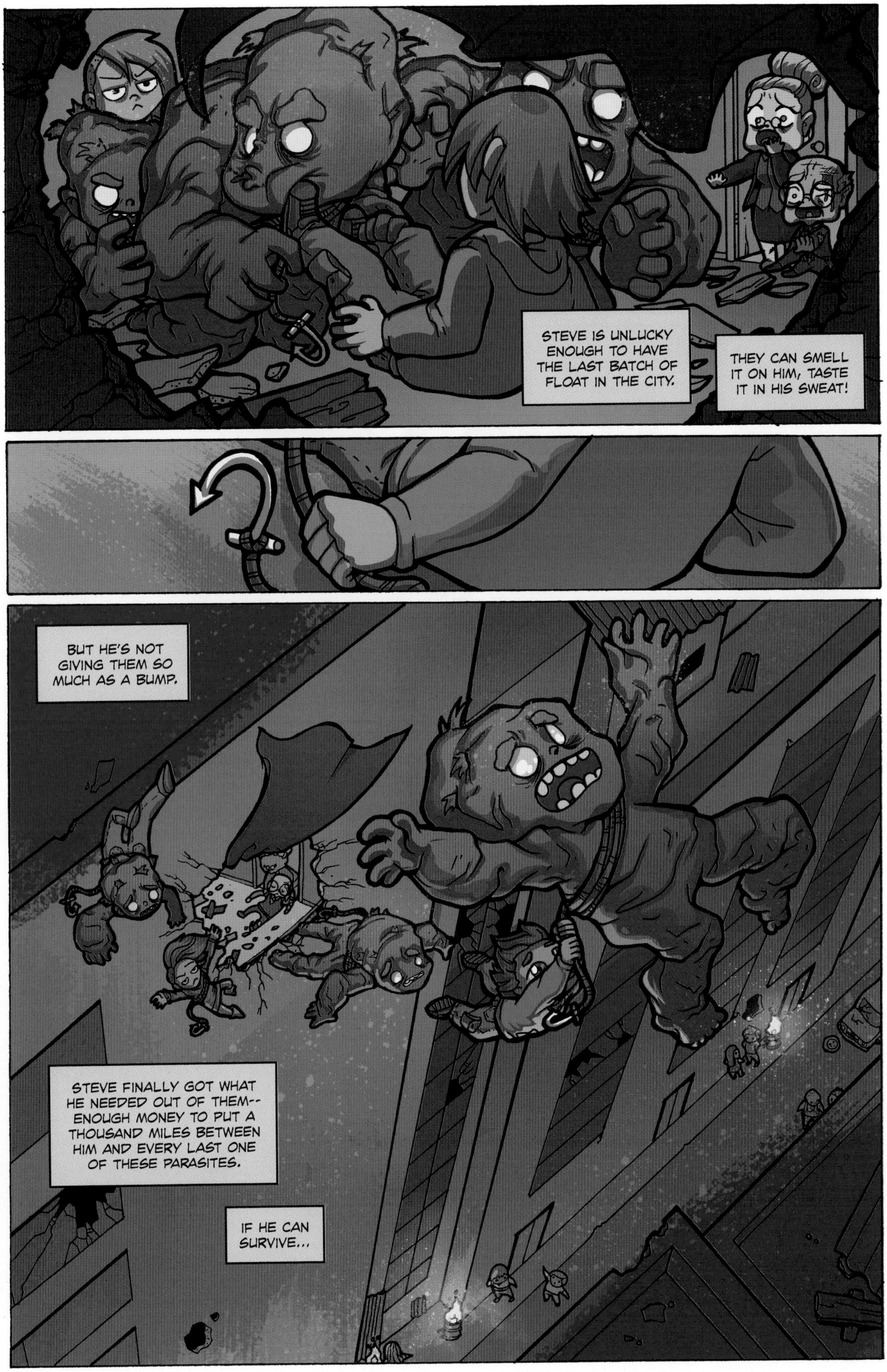
STEVE IS UNLUCKY ENOUGH TO HAVE THE LAST BATCH OF FLOAT IN THE CITY.
THEY CAN SMELL IT ON HIM, TASTE IT IN HIS SWEAT!
BUT HE'S NOT GIVING THEM SO MUCH AS A BUMP.
STEVE FINALLY GOT WHAT HE NEEDED OUT OF THEM-- ENOUGH MONEY TO PUT A THOUSAND MILES BETWEEN HIM AND EVERY LAST ONE OF THESE PARASITES.
IF HE CAN SURVIVE...

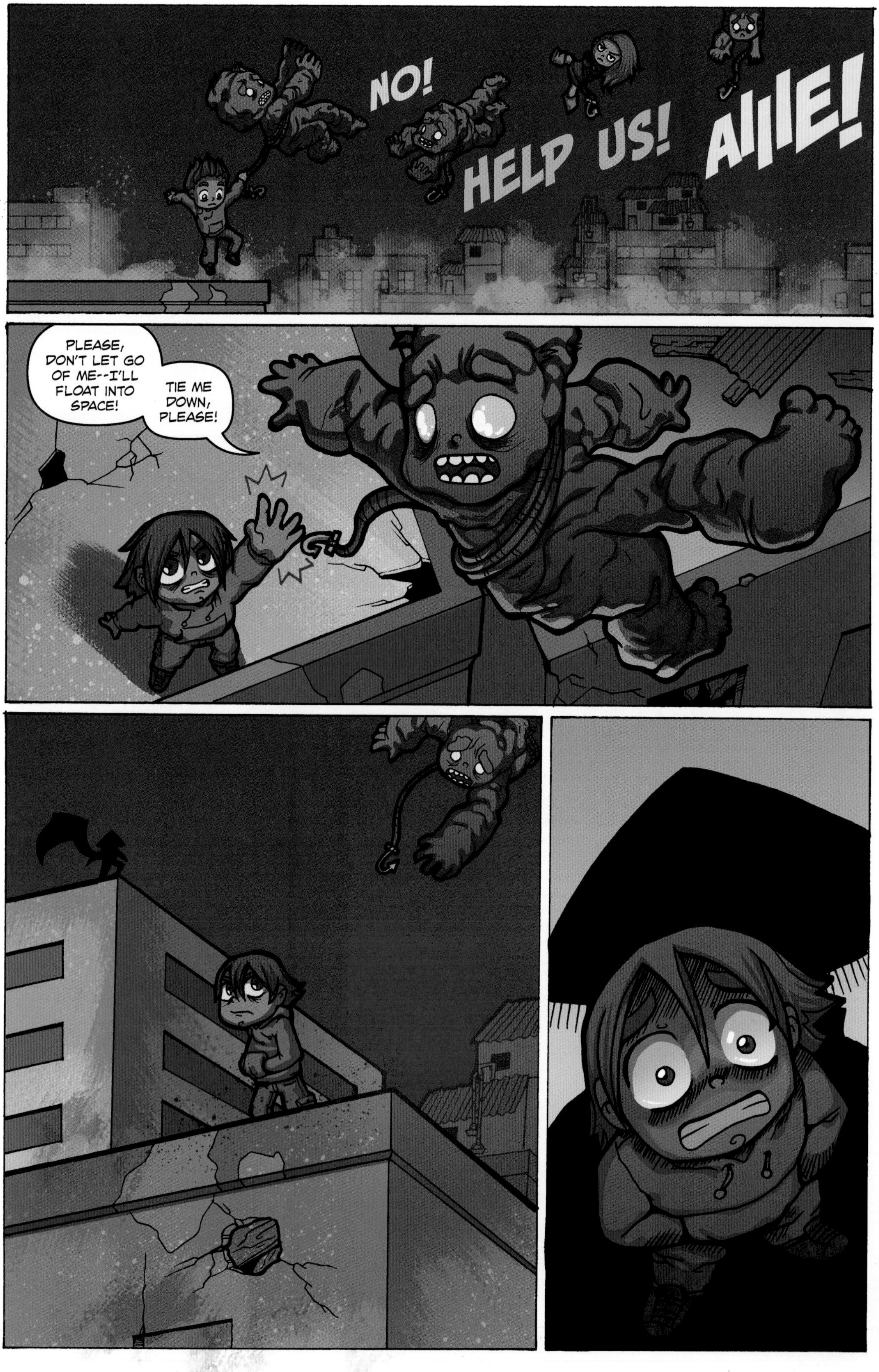
NO!
HELP US!
AIIIE!
PLEASE, DON'T LET GO OF ME--I'LL FLOAT INTO SPACE!
TIE ME DOWN, PLEASE!

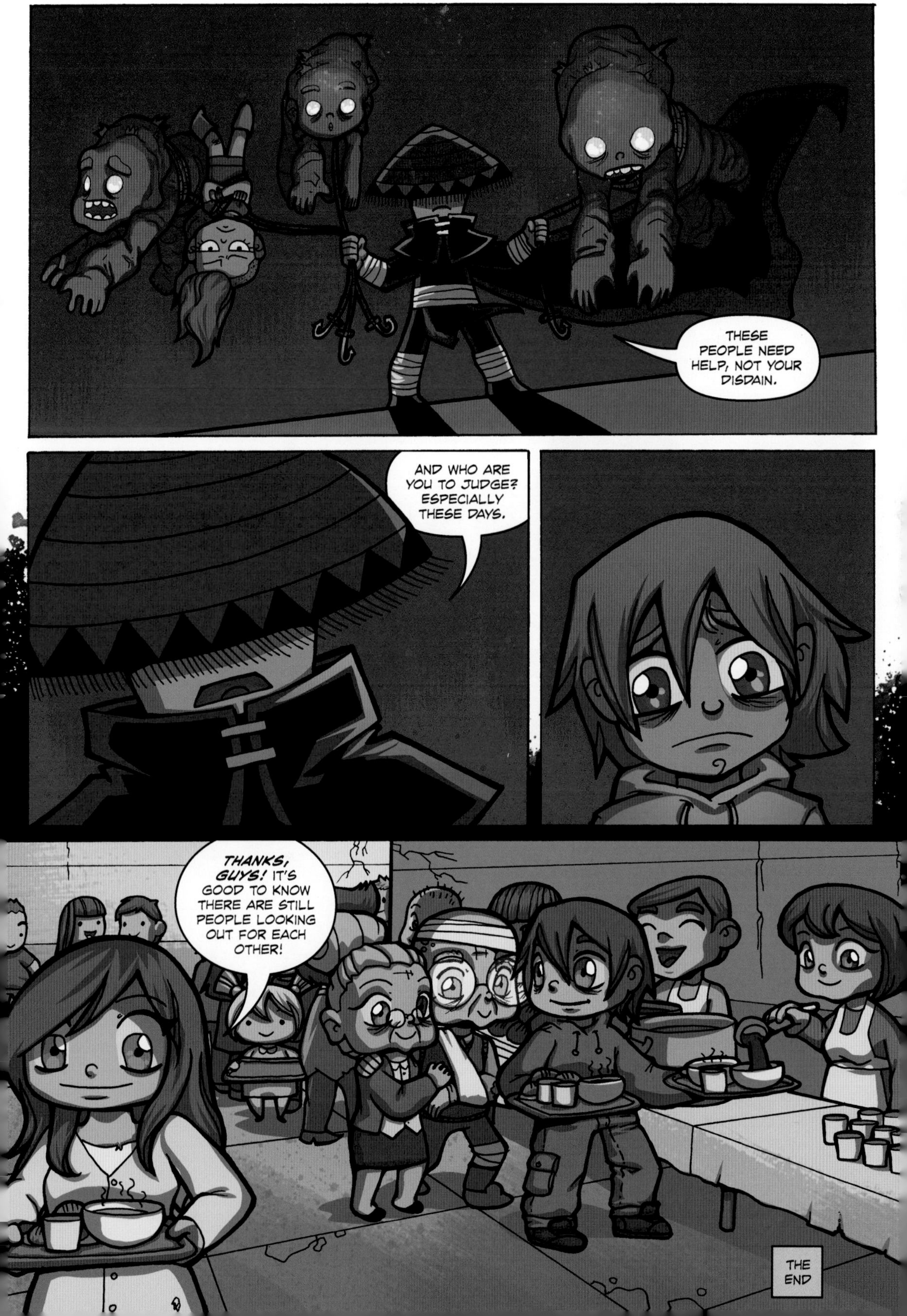
THESE PEOPLE NEED HELP, NOT YOUR DISDAIN.
AND WHO ARE YOU TO JUDGE? ESPECIALLY THESE DAYS.
THANKS, GUYS! IT'S GOOD TO KNOW THERE ARE STILL PEOPLE LOOKING OUT FOR EACH OTHER!
THE END

LITTLE BROTHER, BIG BROTHER

STORY Michael Avon Oeming
ART Taki Soma
COLORS Nick Filardi
LETTERS Aaron Walker

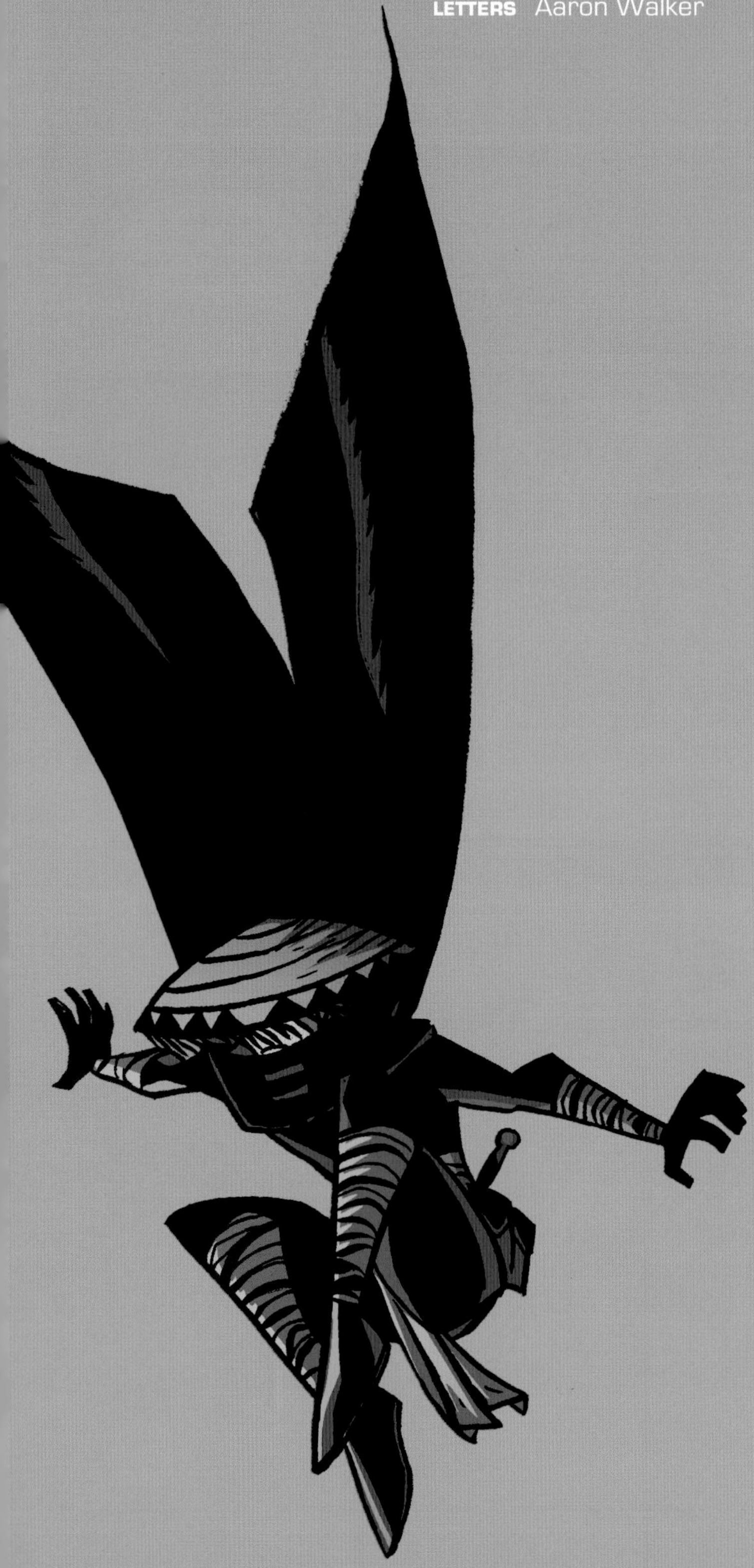

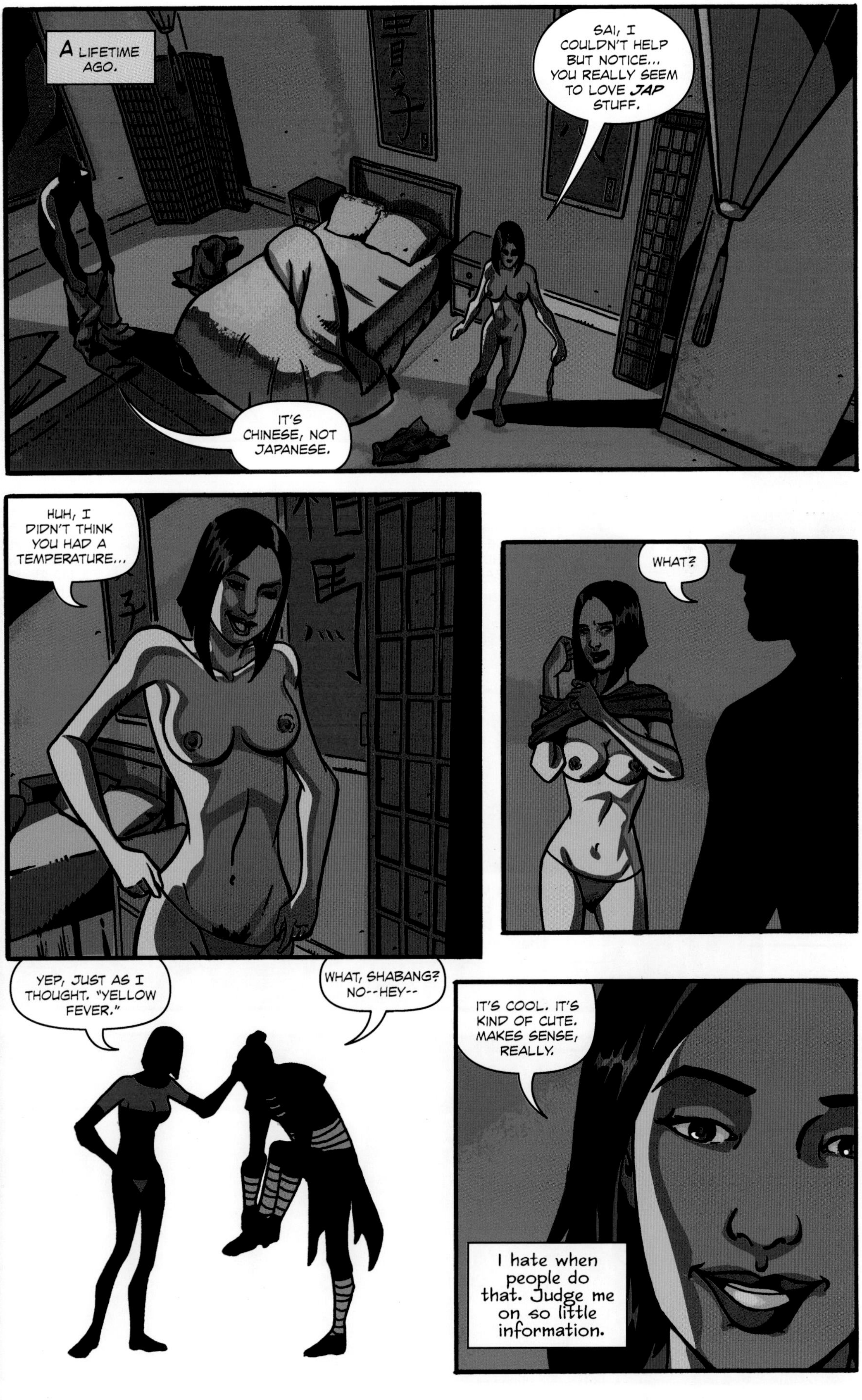
A LIFETIME AGO.
SAI, I COULDN'T HELP BUT NOTICE... YOU REALLY SEEM TO LOVE JAP STUFF.
IT'S CHINESE, NOT JAPANESE.
HUH, I DIDN'T THINK YOU HAD A TEMPERATURE...
WHAT?
YEP, JUST AS I THOUGHT. "YELLOW FEVER."
WHAT, SHABANG? NO--HEY--
IT'S COOL. IT'S KIND OF CUTE. MAKES SENSE, REALLY.
I hate when people do that. Judge me on so little information.

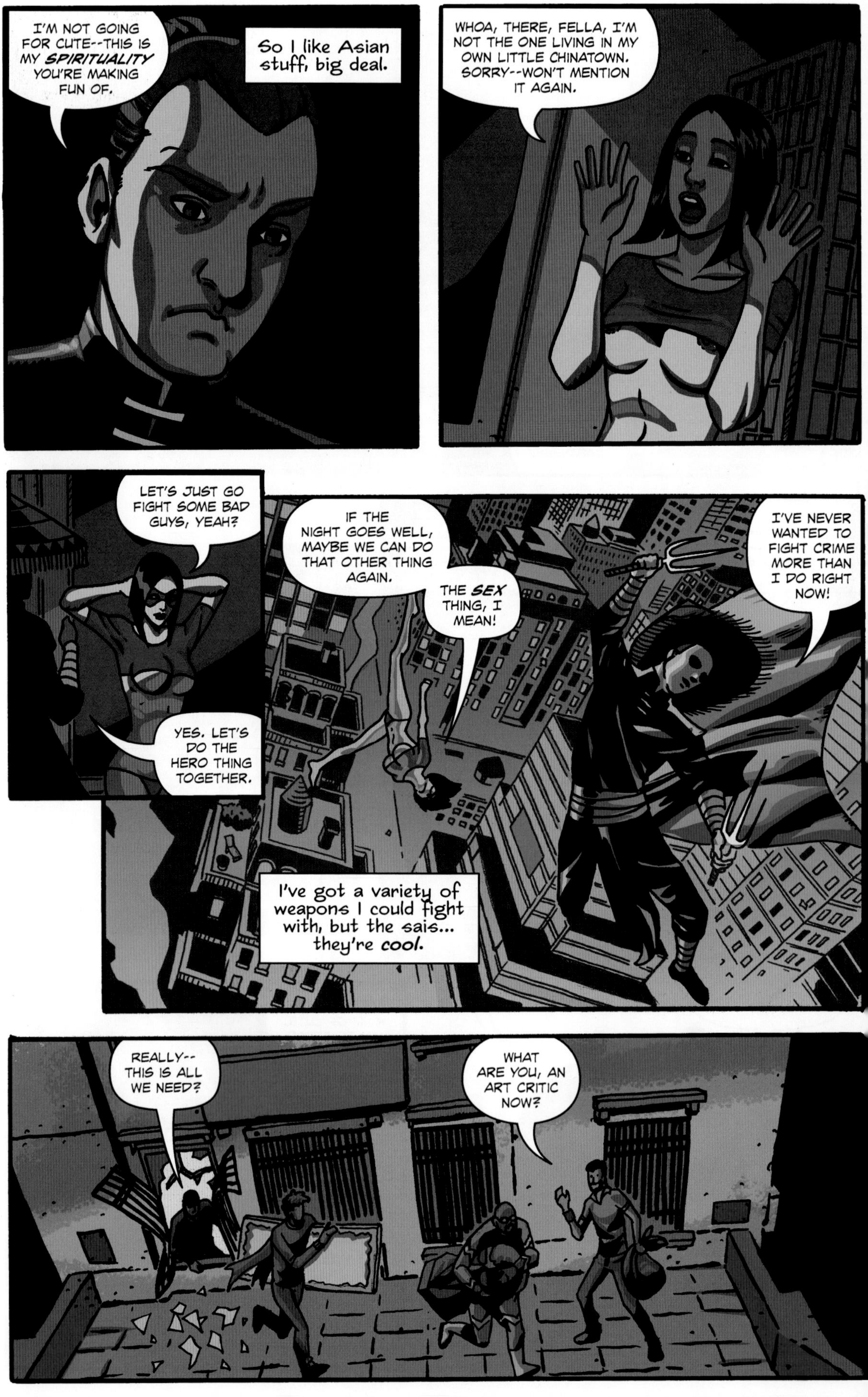

I'M NOT GOING FOR CUTE--THIS IS MY SPIRITUALITY YOU'RE MAKING FUN OF.
So I like Asian stuff, big deal.
WHOA, THERE, FELLA, I'M NOT THE ONE LIVING IN MY OWN LITTLE CHINATOWN. SORRY--WON'T MENTION IT AGAIN.
LET'S JUST GO FIGHT SOME BAD GUYS, YEAH?
YES. LET'S DO THE HERO THING TOGETHER.
IF THE NIGHT GOES WELL, MAYBE WE CAN DO THAT OTHER THING AGAIN.
THE SEX THING, I MEAN!
I'VE NEVER WANTED TO FIGHT CRIME MORE THAN I DO RIGHT NOW!
I've got a variety of weapons I could fight with, but the sais... they're cool.
REALLY-- THIS IS ALL WE NEED?
WHAT ARE YOU, AN ART CRITIC NOW?

IT'S ON OUR SHOPPING LIST, JUST FUCKING-- OH SHIT!

OW! POWERED JERK!

POK

My **brothers** liked them. Sais, nunchucks, throwing stars--cool shit like that.

My brothers who used to beat the **crap** out of me, that is.

But I learned to dodge. After a while none of them could even come *close* to hitting me.

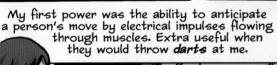

My first power was the ability to anticipate a person's move by electrical impulses flowing through muscles. Extra useful when they would throw **darts** at me.

I know your move before you do.

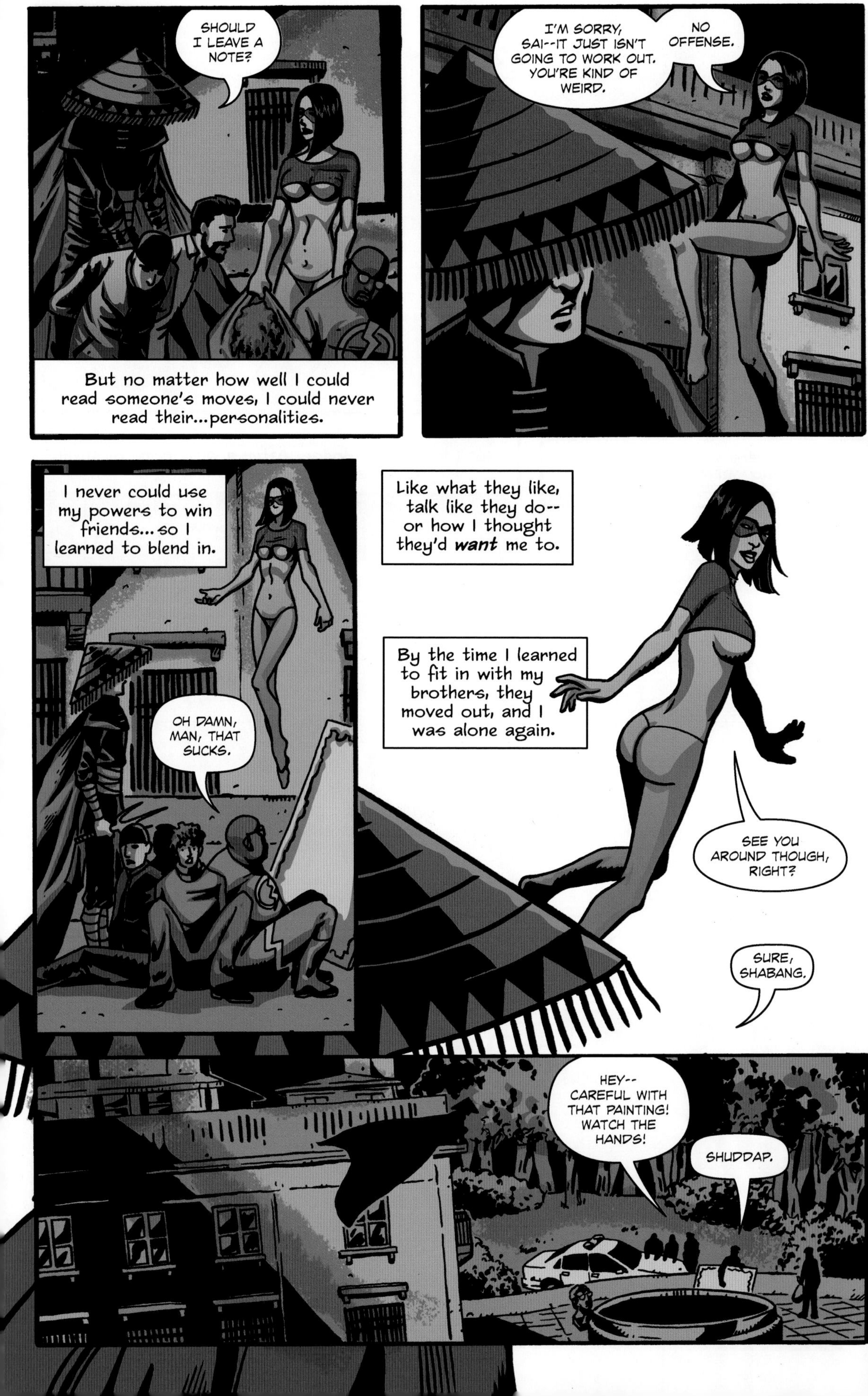
SHOULD I LEAVE A NOTE?
But no matter how well I could read someone's moves, I could never read their...personalities.
I'M SORRY, SAI--IT JUST ISN'T GOING TO WORK OUT. YOU'RE KIND OF WEIRD.
NO OFFENSE.
I never could use my powers to win friends... so I learned to blend in.
OH DAMN, MAN, THAT SUCKS.
Like what they like, talk like they do-- or how I thought they'd *want* me to.
By the time I learned to fit in with my brothers, they moved out, and I was alone again.
SEE YOU AROUND THOUGH, RIGHT?
SURE, SHABANG.
HEY-- CAREFUL WITH THAT PAINTING! WATCH THE HANDS!
SHUDDAP.

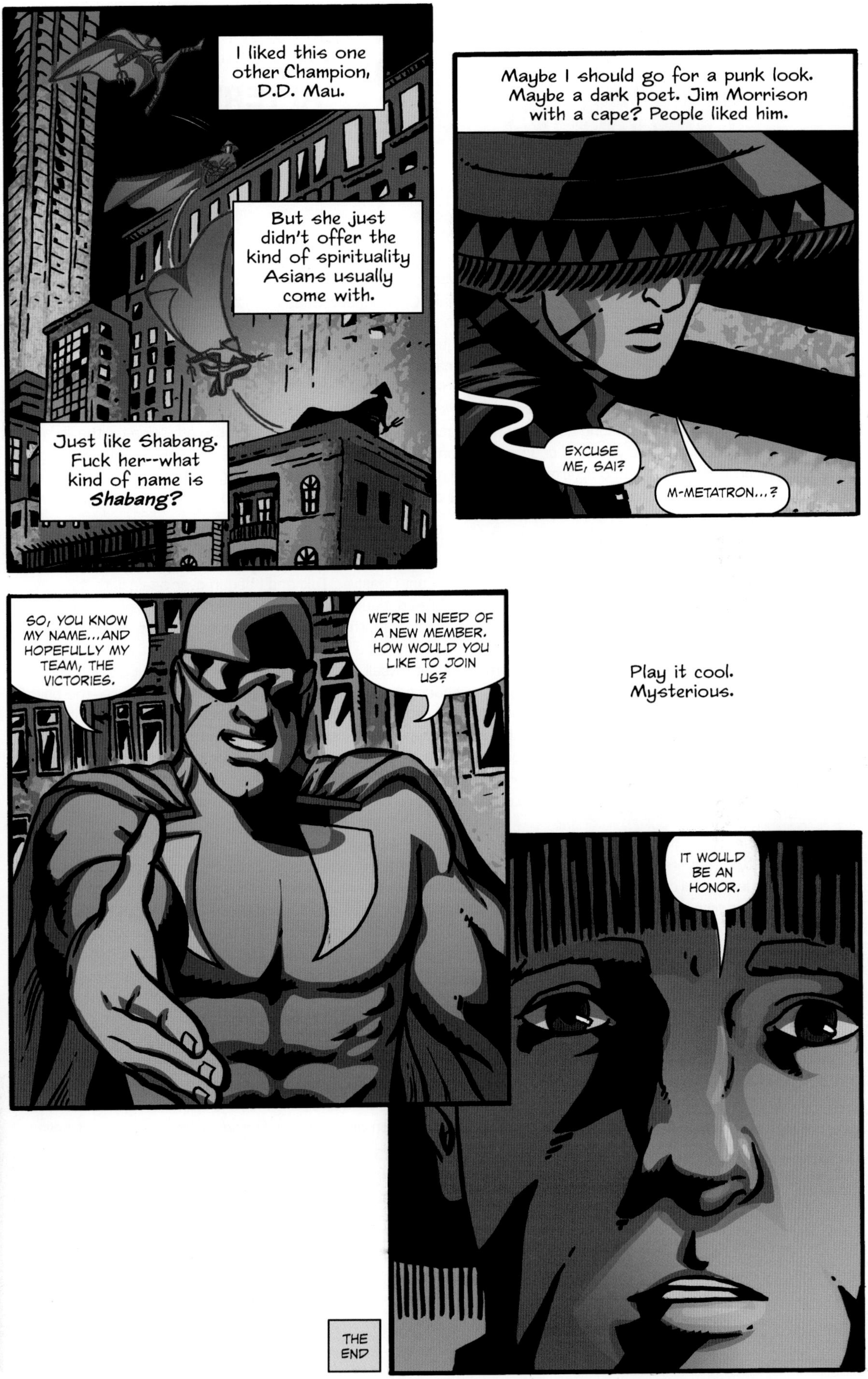
I liked this one other Champion, D.D. Mau.
But she just didn't offer the kind of spirituality Asians usually come with.
Just like Shabang. Fuck her--what kind of name is *Shabang?*
Maybe I should go for a punk look. Maybe a dark poet. Jim Morrison with a cape? People liked him.
EXCUSE ME, SAI?
M-METATRON...?
SO, YOU KNOW MY NAME...AND HOPEFULLY MY TEAM, THE VICTORIES.
WE'RE IN NEED OF A NEW MEMBER. HOW WOULD YOU LIKE TO JOIN US?
Play it cool. Mysterious.
IT WOULD BE AN HONOR.
THE END

THE VICTORIES AFTERWORD

MICHAEL AVON OEMING'S

I'd like to begin with thanking some people for their work on *The Victories*. First has to be the editor and the assistant editors: Scott Allie, Shantel LaRocque, and Daniel Chabon. Scott has been the best story editor I've ever worked with, pushing me when needed and stepping back when I growl at him. We worked very closely together on the scripts, especially the dialogue, and the book just wouldn't be the same without him. The daily grind for editors sees no end, and Shantel and Daniel were amazing with helping me along the way with the tons of little things—especially resending me PDFs I never properly saved! Nick Filardi, my "other wife," colors most of my work—*Powers*, *Takio*, and other works, including *The Victories*. Every time, he finds a different approach to making me look good! Colorists are unsung heroes of the pages, and Nick deserves much more attention for the library of styles he has built over the years. Of course, Taki Soma, my actual wife and creative partner in so many things, saw this all build from the ground up, from the crazy in my head to the crazy on the page. A great artist and writer in her own right, Taki is always great to bounce ideas off, only to have them returned improved. Thank you, love!

The Victories came out of a tough time for me. A lot of my life was catching up with and overwhelming me, things from both the past and the present. I had moved from New Jersey to Seattle, where I began working on Valve video games full time. My son and family stayed on the East Coast as Taki and I began over again with this new working opportunity. I was working full time at Valve while continuing to work full time on comics at home. Long story short, the pressures of being a long-distance/seasonal father, two full-time jobs, relocating, and lots of drinking all caught up with me. I started to go to therapy and found a really great shrink who helped me sort things out. During my sessions I came to understand more about myself. Since I'm always thinking about stories, those insights quickly worked their way into writing ideas about a hero whose pain was part of his powers—the best things about being a hero were always tied in with the most painful things in his life. I was able to draw a lot from myself and also from my mother—hey, I said I was in therapy; of course my mother came up! The first idea that came out of this was *Wild Rover* (which appeared in *Dark Horse Presents*), an homage to my mother's struggle with drinking in which an alcoholic "hero" had to literally fight his demons. We last left him to fight the Scotch demons of the Highlands and Europe. I hope to return to that story one day.

But at the same time, I developed *The Victories*, which originally was about one character and those therapy sessions—Faustus. That first series was planting seeds for an ongoing, but it largely focused on Faustus. Rereading the first issue, I wish I'd pushed the larger picture a little more. It ends with Faustus self-imploding, but I wish I'd given a clearer vision of what the series actually was about. It put off some people who just thought I was trying to be dark and brooding for no reason. But we were all happy with how the first series wrapped, so we went right into the ongoing *Victories* series, where I was able to really explore the other characters and the larger story (which I felt tied into the more personal stories)—my idea that conspiracies are really just society's anxieties manifesting. On a personal level, when horrible things happen to us, we ask, "Why?" and we look for reasons. I think this happened to our country beginning with the Kennedy assassination. How could such a horrific thing happen, on television and later revealed in the Zapruder film? There had to be a reason, and it had to be larger than one lone nut. It was too horrible for any explanation. That anxiety extends to a cosmic anxiety when we're faced with something like the pyramids or the ruins of Puma Punku. It's too astounding to have a realistic explanation; it has to be bigger than us. These themes of "magical thinking," both cosmic and personal, are intertwined, and I wanted to explore them here, wrapped in capes and masks. My version of the *Super Friends*, where you almost never see them out of their costumes, where the masks are the true faces, the costumes are the real skin against their existential crises.

I hope you enjoyed my bit of therapy.

Michael Avon Oeming
July 14, 2014
Portland, Oregon

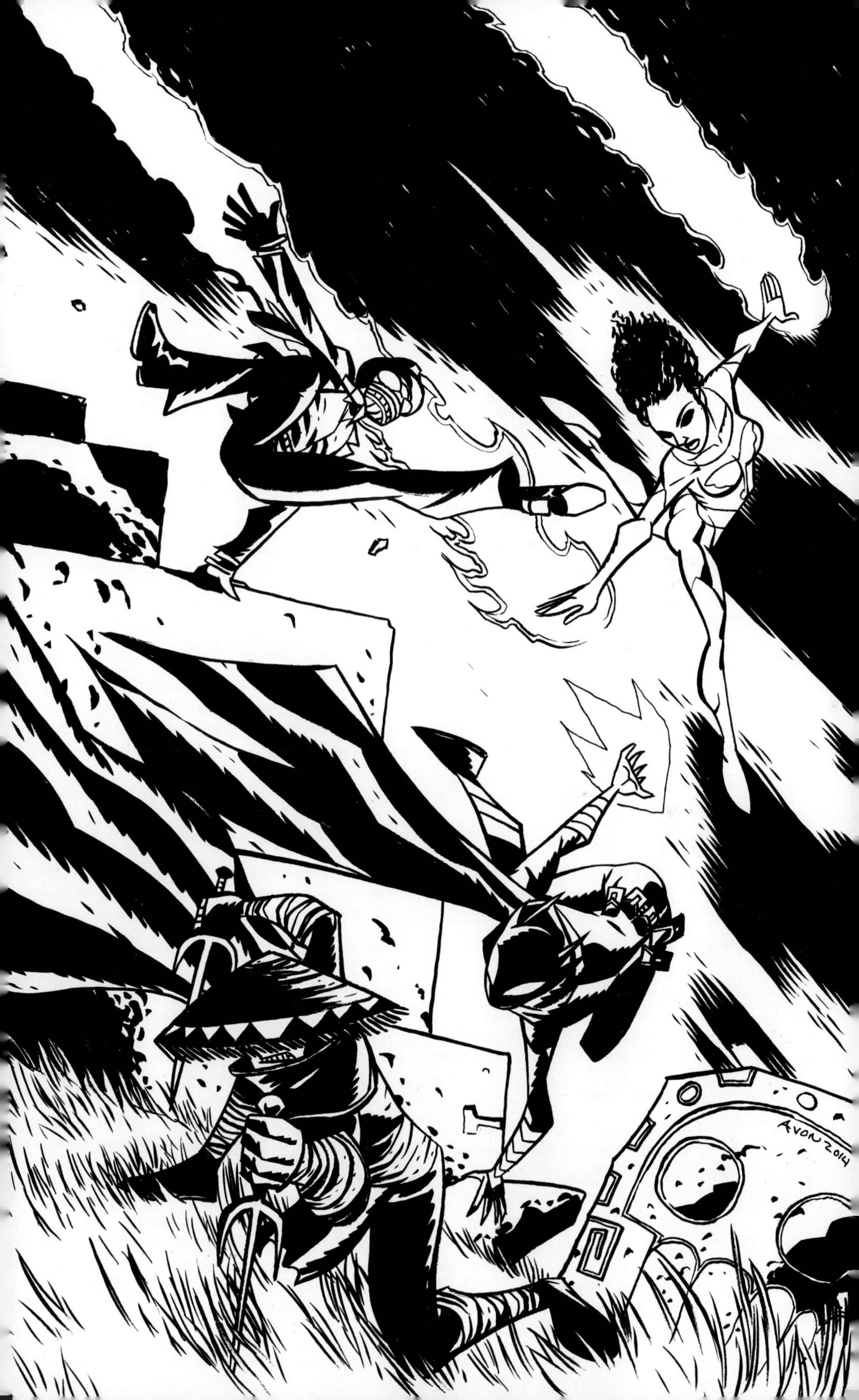
AVON 2014

MORE FROM
MICHAEL AVON OEMING

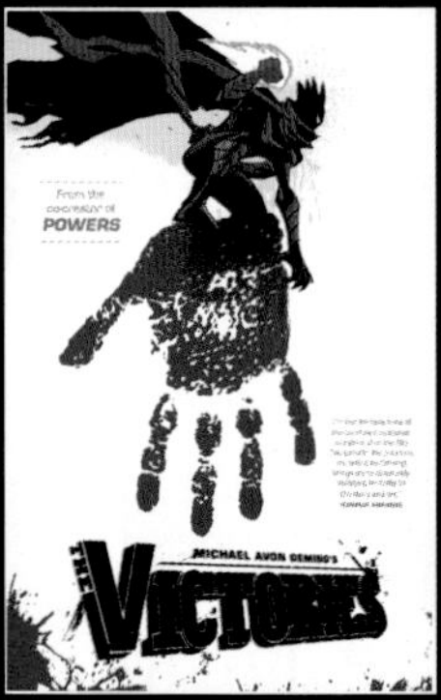
From the cocreator of POWERS
MICHAEL AVON OEMING'S
VICTORIES

THE VICTORIES
Michael Avon Oeming and Nick Filardi

The Victories: heroes sworn to protect us from crime, corruption, and the weird designer drug known as Float.

VOLUME 1: TOUCHED
ISBN 978-1-61655-100-1 | $9.99

VOLUME 2: TRANSHUMAN
ISBN 978-1-61655-214-5 | $17.99

VOLUME 3: POSTHUMAN
ISBN 978-1-61655-445-3 | $17.99

VOLUME 4: METAHUMAN
ISBN 978-1-61655-517-7 | $17.99

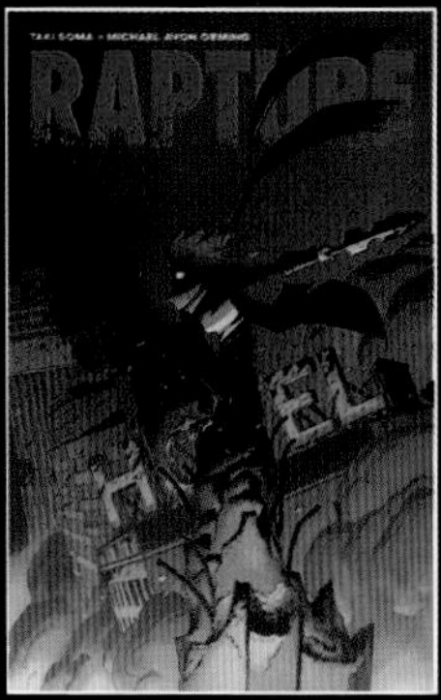

RAPTURE
Michael Avon Oeming and Taki Soma

After warring for a century, Earth's greatest champions and villains suddenly disappear. Amid the wreckage, two lovers, Evelyn and Gil, find themselves separated by a continent and will do anything to find each other again. But when Evelyn becomes a champion with an angelic spear, she finds her love for Gil clashing with her newfound power.

ISBN 978-1-59582-460-8 | $19.99

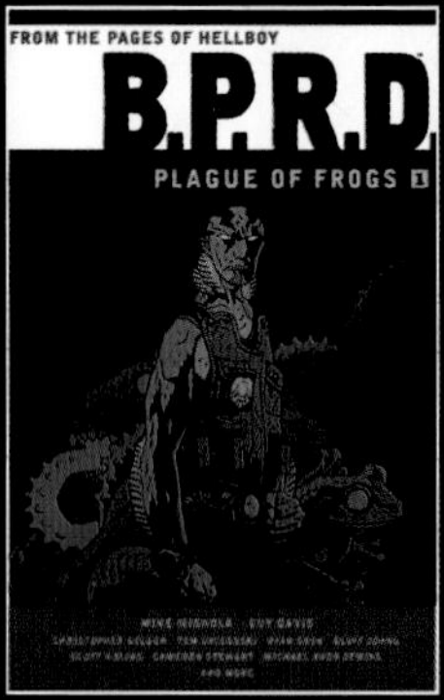
FROM THE PAGES OF HELLBOY
B.P.R.D
PLAGUE OF FROGS 1

B.P.R.D.: PLAGUE OF FROGS HARDCOVER COLLECTION VOLUME 1
Mike Mignola, Christopher Golden, Geoff Johns, Michael Avon Oeming, and others

Abe Sapien leads Liz Sherman and a bizarre roster of special agents in defending the world from occult threats, including the growing menace of the frog army first spotted in *Hellboy: Seed of Destruction*.

ISBN 978-1-59582-609-1 | $34.99

CONAN: THE DAUGHTERS OF MIDORA AND OTHER STORIES
Jimmy Palmiotti, Ron Marz, Michael Avon Oeming, and others

A must-buy for any Conan fan! Collects *Conan and the Daughters of Midora*, *Conan: Island of No Return* #1–#2, and stories from *MySpace Dark Horse Presents* #11 and *USA Today*.

ISBN 978-1-59582-917-7 | $14.99

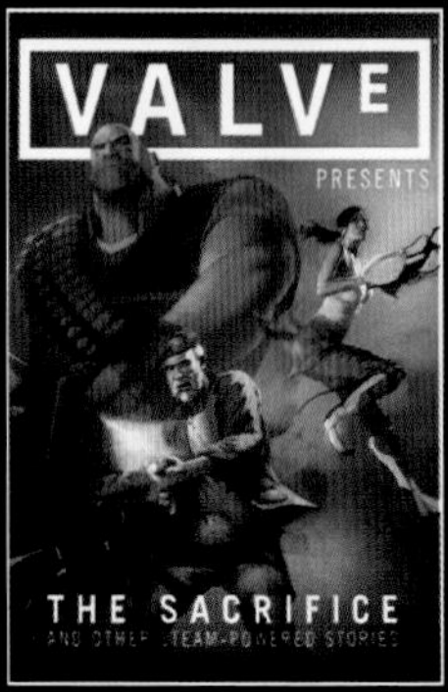
VALVE
PRESENTS
THE SACRIFICE
AND OTHER STEAM-POWERED STORIES

VALVE PRESENTS: THE SACRIFICE AND OTHER STEAM-POWERED STORIES
Michael Avon Oeming and others

Valve joins with Dark Horse to bring three critically acclaimed, fan-favorite series to print, with a hardcover collection of comics from the worlds of *Left 4 Dead*, *Team Fortress*, and *Portal*.

ISBN 978-1-59582-869-9 | $24.99

WILD ROVER FEATURING THE SACRIFICE ONE-SHOT
Michael Avon Oeming and Victor Santos

Shane's an alcoholic. But his curse goes deeper than that—Shane needs to overcome the black magic at the heart of his addiction by killing a liquor demon if he hopes to reclaim his soul.

$2.99

AVAILABLE AT YOUR LOCAL COMICS SHOP OR BOOKSTORE! • To find a comics shop in your area, call 1-888-266-4226.
For more information or to order direct visit DarkHorse.com or call 1-800-862-0052 Mon.–Fri. 9 AM to 5 PM Pacific Time. Prices and availability subject to change without notice.